P9-CDL-060

Uncle John's

BATHROOM READER

by
The Bathroom Readers'
Institute

St. Martin's Press
New York

"Flipper" originally appeared in *Animal Superstars*. Copyright © 1985, by John Javna. Reprinted by permission of the author.

"Politics of Oz" originally appeared in *The Utne Reader*, July/August 1988. Copyright © 1988, by Michael Dregni. Reprinted by permission of the author.

"Doo-Wop Sounds" originally appeared in *The Doo-Wop Sing-Along Songbook*. Copyright © 1985, by John Javna. Reprinted by permission of the author.

"Caveat Eater" Copyright © 1988, by David Goines. Reprinted by permission of the author.

"7 Cool Flicks," "10 Cool Books," and "The Hipster Saint" originally appeared in *The Catalog of Cool*. Copyright © 1982, by Gene Sculatti. Reprinted by permission of the author.

"Congressional Wit," and "Party Lines" originally appeared in *Will the Gentleman Yield?* Copyright © 1988, by Bill Hogan and Mike Hill. Reprinted by permission of the publisher.

"Riddles" originally appeared in *Riddles*. Copyright © 1983, by Mark Bryant. Reprinted by permission of the publisher.

UNCLE JOHN'S BATHROOM READER. Copyright © 1988 by The Bathroom Readers' Institute. All rights reserved. Printed in the United States of America. No part of this book may be used or reproduced in any manner whatsoever without written permission except in the case of brief quotations embodied in critical articles or reviews. For information, address St. Martin's Press, 175 Fifth Avenue, New York, N.Y. 10010

Produced and Packaged by Javnarama
Design by Javnarama

Library of Congress Cataloging-in-Publication Data

Bathroom Reader's Institute (New York, N.Y.)
    Uncle John's Bathroom Reader.

    1. Wit and humor. I. Title.
PN6153.B28 1988 818'.5407   88-30519
ISBN 0-312-02663-3

15 14

Cover created by Michael Brunsfeld
Cover art by Blake Thornton

"Our Anthem," "Louie, Louie," "Sounds of Silence," "Weird Inspirations," "One-Liners," "Rock Characters," "Five Beatles Songs," Dead Man's Curve," and "The Magic Dragon" originally appeared in *Behind the Hits*, Copyright © 1985, by Bob Shannon and John Javna. Reprinted by permission of the authors.

"Elvis' Toothbrush" and "Celebrity Mania" originally appeared in *Meet the Stars*, Copyright © 1985, by Missy Laws. Reprinted by permission of Ross Books.

"M*A*S*H," "Andy Griffith Show," "Just the Facts," "I Love Lucy," "Star Trek," "Perry Mason," "Gilligan's Island," and "The Twilight Zone" originally appeared in *Cult TV*. Copyright © 1985, by John Javna. Reprinted by permission of the author.

"The Fabulous '60s," and "Birth of the Bikini" originally appeared in *60s!*. Copyright © 1983, by John Javna and Gordon Javna. Reprinted by permission of the authors.

❧ THANK YOU ❧

The Bathroom Readers' Institute sincerely thanks the people whose advice and assistance made this book possible.

John Javna
Gordon Javna
Bob Shannon
Stuart Moore
Rachel Blau
Andrea Sohn
Gordon Van Gelder
Co-op Type
Byron Brown
Donna McCrohan
Max Allan Collins
Eric Lefcowitz
Cynthia Robins
Peter Handel
Penelope Houston
Gene Sculatti
Michael Dregni
David Goines
Dr. Lisa Berlin
Jeff Abrahams

Steve Gorlick
Leslie Boies
Jack Mingo
Franz Ross
Sam Javna
Charlie Weimer
Stephen Louis
Carla Small
Lorrie Bodger
Gideon Javna
Dayna Macy
Reddy Kilowatt
Gene Novogrodsky
Bob Migdal
Betsy Joyce
Greg Small
Adrienne Levine
Jay Nitschke
Mike Goldfinger
Doug Burnet

INTRODUCTION

There are two kinds of people in the world—people who read in the bathroom, and people who don't.

People who *do*, share a few of the subtler joys and frustrations of life—e.g., the joy of discovering a really interesting article in the latest issue of a favorite magazine as you head to the head, or the frustration of trying to find something suitable to read…at the last minute. This isn't something we talk about, but it's understood.

People who *don't* read in the bathroom haven't got a clue about why people who do, do. This book isn't for them.

Uncle John's Bathroom Reader is the first book especially for people who love to read in the bathroom. It was conceived in 1987, when a group of socially active citizens in Berkeley, California realized that the publishing industry had plenty of books for every room of the house (bedside readers, cookbooks, coffee-table books, etc.) *except* the bathroom—where up to 60% of Americans read. It was clearly time for bathroom readers to come out of the water closet and "Say it loud, I read in there and I'm proud!"

Consequently, they formed The Bathroom Readers' Institute to fight for the rights of bathroom readers everywhere.

Under their sensitive guidance, *The Reader* has been specially designed with the needs of bathroom readers in mind: It's full of brief but interesting articles that can be read in a few seconds, or a few minutes. It covers a variety of subjects (so a reader never has to settle for the "same old thing"). And it's arranged so a reader can just flip it open to any page; no planning, no searching. We hope you enjoy it. As we say at the Bathroom Readers' Institute: "Go With the Flow."

CONTENTS

NOTE:
Because the B.R.I. understands your reading needs, we've
divided the contents by length as well as subject.

Short—a quick read
Medium—1 to 3 pages
Long—for those extended visits when something
a little more involved is required.

OUR ANTHEM

Ever have people banging on the bathroom door, telling you to "hurry up and get out of there"? Then you'll be glad to know your response has already been immortalized in a classic soul tune. From Behind the Hits, *by Bob Shannon.*

In the '60s, Memphis' Stax Records had the most talented lineup of studio musicians and singers in the south. There was Otis Redding, Rufus Thomas, Booker T. and the M.G.'s, Carla Thomas, Eddie Floyd, and Sam and Dave.

Sam Moore and Dave Prater joined the Stax family in 1965. They were assigned to the writing/production team of Dave Porter and Isaac Hayes, and the partnership clicked big, producing a string of near-perfect Soul masterpieces. First to hit the charts was "You Don't Know Like I Know"; and their first big hit was "Soul Man." In between was a song that almost made the pop Top 20—a record that would have been a much bigger hit if it hadn't been for radio censorship.

White Top 40 stations were just getting used to playing black Soul records in 1966 when "Hold On, I'm Comin'" was released. Because of its suggestive title, many radio stations refused to air it at all. And those that did often made the situation worse as deejays drooled over the sexual implications of the song. In reality, the lyrics were simply about one lover giving the other support "when times are bad." "Coming" just meant "coming to the rescue." Sam and Dave's macho, boastful delivery and sly laughs throughout the song didn't help their case, although they helped to make it a great record. Stax changed the title to "Hold On, I'm A-Comin'" to placate the FCC, but the damage was already done.

If only the radio jocks had known the true story of its conception! You see, Hayes and Porter were in the studio, writing some songs. Porter left for a minute, and when he didn't come back, an impatient Hayes went looking for him. His room-to-room search finally ended up at—you guessed it—the men's room door. Porter was taking his time in there, and Hayes yelled at him to hurry up. Porter's irritated reply: "Hey man, hold on. I'm comin'." And a song was born.

The most valuable bathtub in the world is valued at $5 million. It is solid gold.

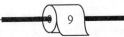

BATHROOM LORE

It seems appropriate to begin this volume with a little background on the room you're probably sitting in right now.

THE FIRST BATHROOM

The idea of a separate room for the disposal of "bodily waste" goes back at least 10,000 years (8,000 B.C.). On Orkney, an island off the coast of Scotland, the inhabitants combined stone huts with a drainage system that carried the waste directly into a nearby stream.

THE FIRST SOPHISTICATED PLUMBING

• Bathtubs dating back to 2000 B.C. have been found on the island of Crete (where there's also evidence of the first flush toilet). Considering they were built almost 4,000 years ago, the similarity to modern baths is startling.
• Around 1500 B.C., elite Egyptians had hot and cold running water; it came into their homes through a system of copper tubing or pipes.

THE FIRST SOCIAL BATHING

The ancient Romans took their bathing seriously, building public facilities wherever they settled—including London. The more elaborate of these included massage salons, food and wine, gardens, exercise rooms, and in at least one case, a public library. Co-ed bathing was not uncommon, nor frowned upon.

BACK TO FILTH

• As Christianity became increasingly powerful, techniques of plumbing and waste disposal—and cleanliness in general—were forgotten; only in monasteries was this knowledge preserved.
• For hundreds of years people in Europe basically stopped washing their bodies, in large part because nudity—even for reasons of health or hygiene—was regarded as sinful by the Church.

The first shopping center was built in Baltimore, MD, in 1896.

- In some cases a reverence for dirt arose in its place. St. Francis of Assisi, for example, believed "dirtiness was an insignia of holiness."
- Upper-class citizens tried to cover up the inevitable body odors with clothes and perfume, but the rest of the population suffered with the rank smells of filth.

CHAMBER POTS AND STREET ETIQUETTE
- Until the early 1800s, Europeans relieved themselves in chamber pots, outhouses, streets, alleys, and anywhere else they happened to feel like it.
- It was so common to relieve oneself in public that people were concerned about how to behave if they noticed acquaintances "urinating or defecating" on the street. Proper etiquette: Act like you don't see them.
- Chamber pots were used at night, or when it was too cold to go outside. Their contents were supposed to be picked up once a day by a "waste man," who carted the community's leavings to a public cesspool.
- But frequently, the chamber pot was surreptitiously dumped at night, which made it dangerous to go strolling in the evening.

DISEASE AND CHANGE
The lack of bathing took an enormous toll on the European population of the Middle Ages, as epidemics caused by unsanitary living conditions became matter-of-fact. But in the 1830s, a London outbreak of Cholera—a disease the English believed could only be contracted by inferior races—finally convinced the English government to put its power behind public sanitation. Over the next 50 years, the British constructed major new public facilities that set the pace for the rest of the world.

THE MODERN FLUSH TOILET
The modern flush toilet was invented by an Englishman named Alexander Cumming in 1775. Cumming's toilet emptied directly into a pipe which then carried the undesirable matter to a cesspool. Other toilets had done this, too; but Cumming's major improvement was the addition of a "stink trap" that kept water in the pipe, and thus blocked odor.

THOMAS CRAPPER
It is widely believed that an Englishman named Thomas Crapper invented the toilet. Not true. That was a hoax.

HEAD FOR THE JOHN
• In the mid-1500s in England, a chamber pot was referred to as a *Jake*. A hundred years later, it became a *John*, or *Cousin John*. In the mid-1800s, it was also dubbed a *Joe*.
• That still may not be the source of the term *John* for the bathroom—it may date to the 1920s, when Men's and Ladies' rooms became common in public places. They were also referred to as *Johns* and *Janes*—presumably after John and Jane Doe.
• The term *potty* comes from the pint-sized chamber pot built for kids.

BATHROOMS
• The bathroom we know—with a combination toilet and bath—didn't exist until the 1850s. And then only for the rich.
• Until then, the term bathroom—which came into use in the 1820s or 1830s—meant, literally, a room with a bathtub in it.

A FEW AMERICAN FIRSTS
• First American hotel with indoor modern bathrooms: The Tremont House in Boston, 1880s.
• First toilet in the White House: 1825, installed for John Quincy Adams (leading to a new slang term for toilet—a *quincy*).
• First city with modern waterworks: Philadelphia, 1820.
• First city with a modern sewage system: Boston, 1823.

THE FIRST TOILET PAPER
• Toilet paper was introduced in America in 1857, as a package of loose sheets. But it was too much like the paper Americans already used—the Sears catalog. It flopped.
• In 1879, an Englishman named Walter Alcock created the first perforated rolls of toilet paper. He couldn't sell them.
• In 1880, things got rolling. Philadelphia's Scott Brothers saw the potential for a product that would constantly have to be replaced and introduced Waldorf Tissue (later ScotTissue), which was discreetly sold in plain brown wrappers. The timing was right—there were enough bathrooms to make them a success.

Every day, people around the world drink more than 300 million Cokes.

PRIME TIME PROVERBS

TV's comments about everyday life in America. From Prime Time Proverbs, *a forthcoming book by Jack Mingo.*

ON FOOD:
"Why am I bothering to eat this chocolate? I might as well apply it directly to my thighs."
—Rhoda Morgenstern,
Mary Tyler Moore Show

Gracie: "The reason I put the salt in the pepper shaker and the pepper in the salt shaker is that people are always getting them mixed up. Now when they get mixed up, they'll be right.."
—*Burns and Allen*

"Six years, and you haven't learned *anything*—it's *white wine* with Hershey Bars."
—Harvey Barnes,
Making the Grade

ON THE BATTLE OF THE SEXES:
"Early to bed, early to rise, and your girl goes out with other guys."
—Bob Collins,
Love That Bob

"Carmine and I have an understanding. I'm allowed to

date other men, and he's allowed to date ugly women."
—Shirley Feeney,
Laverne and Shirley

ON MARRIED LIFE:
Edith: "Do you like bein' alone with me?"
Archie: "Certainly I like being alone with you. What's on television?"
—*All in the Family*

ON MONEY:
"There are two things [I won't do for money]. I won't kill for it and I won't marry for it. Other than that, I'm open to about anything."
—Jim Rockford,
The Rockford Files

CURRENT EVENTS:
"What's this I hear about making Puerto Rico a steak? The next thing they'll be wanting is a salad, and then a baked potato."
—Emily Litella
(Gilda Radner)
Saturday Night Live

THE FABULOUS '60S

Odds and ends about America's favorite decade, from 60s!, by John and Gordon Javna.

CUT 'EM SOME SLACKS. It wasn't considered "lady-like" to wear pants in the '60s. In 1968, for example, *Women's Wear Daily* polled several employers about it. Some of the comments: Macy's, New York: "We don't allow it"; First National Bank of Boston: "We would allow our women employees to wear pants if they continue to act like women"; Citizens and Southern National Bank, Atlanta: "We would not want to be among the first...."

OFF WITH HER PANTS. In 1969 Judy Carne, a star of "Laugh-In," visited the posh "21" Club wearing a "tunic-topped pants suit." When the management refused to let her in because of its policy against women in pants, she took off her pants, checked them in the checkroom, and sailed off into the dining room wearing only her tunic—barely long enough to be called a micro-mini-skirt. The club changed its policy on pants the next day.

WHICH DOPE? Spiro Agnew's daughter was suspended from school while they investigated her for smoking dope.

FAST FOOD: A few '60s fast-food flops you never ate at: Johnny Carson's "Here's Johnny's!" restaurants; Mahalia Jackson's Glori-Fried Chicken; Mickey Mantle's Southern Cooking; Tony Bennett Spaghetti House; Alice's Restaurants.

TV OR NOT TV? In 1967, a lady went on "Let's Make a Deal" dressed as a little girl holding a baby bottle. Monty Hall took away her baby bottle and said, "All right, for two hundred dollars, show me another nipple."

WHY WE DON'T OWN THE MOON: The U.S. waived any claim to the moon by signing the Treaty on Exploration and Use of Outer Space in 1967. This established the lunar surface as the property of all mankind.

One slice to go: America's first pizzeria opened in New York City in 1895.

FAMOUS
FOR 15 MINUTES

Andy Warhol was prophetic when he said, "In the future, everyone will be famous for 15 minutes." Here are a few examples of what we have to look forward to.

THE STAR: Annabella Battistella, a.k.a Fanne Foxe, "The Argentine Firecracker," voluptuous Latin "exotic dancer."

THE HEADLINE: "Stripper sinks political career."

WHAT HAPPENED: Late one night in October 1972, a suspicious Washington, D.C. cop pulled over an erratically moving vehicle. The inebriated driver turned out to be Congressman Wilbur Mills of Arkansas, a 36-year veteran of the House and chairman of its powerful Ways and Means Committee. In the car with him were his next-door neighbor, 38-year-old Annabella Battistella (a stripper known on stage as Fanne Foxe), and some friends—all headed home after a night of carousing. At some point during the confrontation—no one is sure exactly why—Annabella suddenly ran screaming from the car and jumped or slipped into the Tidal Basin, a shallow section of the Potomac river. The event became front page news, and it was revealed that the staid Mills—happily married for 40 years—had been having an affair with Fanne.

Shock waves rippled through Washington, but Fanne cashed in immediately, booking a tour of East Coast strip joints as "the Washington Tidal Basin Girl" ("You've read about her, now see her in person!"). She claimed to be making $3,000 a week, and that a "big toy company" was planning a Fanne doll. She even got the Harvard Republican Club's "Newcomer of the Year" award.

THE AFTERMATH: Mills' career was jeopardized, but it seemed as though he'd pull through—until two months later, when he suddenly appeared onstage in a seedy Boston strip joint, and gave Fanne a kiss. That was it. "I'm a sick man," he told colleagues when they challenged his authority. Mills was hospitalized, and Fanne continued to take it off, but faded into obscurity.

Walter Cavanaugh, "Mr. Plastic Fantastic," has 1,196 different valid credit cards.

THE STAR: Scott Halprin, a San Francisco teenager.

THE HEADLINE: "Rock Star for a Night: Kid From Audience Steps Forward."

WHAT HAPPENED: In 1973 the Who were in San Francisco playing the first show of what was to be a major U.S. tour. As the opening bars of "Won't Get Fooled Again" burst from the massive sound system at the Cow Palace, the group's unpredictable drummer, Keith Moon, suddenly slumped over, totally out of it, unable to hit another cymbal. Moon was escorted offstage and returned shortly after, seemingly revived. But a few minutes later, he collapsed again, this time completely unable to continue.

In a bizarre fantasy-come-true, the Who's leader, Pete Townsend, went to the edge of the stage and asked for volunteers. A 19-year-old named Scott Halprin bounded forward...and soon he found himself playing "Magic Bus" and "My Generation." "It happened really quick," said Halprin later. "I didn't have time to think about it and get nervous. I really admired their stamina...I only played three numbers and I was dead."

THE AFTERMATH: Keith Moon recovered (at least for a few more years). Halprin didn't become a star, but he was the subject of a small piece in *Rolling Stone*. "That drummer," said lead singer Roger Daltry, "was really good."

THE STAR: Peg Entwistle, aspiring actress.

THE HEADLINE: "Starlet Plunges to Death in Desperate Dive."

WHAT HAPPENED: Young Peg Entwistle had been a success on the Broadway stage, and she arrived in Hollywood expecting to build a career in motion pictures. Unfortunately, it didn't work out. So in September of 1932, she decided to end it all. She did it in the grand Cecil B. DeMille style: she climbed to the top of the 50-foot-high H in the "Hollywood" sign above the city, and leaped to her death. It made national news, although it was a little too late to do her career any good.

AFTERMATH: Hollywood, "the city of broken dreams," had a new fad. Disappointed would-be movie stars continued to take their own lives by jumping off the sign.

The biggest recorded bubble ever blown with bubble gum was 22 inches in diameter.

THE STAR: Sacheen Littlefeather, a Native American political activist, and an Oscar stand-in for Marlon Brando.

THE HEADLINE: "Brando Refuses Oscar, Sends Surrogate in Protest Over Indian Rights."

WHAT HAPPENED: In 1972, Marlon Brando was nominated for a Best Actor Oscar for his role in *The Godfather*. Brando was becoming increasingly politicized and at the time, the plight of the American Indians was his primary interest. So he arranged to have a young activist named Sacheen Littlefeather accept the award (if he won) in his place, handing her a three-page speech to read. When the time came, dressed in full Indian regalia, Ms. Littlefeather shocked the audience and TV network—and Roger Moore, the man trying to present it—by refusing the award for Brando and reading a short speech (the Academy refused to allow the long one) which decried the treatment of the Indian in Hollywood films.

AFTERMATH: Littlefeather had regularly played bit parts in films herself, but after the incident found herself blacklisted for several years. She was also harassed by both the FBI and unknown individuals. She is still an activist, but feels bitter about the experience.

THE STAR: Eddie Gaedel, a 3' 7" midget.

THE HEADLINE: "Small Man in Big Leagues: A Veeck Stunt."

WHAT HAPPENED: It was a Sunday doubleheader with the Detroit Tigers on August 19, 1951, and the St. Louis Browns were celebrating the 50th anniversary of the American League. Between games, Brown owner Bill Veeck wheeled a huge cake out onto the field, and out popped Eddie Gaedel, wearing a Browns uniform with the number 1/8 on it. During the first inning of the next game, Gaedel popped out of the dugout and informed the umpire he was pinch hitting. Challenged, Veeck produced a valid contract. Pitching is difficult as it is, but a 3'7" person has a strike zone of about 18 inches. Gaedel walked on four straight pitches. He then left for a pinch-runner.

AFTERMATH: Gaedel made a quick 100 bucks for his appearance, and American League president Will Harridge issued a solemn declaration barring midgets from baseball, and warning Veeck not to try any similar stunts.

Life span: The oldest known goldfish lived to 41 years of age. Its name was Fred.

WORDPLAY

Here are the origins of a few common phrases.

FALL GUY

Meaning: Someone who takes the blame.

Background: The first people to "fall" were Adam and Eve, who fell from grace and were booted out of Eden. In England, this gave rise to the term "take a fall," meaning "to be arrested," often in conjunction with taking the rap for someone else. Someone who took a fall was known as a "fall guy."

BETWEEN A ROCK AND A HARD PLACE

Meaning: In trouble, stuck with two undesirable choices.

Background: This is an updated version of an expression dating back to the Ancient Greeks, "between Scylla and Charybdis." The former was a large rock that endangered seamen in the Straits of Messina, the latter was a potentially fatal whirlpool on the opposite side. Sailors tried to avoid sailing between them. It is speculated that Charybdis is known as "a hard place" partly because it's so hard to pronounce.

KEEP YOUR SHIRT ON

Meaning: Stay calm.

Background: Probably from the age-old response to a challenge to fight. You rip your shirt off to fight, and you keep it on if you're avoiding one.

SWAN SONG

Meaning: A final, best performance.

Background: Though in actuality swans don't make many sounds, in legends the bird was believed to give a final, wonderful song just before it died.

STOOL PIGEON

Meaning: An informer, a traitor.

Background: To catch passenger pigeons (now extinct), hunters would nail a pigeon to a stool. Its alarmed cries would attract other birds, and the hunters would shoot them by the thousand. The poor creature that played the traitor was a "stool pigeon."

Weighty stuff: The heaviest dog on record was a St. Bernard that weighed 310 pounds.

THE TWILIGHT ZONE

*Picture, if you will, a 5-foot, 5-inch ex-boxer who produced,
created, and often wrote what may be the
best television program in history.
From Cult TV, by John Javna.*

You're traveling through another dimension, a dimension not only of sight and sound, but of mind; a journey into a wondrous land whose boundaries are that of the imagination. That's the signpost up ahead! Your next stop...the Twilight Zone!"

HOW IT STARTED
In the mid-'50s, Rod Serling was an award-winning writer for the celebrated TV anthology series, "Playhouse 90." However, he became frustrated with the inane changes sponsors insisted on making to his scripts. One sponsor (an auto maker) demanded that the Chrysler building be painted out of a scene. Another (a tobacco company) deleted the word "lucky" from a script because Lucky Strikes weren't their brand. And when an insurance company refused to allow a central character to commit suicide, Serling quit. People were shocked that the outspoken playwright left a cushy job at one of TV's most prestigious programs to write and produce his own "fantasy" show. But Serling knew exactly what he was doing. By operating under the cover of fantasy, Serling could get his message across without getting it censored.

In 1957, he reworked a script that had aired years before on a local Cincinnati station, and presented it to CBS as the "Twilight Zone" pilot. CBS wasn't interested, but Desilu Productions aired it as an episode of "Desilu Playhouse." It generated more viewer response than any other show that season, and CBS decided to take another look. They requested a second script from Serling ("The Happy Place"), which was deemed too depressing. So he wrote a third, this time keeping the concept simple and straightforward. In February, 1959, "Where Is Everybody" was accepted by CBS as a pilot; in March, Gener-

According to *Guinness,* an Arkansas boy grew a 260-lb. watermelon in 1985.

al Foods bought it; and on October 2, 1959, living rooms across America entered "The Twilight Zone."

INSIDE FACTS

The Amazing Serling: In real life, Rod Serling was a nervous wreck in front of the camera. It was his idea to introduce and close the episodes himself, but he remained an uneasy, sweating mess right through the last show. "Only my laundress really knows how frightened I am," he said of his appearances.

He was incredibly productive. He worked 18-hour days, and could turn out a completed "Twilight Zone" script in around 35 hours—much of it dictated into a tape recorder while he sat by the swimming pool of his L.A. home. In the first season, he wrote a phenomenal 80% of the scripts; by the fifth season, he was still producing about 50% of them.

Sadly, Serling died during open heart surgery in 1975. He was 50 years old.

Calling All Writers. One of Serling's biggest complaints about network procedure was that new talent was constantly being smothered by the system. So he invited amateur writers to send in their manuscripts if they thought they were good enough. It was an interesting lesson—he received 14,000 scripts in five days. Of the 500 that Serling and his staff got around to reading, only two of those were of "professional quality." Did he use those two? He couldn't—they "didn't fit the show."

Name Game. Fans think that Rod Serling invented the term "Twilight Zone." So did Serling. He'd never heard anyone use it before, so he assumed he'd created it. He was in for a surprise: after the show debuted, he was informed that Air Force pilots used the phrase to describe "a moment when a plane is coming down on approach and it cannot see the horizon."

Belated Thanks. Although it was considered a "prestige" show, "The Twilight Zone" never had good enough ratings to excite advertisers. Sometimes, in fact, sponsors didn't even understand what the show was about. In the first season, one of the sponsors called up CBS every Monday to demand an explanation of Friday's show. "And then," said Serling, "he demanded an explanation of the explanation."

According to one survey, 2/3 of the men in America believe in love at first sight.

THE WRONG IDEA

Some words try their best to mislead you.

French Fries actually came from Belgium, not France.

Fairy tales are seldom about fairies.

One horsepower represents the amount of power it takes to move 550 pounds one foot in one second. Actually, it would take one-and-a-half horses to pull off this feat.

Your **funny bone** is a nerve, not a bone.

Fabric softeners grease and lubricate the fibers of material to make it feel soft—they do not actually soften them.

Great Danes hail from Germany, not Denmark.

Brazil nuts are seeds, not nuts (but they do come from Brazil).

Shooting stars are meteors, not exploding stars.

Hardwood comes from deciduous trees. **Softwood** comes from evergreen trees.

But the terms "hard' and "soft" have nothing to do with how tough or weak the wood really is. Balsa wood, for example—which you can practically cut with fingernails—is technically a hardwood.

Your **backbone** is actually thirty-three different bones.

Rice Paper has absolutely no rice in it.

Moth-holes in sweaters are created by larvae before they become grown-up moths.

Mountain Goats do live in the hills, but they aren't goats—they're small antelopes.

Coconuts are really giant seeds, not nuts.

10-gallon hats are for oversize heads, but they only hold about a gallon of liquid.

Electric eels are capable of producing a whopping 650 volts—but they aren't eels.

Around 3/4 of all Americans say they are content with their lives.

BRAINTEASERS

*We've included a few simple logic problems in the book.
For obvious reasons, they don't require heavy math
or pencil and paper. Answers are on p. 223.*

My Uncle Gordon is quite absent-minded. One day I
ran into him on the street. He was mumbling to himself, and seemed quite perplexed.

"What's the matter, Uncle Gordon?" I asked.

"Hmm? Oh, it's you, nephew. I was just trying to figure out
what day today is."

"Well that's easy enough," I replied, a little relieved that it
wasn't anything serious. "Today is—"

Uncle Gordon cut me off.

"Now, I now that the day before the day after tomorrow will
be Saturday. And the day after the day before yesterday was
Thursday. But what is today?"

Can you help him?

Uncle Gordon and I were sitting on a park bench together. I
was reading a book, and Gordon was reading the newspaper.

"Well, well," he mused. "Here's a little poem I don't understand" And he recited it:

"A box without hinges, key or lid.
Yet golden treasure inside is hid."

"It's a riddle," I explained.

"But what's the answer?" he demanded.

Do you know?

Uncle Gordon was puzzled by a math problem: "If one car
starts from New York at 11 A.M. and travels 55 m.p.h, and another car starts from Boston at 1.P.M. and travels 60 m.p.h.,
which car will be nearer New York when they meet?"

"But Uncle Gordon, " I chided him, "That's easy."

You know the answer, of course.

The first beer can was used by Kreuger Beer, and introduced in 1935.

A FOOD IS BORN

*These foods are common, so you've probably never even
wondered where they came from. Here
are the answers anyway.*

BAGELS. According to *The Bagels' Bagel Book:* "In
1683 in Vienna, Austria, a local Jewish baker wanted to
thank the King of Poland for protecting his countrymen
from Turkish invaders. He made a special hard roll in the
shape of a riding stirrup—'Beugel' in Austrian—
commemorating the king's favorite pastime, and giving the bagel its distinctive shape."

MAYONNAISE. Originally brought to France by Duke Ri-
chelieu, who tasted it while visiting Mahon, a city on the island
of Minorca. It was eventually dubbed Mahonaisse by French
chefs, and considered a delicacy in Europe. In America, it became known as mayonnaise, but for over a century was still regarded as suitable for only the most elegant meals. Finally, in
1912, Richard Hellman, a German immigrant, began packing it
and selling it in jars from his New York deli. This trans-
formed mayonnaise from a carefully-prepared treat for the
select few, to a mass-merchandised condiment.

GATORADE. According to *60s!*, by John and Gordon Javna:
"In 1965, Dr. Robert Cade was studying the effects of heat ex-
haustion on football players at the University of Florida
(whose team name is the Gators). He analyzed the body liq-
uids lost in sweating and within three minutes came up with the
formula for Gatorade. Two years later, Cade sold the formula
to Stokely-Van Camp. Soon, annual sales were well over $50
million and Gatorade could be found on the training tables of
over three hundred college sports teams, a thousand high
school squads, and all but two pro football teams."

7-UP. According to *Parade* magazine: "In October 1929, just
before the stock market crash, St. Louis businessman Charles
L. Grigg began marketing a beverage called Bib-Label Lithi-

The TV dinner was introduced in 1954.

ated Lemon-Lime Soda. His slogan: 'Takes the "Ouch" out of grouch.' The drink was a huge success during the Depression, perhaps because it contained lithium, a powerful drug now prescribed for manic-depressives....The drink's unwieldy name was later changed to 7-UP. The '7' stood for its 7-ounce bottle, the 'UP' for 'bottoms up,' or for the bubbles rising from its heavy carbonation, which was later reduced. The lithium was listed on the label until the mid-'40s."

CHEWING GUM. American Indians chewed resin from freshly cut spruce bark, and colonial settlers occasionally chewed "a limp paraffin," but it wasn't until the late 1860s that chewing gum become a commercial success. A Staten Island inventor named Thomas Adams noticed that his visiting neighbor from Mexico—the deposed dictator Santa Ana— "seemed to enjoy chewing...lumps of gum from the sapodilla plant, now known as chicle"....Adams decided chicle was better than paraffin, and went to market with "Adams New York Gum—Snapping and Stretching." Later, he tried adding flavors and found that licorice tasted best. Still later, he invented a "gum-making machine" that made mass production possible.

POPSICLES. Eleven-year-old Frank Epperson accidentally left a mixture of powdered soda mix and water on his back porch one winter night in 1905. The next morning, Frank found the stuff frozen, with the stirring stick standing straight up in the jar. He pulled it out, and had the first "Epperson icicle"— or "Epsicle." He later renamed it "Popsicle," since he'd made it with soda pop. It was patented in 1923, eighteen years later.

THE ICE CREAM CONE. It happened at the 1904 World's Fair in Saint Louis (where the hot dog and the hamburger were also popularized). An ice cream vendor who was selling cups of the frozen dessert had so many customers in the hot weather that he ran out of cups. In desperation, he looked around to see if another nearby vendor might have some spare containers, but all he could find was a waffle concession. He quickly bought some waffles and began selling them wrapped around a scoop of ice cream. The substitute became even more popular than the original, and it spread around the country.

Patty Hearst's prison T-shirt: "Being kidnapped is always having to say you're sorry."

7 COOL FLICKS

7 unsung cool films recommended by Gene Sculatti, author of The Catalog of Cool.

CAGED MEN (1973). Wrestling great Abdullah the Butcher and his (real life) midget manager make screen debuts, playing desperate lifers trying to grow pot in a jail greenhouse. Hammerlocks and hopheads.

CHE! (1969). Unwatchable, even within its genre (bogus "revolutionary" films of the late sixties), but singularly brilliant for its perverse casting: Jack Palance as Fidel Castro. Arriba!

DECOY FOR TERROR (1970). Beatnik artist murders his models ("They always *move!*") by freezing them. Cool climax: a power outage causes one, frozen posed with a bow and arrow, to release the arrow, killing artist who's just finished his masterpiece. Neil Sedaka sings "Do the Waterbug" (Do the Cow/If you want to right now...").

HIT LADY (1964). Women's lib comes knocking in sharp threads: Yvette Mimeux as a bikini-clad mob assassin. Groovy.

KITTEN WITH A WHIP (1964). Ann-Margaret, as a delinquent-on-the-run, holes up with Senator John Forsythe and threatens to cry rape if he chucks her.

R.P.M. (1970). The only thing that could beat Ann-Margaret playing a campus radical is Anthony Quinn as a left-leaning, motorcycle-riding professor named Taco. R.P.M. offers both.

THUNDER ROAD (1958). Flickdom's granddaddy of cool, bad Bob Mitchum in a barbiturate-soaked performance....When some creep tries running moonshiner Mitch off the road, Mr. Heavylids cooly removes the old cig from his lip and flicks it across his car, out the window, and into the creep's car. It lands on his lap and he drives screaming to his death over an embankment. Mitchum never changes his expression.

In 1987, a 1,400-year-old lump of still-edible cheese was unearthed in Ireland.

TOY ORIGINS

You've loved them. You've played with them.
You've probably lost parts to them.
Now, here's where they came from.

SCRABBLE. Created in 1931 by an out-of-work architect named Alfred Botts. He hoped he could support his family by inventing a successful word game, but before the game was refined, he had his job back. That was just as well; when he finally showed his hand-made "Criss-Cross" to toy companies, they insisted it had no potential—it was too intellectual.

In 1948, Botts and a friend went into business manufacturing the game—now called Scrabble—in an old schoolhouse. It was an unsophisticated cottage industry that enabled the friend to barely eke out a living. But in the summer of 1952, for no apparent reason, Scrabble suddenly became a fad. In two years, the partners went from selling less than ten thousand games a year to selling more than four million. To meet the growing demand, the rights were sold to Selchow-Righter, and thirty years later, Scrabble ranks as the second-best selling game in history.

LINCOLN LOGS. In 1916, Frank Lloyd Wright went to Tokyo to supervise construction of the Imperial Palace Hotel, a magnificent building, assembled with an inner frame of wood so it would withstand earthquakes better. Wright brought his son John with him, and as John watched workers move the huge timbers required for the structure, he came up with an idea for a wooden construction toy. When he returned to America, John created Lincoln Logs.

SILLY PUTTY. In 1945, an engineer at a General Electric laboratory in New Haven, Connecticut, was assigned the task of trying to create synthetic rubber. One day he combined boric acid with silicone oil. The result: a bizarre substance with a variety of fascinating properties (it bounced, stretched, and could be broken with a hammer), but no practical use. It became a New Haven conversation piece.

#1 Dead entertainer: In 1988, Elvis earned an estimated $15 million.

Several years later, a marketing man named Peter Hodgson saw a group of adults playing with the stuff at a cocktail party. Hodgson was putting together a mail order catalog for a toy store at the time, and decided to include this "nutty putty" in it. The response was amazing. Even without a photo, the "putty" outsold everything in the catalog except crayons. Hodgson knew he had a winner—so he bought $147-worth of putty from G.E., and packaged it in little plastic eggs. In the first five years, over 32 million containers of the stuff were sold worldwide.

RUBIK'S CUBE. Devised by Hungarian mathematician Erno Rubik in 1974 as an aid for teaching math concepts to his students. Rubik realized the puzzle's possibilities as a toy, and ended up selling two million of the cubes in Hungary alone—a total of one cube for every five Hungarians. In 1980, the Ideal Toy Corporation bought the rights, and the puzzle became a world-wide craze. Rubik reportedly became "the first self-made millionaire in a Communist country."

SLINKY. Richard James, a marine engineer, was trying to invent a spring that could be used to offset the effects of a boat's movement on sensitive navigational instruments. One day he knocked a sample spring off a high shelf—but instead of simply falling, it uncoiled like a snake and "crawled" down to the floor. James realized he had a toy product, gave it a name, and formed the James Toy Company to manufacture it.

TINKER TOYS. Charles Pajeau, an Evanston, Illinois stoneworker, conceived of Tinker Toys in 1913 after observing some kids playing with "pencils, sticks, and empty spools of thread." He designed it in a garage in back of his house, and brought the finished toy—packed in its famous cannister—to the 1914 American Toy Fair. But the public wouldn't buy it. So Pajeau had to prove his marketing genius again; at Christmastime, he dressed some midgets in elf costumes and had them play with Tinker Toys in the windows of New York's Grand Central Station and Chicago's Marshall Field's department store. The publicity this stunt attracted made all the difference—a year later, over a million sets had been sold.

WILL ROGERS SAID...

A tiny piece of the rich legacy left by America's national humorist during the '20s and '30s.

"You can't say civilization don't advance, for in every war they kill you a new way."

"Half our life is spent trying to find something to do with the time we have rushed through life trying to save."

"Being a hero is about the shortest-lived profession on earth."

"I don't make jokes—I just watch the government and report the facts."

"Everybody is ignorant, only on different subjects."

"Everything is funny as long as it's happening to somebody else."

"The American people are generous and will forgive almost any weakness with the exception of stupidity."

"I guess the truth can hurt you worse in an election than about anything that could happen to you."

"American people like to have you repent; then they are generous."

"Income Tax has made more liars out of the American people than golf."

"Nobody wants to be called common people, especially common people."

"Lord, the money we do spend on Government and it's not one bit better than the government we got for one third the money twenty years ago."

"It must be nice to belong to some legislative body and just pick money out of the air."

"Half the people in the U.S. are living on interest paid by people who will never get the last mortgage paid."

"No man is great if he thinks he is."

"A remark generally hurts in proportion to its truth."

The first scheduled TV broadcast, in 1931, featured George Gershwin and Kate Smith.

MYTH AMERICA

You've believed these stories since you were a kid.
Most Americans have, because they were taught to us
as sacred truths. Well, sorry. Here's another look.

SAVAGES
The Myth: "Scalping" was a brutal tactic invented by the Indians to terrorize the settlers.
The Truth: Scalping was actually an old European tradition dating back hundreds of years. Dutch and English colonists were paid a "scalp bounty" by their leaders as a means of keeping the Indians scared and out of the way. Finally the Indians caught on and adopted the practice themselves. The settlers apparently forgot its origins and another falsehood about Indian cruelty was born.

MOTHER OF THE FLAG
The Myth: Betsy Ross, a Philadelphia seamstress, designed and sewed the first American flag at the behest of the Founding Fathers.
Background: This story first surfaced in 1870 when Betsy Ross's grandson told a meeting of the Pennsylvania Historical Society that his grandmother had been asked to make a flag for the new nation. The tale must have touched a nerve, because it quickly spread and soon was regarded as the truth.
The Truth: While Betsy Ross did in fact sew flags for the Pennsylvania Navy, there is no proof to back up her grandson's tale. Ironically, no one is sure who designed the flag. The best guess is that the flag's design is derived from a military banner carried during the American Revolution.

MIDNIGHT RAMBLER
The Myth: Paul Revere made a solitary, dramatic midnight ride to warn patriots in Lexington and Concord that the British were coming.
Background: Revere's effort was first glorified in Henry Wadsworth Longfellow's poem, "The Midnight Ride of Paul

---

The #1 nonfiction book of 1959: Pat Boone's *Twixt Twelve and Twenty* (advice to teens).

Revere." Longfellow may have written the ode out of guilt—his grandfather had tried to court-martial Revere during the Revolutionary War. The charge: "Unsoldierly behavior tending toward cowardice." (Revere was not convicted.)

The Truth: Paul Revere was actually one of two men who attempted the famous ride...and it was the other one, William Dawes, who made it to Concord. Revere didn't make it—he was stopped by British troops. As for Revere's patriotic motives: According to Patricia Lee Holt, in *George Washington Had No Middle Name*, "Paul Revere billed the Massachusetts State House 10 pounds 4 shillings to cover his expenses for his ride."

INDIAN MADE

The Myth: Pochahontas and Captain John Smith were in love. When her father tried to chop Smith's head off, Pochahontas put her own neck on the line and begged her father to spare her beloved.

Background: John Smith told people this had occurred.

The Truth: Smith probably made it up. He did know Pochahontas in Jamestown, but they weren't an item. All that's known about her is that "she apparently entertained the colonists by performing cartwheels in the nude."

AMERICUS THE BEAUTIFUL

The Myth: Amerigo Vespucci, a Florentine navigator, made four trips to the New World from 1497 to 1502. The newly discovered land was named America in his honor.

Background: Vespucci wrote an account of his four voyages. An Italian mapmaker was so impressed by it that he put "Americus's" name on the first known map of the New World.

The Truth: America is named after a probable fraud. Scholars doubt Vespucci really made those trips at all.

THANKSGIVING

The Myth: The Pilgrims ate a Thanksgiving feast of turkey and pumpkin pie after their first year in the New World, and we've been doing it ever since.

The Truth: Thanksgiving didn't become a national holiday until Abraham Lincoln declared it in 1863, and the Pilgrims ate neither the bird we call turkey, nor pumpkin pie.

About 1/6 of the male population in America weighs over 200 lbs.

MOVIE OF DOOM

Getting a job in a movie can be hazardous to
your health—in unexpected ways.

THE VICTIMS: More than 90 of the 220 people working on the film *The Conqueror*, including director Dick Powell, stars John Wayne, Agnes Moorhead, and Susan Hayward, and dozens of secondary players and crew members.

THE CIRCUMSTANCES

On May 19, 1953, the U.S. government tested a powerful A-bomb at Yucca Flats, Nevada. In St. George, Utah, 100 miles to the west, people were fascinated by the event. As *Macleans* magazine described it: "Some of the people went up on the hillside outside town to watch the blast, because nobody told them not to. A few hours later, grey ash began to sift over the Black Hill west of the city; it drifted across the lawns, clung to laundry on the lines, burned the skin of people in the streets....The town's citizens were merely instructed to wash the ash off their automobiles. They were urged not to worry."

A year later, the cast and crew of the film *The Conqueror*, a schlock version of the life of Genghis Khan (John Wayne was Genghis), arrived in St. George to film on location at a nearby desert. They—and the fulltime residents of St. George—were unaware that radiation levels were extraordinarily high in the area...and that, in fact, the entire perimeter may have been contaminated by fallout.

The result: Wayne and almost 100 others—about 45% of the people associated with the filming—died of cancer over the next 30 years. Residents of St. George also had an unusually high incidence of cancer.

UNANSWERED QUESTIONS

• Was the cancer caused by the cumulative, long-lasting effects of low-level radiation?
• Was the area contaminated?

The first city in history to boast a million inhabitants was London, in 1811.

• Did the government know about it, and intentionally conceal the information?

POSSIBLE CONCLUSIONS
• Government officials were as naive as the citizens of St. George, believing that it was adequate (as they told one St. George resident) to take a shower and change one's clothes when exposed to low-level radiation.

• The low-level radiation didn't cause the cancer that killed so many of the cast and crew of *The Conqueror*. Certainly, not all of them blamed atomic testing for it. (Wayne, a fervent anti-communist, never did. On the other hand, actress Jeanne Gerson, asserting she was the last of the film's stars still living, sued the government when she, too, contracted cancer at age 76.) Still, while no definite link has been (or can be) proven, the situation is highly suspicious; about 45% of the crew contracted cancer, a rate which far exceeds any reasonable statistical probability.

• The government knew it was endangering the lives of American citizens—it had essentially doomed the people working on the movie—but felt it was worth the sacrifice of a few lives to further their knowledge of nuclear power. Considerable evidence which points to this conclusion is coming to light. "Documents made public in 1979," says *Macleans*, "show a long-term pattern to confuse and mislead the public about the dangers of fallout."

For example: An official memo written in 1953—the year of the Yucca Flats test—insisted that "people have got to learn to live with the facts of life, and part of the facts of life is fallout." Another said, "We must not let anything interfere with these tests—nothing." And a subsequent study in 1963 which indicated serious health risks to people exposed to high levels of radiation was suppressed by the Atomic Energy Commission because, one official wrote, "The public would know they have not been told the truth."

So it may, in fact, be true that the U.S. government was responsible for the death of Duke Wayne. And the 1954 B-film, which he reluctantly took on, turned out to be a bomb in more ways than one.

The first heart transplant took place on December 3, 1967.

THE JAVA JIVE

*This might well be the B.R.I. membership's favorite drink.
But did you know...*

• Americans drink about 400 million cups of coffee per day—or 146 billion cups every year.

• Coffee has absolutely no nutritional value.

• Legend has it that coffee was discovered over 1,000 years ago, when an Abyssinian goatherder noticed his goats prancing on their hind legs after sampling the fruit of a wild coffee tree. He tried the raw berries himself and began dancing wildly.

• Four out of five adults in the US drink coffee. They put away an average of two cups a day, which adds up to about a third of the world's supply.

• The coffee tree is really an evergreen shrub. It grows to about 25 feet high.

• Per capita, Finns drink the most coffee in the world.

• Hot Water Politics:
Tea was the most popular drink in the Colonies until 1773, when King George III levied a tax on it. After the Boston Tea Party, coffee be-

came the drink of preference, and much of the Revolution was planned in the patriots' favorite new type of meeting place—the coffee house.

• Over 10,000 different studies have analyzed the medical effects of caffeine—and there still are no conclusive results.

• Caffeine is tasteless.

• An average cup of coffee contains 100 milligrams of caffeine; a cup of espresso has 200.

• Signs of caffeine overdose:
1) Cold Sweat
2) The Shakes
3) Heart Palpitations, plus a feeling of Impending Doom

• The symptoms of caffeine withdrawal:
1) Headaches
2) Nervousness
3) Irritability

• Researchers believe that heavy coffee drinkers use the drug to treat themselves for the most common psychiatric condition: depression.

PRESIDENTIAL AFFAIRS

Until details of John Kennedy's private life began to sur-
face, Americans believed their presidents were above
"playing around." Now we know better. Some samples:

T HOMAS JEFFERSON
The egalitarian aristocrat of Virginia who theoretically
opposed slavery, yet owned dozens of slaves, was quite
fond of one in particular—the light-skinned Sally Hemings.
Jefferson fathered five children with Hemings, four of whom
survived. The children apparently passed into the white community with little trouble, and Jefferson's will directed that after his death they be "freed." They were. One son, Madison
Heming, resembled Jefferson closely, and reportedly wrote
about his life at Monticello in 1873.

WARREN HARDING

One of America's most inept chief executives, he was so indis-
creet with his affairs that some historians speculate that his
wife retaliated by poisoning him while he was in office.

Harding carried on long liaisons with at least two different
women. One, a Mrs. Phillips, was the wife of a department
store owner in Marion, Ohio. She tried to cash in on her relationship with Harding when he was nominated for president by
the Republicans, and was probably sent to Japan with a huge
chunk of cash in exchange for maintaining her silence.

Harding's romantic poetry to her was discovered after her
death. An excerpt: "I love you more than all the world. Posses-
sion wholly imploring. Mid passion I am oftimes whirled, oftimes admire—adoring. Oh God! If fate would only give Us
privilege to love and live!"

Another of Harding's lovers, Nan Britton, wrote a book in
1927 in which she claimed to have given birth to his daughter in
1919. Her story is less documented than Mrs. Phillips's, but is
regarded by historians as probably true.

DWIGHT D. EISENHOWER

This paragon of middle-American virtue gave in to temptation
during World War II. While his wife, Mamie, followed his

According to Gallup, pepperoni is America's favorite pizza topping.

career from the states, another woman—Kay Summersby—
kept him company. Eisenhower was the head of the Allied
forces in Europe; Kay was his driver for over three years. In
her 1977 book, *Past Forgetting: My Love Affair with Dwight D.
Eisenhower*, Summersby (a former British model) details what
actually happened between the two during the war. Apparently, she and Eisenhower tried on several occasions to consum-
mate their affection for each other—but Ike was unable to
really "rise" to the moment. An unhappy marriage had apparently stripped the 5-star General of his libido and work was
the substitute he used in its place.

LYNDON BAINES JOHNSON
LBJ had no such problem; as his former press secretary,
George Reedy, commented in a Johnson biography: "[LBJ] had
the instincts of a Turkish sultan in Istanbul." One tale: In 1950
one of his many sexual partners became pregnant. According
to the woman, Madeline Brown, Johnson quietly took care of
her—both before and after the birth of a son named Steven.
For twenty-one years the two carried on, with Johnson setting
her up in an apartment for discreet get-togethers.

JOHN KENNEDY
The stories about JFK's sexual exploits are too numerous to re-
count. He chased women like a man possessed, but his family
name and connections helped keep that part of his personal
life out of the news until years after his death. Movie stars,
White House workers, "staff" members and gangsters' girl-
friends were all the subject of Kennedy's penetrating life-
style. Some reports now acknowledge that often two women
were included in the fun.

FRANKLIN ROOSEVELT
The love of FDR's life apparently wasn't Eleanor, but a woman named Lucy Mercer, Eleanor's one-time social secretary.
Their affair was discovered by Mrs. Roosevelt, who confronted
FDR with the information. He promised to end the relationship, but it is reported that Mercer was with him when he died
in 1945—almost 30 years after the relationship had begun.

Elvis collected statuettes of Joan of Arc and Venus de Milo.

BRAIN TEASERS

*These simple logic problems have appeared in
American game books in various forms for almost a
century. We confess that they're not as hard as they
first seem to be—we've stayed away from heavy
math problems and—for obvious reasons—
anything you'd need a pencil to solve.*

A man needs something specific for his house, so he goes
to a hardware store to purchase it. When he asks the
clerk the price, the clerk answers that "the price of
one is fifty cents, the price of thirty is one dollar, and the price
of one hundred forty-four is one dollar and fifty cents."
What is the man buying?

Two boys were playing on a tool shed roof when the roof collapsed with a crash. The boys fell uninjured to the floor below, but when they picked themselves up, the face of one boy
was covered with dirt and the other boy's was still clean. Instantly, the boy with the clean face ran off to wash his face,
while the one with the dirty face remained placidly behind.
Why did the boy with the clean face act as he did?

A tree has one blossom on it at the beginning of June. The
blossoms double in area every 24 hours. It takes the entire
month for the tree to be covered completely with blossoms.
On what date will the tree be half-covered?

You have one match. You enter a room that contains a wood-
burning stove, a kerosene lamp and a fireplace. Which should
you light first?

There is a town in Newfoundland, Canada called Dildo.

WORD PLAY

While you're sitting there, you might like to improve your
vocabulary a bit. Here are some
obscure words and definitions to study.

Peccadillo: A slight or trifling sin; a fault

Sesamoid: Having the shape of a sesame seed

Anserine: Gooselike, as in goose bumps on skin

Wanion: Disaster or bad luck

Joad: A migratory worker

Pettifogger: An inferior lawyer

Feverwort: A weedy herb

Squamous: Covered with scales

Cachinnate: To laugh noisily

Erubescence: Process of turning red, blushing

Histoplasmosis: A respiratory illness caused by inhaling festered bat dung

Paraselene: A mock moon appearing on a lunar halo

Yerk: To tie with a jerk

Bilbo: A finely tempered Spanish sword

Verisimilitude: Appearance of truth

Salubrious: Wholesome

Fecund: Fruitful

Epistemology: A school of philosophy that includes the study of the nature of human knowledge

Yowie: A small ewe

Parsimony: Stinginess

Holm: An island in a river

Coriaceous: Tough, leathery texture

Mullion: A vertical dividing piece between window lights or panels

Sippet: A triangular piece of toasted or french bread used to garnish a dish of hash

Infrangible: Not breakable

Sudorific: Causing perspiration

Cerulean: Sky blue

Pomology: The study of fruit

Rusticate: To send into the country

Agnomen: An added name due to some special achievement

Saponification: Process of making soap

Motet: A sacred musical composition for several voices

Lycanthropy: The power of turning a human being into a wolf by magic or witchcraft. Wolfman science.

The most common bird in the world is the starling.

GILLIGAN'S ISLAND

*Few TV shows have been both as reviled and beloved as
"Gilligan's Island"—sometimes by the same people. Two
unanswered questions remain about this program:
1) Where did they get all those clothes?
2) How did they last for three years without sex?*

HOW IT STARTED

In 1963, veteran TV writer Sherwood Schwartz ("The
Red Skelton Show", "I Married Joan") was ready to
break away from writing other people's shows and create his
own sitcom. A literate man with degrees in zoology and psy-
chology, Schwartz had an idea for a meaningful show: He'd
take representative members of American society, strand them
on an island (this was inspired by Defoe's *Robinson Crusoe*),
and their interaction would be a microcosm of life in the U.S.

How this idea turned into "Gilligan's Island" is anyone's
guess. In the end, Sherwood's castaways were more caricatures
than characters. He called them *clichés*: "The wealthy, the Hollywood glamour girl, the country girl, the professor, the misfit,
and the resourceful bull of a man." He added, "Anybody who
is watching can identify with someone." Yes, but would they
want to?

Schwartz brought his concept to CBS and United Artists; both
agreed to finance a pilot. But after the pilot was filmed, CBS
started playing with the premise. Network president Jim Au-
brey felt it should be a story about a charter boat that went
out on a new adventure every week. "How would the audience
know what those guys were doing on the island?" he wanted to
know. It looked like Schwartz's original idea was sunk. Then he
had a brainstorm—explain the premise in a theme song! He
wrote his own tune and performed it at a meeting of CBS
brass (probably a first). And on the basis of that song, CBS
ok'd the castaways. Now do we thank them or what?

INSIDE FACTS

Even "Gilligan's Island" wasn't sanitized enough for the censors!

Never mind that there wasn't a hint of sex in three years on a deserted island. CBS censors still objected to Tina Louise's low-cut dresses and Dawn Wells' exposed navel.

•Believe it or not, some viewers took the show seriously. The U.S. Coast Guard received several telegrams from concerned citizens asking why they didn't rescue the Minnow's crew.

•Schwartz picked the name "Gilligan" from out of the Los Angeles phone book.

•Schwartz originally wanted Jerry Van Dyke to play Gilligan. He turned it down in favor of the lead in a different TV series—"My Mother the Car." Another actor wanted to play the Skipper, but was rejected: Carroll "Archie Bunker" O'Connor.

EVERYONE'S A CRITIC
The public loved Gilligan, but most critics hated it. A sample:
•L.A. Times: "'Gilligan's Island' is a show that should never have reached the airwaves, this season or any other."

•S.F. Chronicle: "It is difficult to believe that this show was written, directed, and produced by adults. It marks a new low in the networks' estimation of public intelligence."

THE PILOT FILM
•It was shot in Hawaii, just a few miles from the spot where South Pacific was filmed.

•One of the major problems faced by the production crew during the pilot's filming: frogs. Inexplicably, they piled up by the hundreds outside the doors of the on-site cottages.

•Filming of the pilot was completed on November 22, 1963— the day J.F.K. was assassinated.

ABOUT THE ISLAND
•It was man-made, located in the middle of an artificial lake at CBS's Studio Center in Hollywood, and surrounded by painted landscapes, artificial palm trees, and wind machines.

•At one point, the concrete lake-bottom leaked. So it had to be completely drained, repaired, and filled again.

•It cost $75,000 to build.

Killer Ant: The black bulldog ant of Australia and Tasmania can kill a person.

CRYONICS

*At one time or another, everyone has toyed with the idea of
eternal life—or at least, of being able to put things on hold
and come back, when cures for today's terminal diseases
have been found. Enter the technology of cryonics,
the attempt to preserve human life by
storing bodies at subfreezing temperatures.*

W HAT IT IS
Theoretically, cryonics is a way of putting nature on
ice, of creating suspended animation in human be-
ings by freezing them—a notion that can be traced back to
1964, when physics professor Robert Ettinger wrote and published a book called *The Prospect of Immortality*.

At death, the body is cooled to near freezing and the blood
is removed and replaced with a synthetic solution. Then the
body is placed in a stainless steel tank filled with liquid nitrogen. The reason: when living tissue is cooled at a controlled
rate to the temperature of liquid nitrogen, all molecular and
biological activity stops. Theoretically, with its biological clock
stopped, the tissue stays viable via suspended animation.

The body is kept in the tank at subfreezing temperatures, until the anticipated day when technology makes "re-animation"
possible.

When will that be? According to a committed cryonicist: "The
technology of freezing is still very primitive, and will require
advances in thawing and resuscitation that may not be available for two centuries, if ever."

IS IT STRICTLY FOR LUNATICS?

At first a lot of scientists thought it was a money-making scam
(and many still do), a false hope for people who are unable
to accept the inevitability of their own deaths. But recently theory has given way to practice as biologists at the University of
California have been able to revive ice-cold hamsters and
dogs.

Freezing, said one of the UC scientists, "is nature's way of
saying 'time out.' It's a way of putting life on hold. For in-

---

According to *Billboard*, the #1 song of the '60s was "Theme from a Summer Place."

stance, some frogs go through the winter with 1/3-to-1/2 of their body's water turned into ice. They can go without breathing, eating or even without a heartbeat. In the spring, they thaw out and go on with their lives."

Throughout the years, the basic doctrine of cryonics has not varied: the dead are considered temporarily incurable.

WHAT IT IS NOT

Cryonics shouldn't be confused with cryobiology, a recognized branch of medical research that studies the effects of very low temperatures on living tissue. Cryobiology has enabled scientists and physicians to freeze blood, corneas, bone marrow, sperm and even human embryos for use at a future time. However, organs such as the pancreas, the kidney and the human heart (to be used in transplant surgery) have proven to be unusable if frozen (which makes the whole premise behind cryonics highly suspect).

FREEZER FACTS

• The American Cryonics Society says that its membership numbers 100 people who have committed themselves for freezing after death.

• In three cryonics centers in California and Michigan, the earthly remains of 15 people are on ice. There used to be 45, but 30 of the tanks leaked.

• Freezing doesn't come cheap. The price tag for return in the 21st century varies between $100,000 and $125,000.

• For a reduced price of $30,000 one may have his head frozen instead of his entire body. The head may or may not be grafted onto a healthy body at some future date; the guiding idea is that cloning will make other body parts easy to replicate in the future when the technology is available.

• Cryonicists do have a sense of humor. Their slogan is: "Freeze, Wait, Reanimate." The standard joke is "Many are cold, but few are frozen."

• "There's a poem we like to quote," says one cryonicist:
"I really think that I could freeze,
My mother-in-law with the greatest of ease.

The only thing that gives me pause,
Is what will happen when she thaws."

• **Whoops:** When Saul Kent's mother, Dora, died after years of suffering from arthritis and a degenerative brain disease, he hired Alcor Life Extension Foundation, a cryonics facility in Fullerton, California, to freeze her head until it could be revived and attached to a new body. There was one hitch, however: Dora Kent may not have been dead before her head was removed. Besides, the old woman may not have wanted to be turned into a human ice cube; she never signed the consent forms.

RECENT DEVELOPMENTS: Research physiologists at the University of California at Berkeley froze a three-year-old beagle named Miles and revived him.

•Miles was anaesthetized and placed on a bed of ice until his temperature fell from his normal 100.5 degrees (F) to 68 degrees.

•Next, the pooch, drained of his own blood (which was replaced with a clear, synthetic blood that wouldn't clot in the cold) was frozen.

•Legally "dead" for the hour his body spent at below 50 degrees, Miles was thawed, given back his blood and returned to perfect doggie health.

FOR NOW: While the Miles experiments may lead scientists to give ailing humans "the big chill" until cures for their diseases have been found, experiments with freezing a patient's own blood may alleviate a lot of problems right now. Surgery requires a lot of donated blood (which may or may not be contaminated); with freezing and the use of synthetic blood, a patient's own blood can be recycled.

WHAT ABOUT UNCLE WALT?
The most enticing rumor associated with cryonics is that Walt Disney had his body frozen and is planning to return some day. Is it true? In the book *Disney's World*, an associate reveals: "My information is that he *is* frozen down....[And] if he does come back, there's going to be hell to pay. He wouldn't approve of much that's gone on at the [Disney] Studios...."

Thomas Wedgwood took the world's first photograph in 1802.

FLIPPER

*The most famous aquatic animal superstar is the dolphin
who starred in her own TV series. Here's the inside scoop on
Flipper, from* Animal Superstars, *by John Javna.*

O RIGIN:
"Lassie in a wet suit," as one TV critic jokingly described "Flipper," was exactly what underwater stunt
man Ricou Browning had in mind when he created Flipper in
the early '60s.

"I was watching 'Lassie' on television with my kids one night,"
he says, "and I thought, 'Wouldn't it be great to do an animal
show similar to "Lassie" with a kid and a dolphin?'" He envisioned the story as a book, but the idea was turned down by
every publisher Browning sent it to.

So he tried movie producers instead. At the time, very little
was known about dolphins, and no one knew if they could be
trained to become film performers. But when Browning sent
his ideas to producer Ivan Tors, Tors couldn't resist the challenge. "Let's make a movie of...that story of yours," he told
Browning. The result: two films, a TV series, and the #1
aquatic superstar of all time.

ABOUT THE STAR

Species: Dolphin
- Length: seven feet
- Weight: 300 lb.
- Number of teeth: 84
- Speed: Up to 40 miles per hour
- Favorite foods: Mullets and butterfish
- Sex: Female
- Name: Mitzi was the star of two Flipper films. Suzy
  starred in the TV series—until she became too rough with
  the actors. Then Cathy replaced her.

INSIDE FACTS

- **Secrets of success:** Unlike previous dolphin trainers who
worked on dry land, everyone connected with "Flipper" inter-

acted with the animals in the water. This cut training time from six months per trick to three weeks.
• Flipper's most memorable trick—carrying a boy on her back—was really a "fetch." Browning threw his nine-year-old son in the water and ordered Flipper to retrieve him. She put her fin under his arm, and off they went.

TRICKS AND TRAINING
• **The Trainer**: Although Ivan Tors worked with the dolphins sometimes, Ricou Browning was their trainer. Browning had been a diver on "Sea Hunt," and (are you ready for this?) played the creature in *The Creature from the Black Lagoon*.
• The stars of "Flipper" could learn new tricks in one shot, as long as their human trainers were "smart enough" to communicate what they wanted.
• Each dolphin could learn the 35 basic maneuvers that the role of Flipper required in only six months.
• Essential tricks included "fetching" (Mitzi could fetch up to five things at once), towing a boat with a rope, shaking hands with her flipper, hitting the water with her tail, and letting a person hold her flipper while she swam.

STAR GOSSIP
Ivan Tors had a very special relationship with Suzy, the dolphin who played Flipper on TV—she'd saved his life.
• When Suzy was first being trained, Tors swam out into a lagoon to meet her. But she swam away, refusing to let him near her. Tors chased her until he was exhausted. Then he surfaced to get his breath—and was overwhelmed by a huge wave. As he desperately called for help, he suddenly felt Suzy's dorsal fin underneath him. He grabbed it, and she towed him to safety, winning his gratitude—and a starring role on the show.

SCREEN CREDITS
• 1963: *Flipper* (film). Co-stars: Chuck Connors, Luke Halpin.
• 1964: *Flipper's New Adventures* (film). Co-stars: Brian Kelly, Luke Halpin.
• 1964-67: "Flipper" (TV series). 88 episodes. Co-stars: Brian Kelly, Luke Halpin, Tommy Norden, Pete the Pelican, Spray the Retriever.

Elvis owned 18 TVs, including one installed on the ceiling over his bed.

PRIME TIME PROVERBS

TV comments about everyday life in America.
From Prime Time Proverbs, *by Jack Mingo.*

ON MARRIAGE:

"Son, stay clear of weddings because one of them is liable to be your own."
—**Pappy Maverick,**
Maverick

"Just because I've been married for twenty-five years is no reason to stop being sexy."
—**Ralph Kramden,**
The Honeymooners

Groucho: "Are you married, Georgette?"
Contestant: "Yes, I've been married to the same man for thirty-one years."
Groucho: "Well if he's been married for thirty-one years, he's not the same man."
—***You Bet Your Life***

ON TELEVISION:

"Well, Beaver, this may be hard for you to believe, but life isn't exactly like television."
—**Ward Cleaver,**
Leave It to Beaver

"It's just plain foolishness, squattin' all day in front of that little black box, starin' bleary-eyed at people who ain't more than two inches high. It's a passin' fancy, I tell you, like buggy whips and high button shoes."
—**Grandpa Amos McCoy**
The Real McCoys

Maggie: "It's four o'clock in the morning and you're watching a test pattern."
Dave: "I know, but I want to see how it ends."
—***My Mother the Car***

ON RACE & RELIGION:

"Jesus was a Jew, yes, but only on his mother's side."
—**Archie Bunker,**
All In the Family

"Have you always been a Negro, or are you just trying to be fashionable?"
—**Dr. Morton Chesley,**
Julia

"You keep talking about minorities. Well mister, you're a psycho, and they're a minority, too."
—**Sgt. Joe Friday,** ***Dragnet***

A dragonfly, the fastest flying insect, can move up to 35 m.p.h.

WHAT A DOLL!

Barbie is the product that toymakers dream of. She never
goes out of style...and each succeeding generation
loves to play with her. What a doll!

Children have been playing with dolls for thousands of years, but the most popular doll in the history of the world has only been in existence since 1959. It's Barbie, of course. Since Mattel's buxom fashionplate was first introduced, more than 400 million Barbie dolls have been sold. And the number is growing every day.

Some toys are just toys. But Barbie is a way of life.

From the outset, she encouraged little girls to be good consumers. "Barbie was important not for herself, but for all that could be added to her," explains Thomas Hine in *Populuxe*. "She had party dresses, and gowns for the prom, and a wedding ensemble....She had a boyfriend, Ken, a little sister, and a Corvette. There was always something new to buy for her—a more stylish outfit, a new kind of fashion, a different fantasy."

But Barbie carried other social messages besides the joys of consumerism. The joy of sex, for example. With her large breasts and hourglass figure, Barbie resembled a teenage Jayne Mansfield; she was clearly a traditional sex object. Yet you knew you'd never see Barbie stuck in anyone's kitchen, barefoot and pregnant. It's no coincidence that Barbie debuted at about the same time as The Pill. As much as any child's toy could in 1960, she represented an ideal of sexual freedom.

And how about Barbie's obsession with looks and possessions? Sure, they propagated a shallow set of values to the little girls who adored her. But they also implied independence. Prior to Barbie, every popular doll in America was a baby doll. Barbie signified a change. Girls didn't have to play "mommy" anymore. They had a new kind of role model—a career girl who could be a model, a nurse, a nightclub singer...even an astronaut. Sure, Barbie had expensive taste, but she didn't depend on her boyfriend for anything. In fact, Barbie was the boss in that relationship. It was *Barbie's* Corvette, remember— Ken just went along for the ride.

BARBIE'S ROOTS

The real Barbie (yes, there was one) was the daughter of Ruth and Eliot Handler, who founded Mattel after World War II. The idea for the teenage fashion doll came to Ruth when she noticed that Barbie preferred playing with shapely paper dolls to playing with baby dolls. The Handlers gambled that other modern girls would feel the same way. The Handlers had a son, too, named Ken.

Barbie was introduced at the New York Toy Fair in February, 1959. The first Barbie dolls cost $3—today, in mint condition, they're worth over $1,000. And the figure keeps rising.

Barbie's creators based her appearance on the prevailing standards of beauty in 1959—Brigitte Bardot, with her perky pony tail and knock-out figure, and Grace Kelly's patrician blondness.

She was originally called a three-dimensional fashion drawing. Said Ruth Handler, "Barbie was originally created to project every little girl's dream of the future," and part of that future meant being grown up. Grown up to a little girl, was having breasts. It was no accident that a lingerie line was one of the first sets of Barbie clothes available.

Collectors seem certain that the design for Barbie was lifted from a German doll named "Lilli"—which was, in turn, based on a cartoon character created for the daily newspaper *Bild-Zeitung*. Ironically, the German Lilli was not a wholesome teenager, but a winsome, sexually loose gold-digger. Maybe that explains her body.

ALL DRESSED UP...

Barbie was sold as a teenage fashion model, but her wardrobe was definitely haute couture, or as close to Parisian fashion as one could come with a doll. Whenever new costumes were planned for the doll, Mattel designer Charlotte Johnson and her staff traveled to Europe to see the collections of Dior, Jacques Fath, Balenciaga, Givenchy, Mme. Gres, Balmain and Schiaparelli. Then they adapted what they saw.

Barbie has always been on the top of pop fashion trends. In

the late'50s and early '60s, her wardrobe included white gloves and pillbox hats. By the '70s, she was the prototypical exercise nut in leotards and tights—so she'd look great in her hot pants outfits and fringed suede vests. By 1980, she was a disco singer wearing glitter togs and toting a microphone.

...AND NO PLACE TO GO
Overall, the most popular Barbie outfits are wedding gowns. But although she has all the necessary gear for a fancy wedding (and has for about 30 years), Barbie has never actually taken the plunge. She and Ken haven't even set a date.

•Mattel is the world's largest manufacturer of "women's" clothing. They produce 20 million Barbie outfits a year.

BARBIE FACTS
•In 1987, Mattel sold $450 million worth of Barbie merchandise—that's almost $1 billion on the retail level.

•Barbie's last name is Roberts.

•Barbie is a college graduate. She attended a generic educational institution called State College.

•The Barbie Fan Club has over 600,000 members worldwide.

•Not that you care, but...what would happen if you laid all the Barbie dolls that have been sold since 1959 in a line, head-to-toe? According to Mattel press releases, "that's enough dolls to circle the earth more than three-and-a-half times."

•Some Barbie features over the years: Fashion Queen Barbie had wigs in 1963; in 1966, Barbie's hair and clothes changed color "when swabbed with a special solution"; there was "a motorized stage in 1971, which, when activated, made Live Action Barbie dance"; 1980's Western Barbie winked. And the beat goes on.

BARBIE FLOPS
•Two Barbie flops: "Colored Francy," and "Kissing Barbie." "Kissing Barbie"'s lips moved, but Mattel didn't make a "Kissing Ken," so there was nobody for Barbie to pucker up with.

•In 1986, Mattel tried to introduce a Barbie clothing line for real girls from 7 to 14 years old. Their slogan: "We Girls Can Do Anything." Mattel marketed the clothes in stores like J.C. Penney and K-Mart; but it didn't work.

CUSTOMS

Where did they come from? A few random examples.

TIPPING
Some think it began in the 17th century, when restaurants had boxes labelled T.I.P.—To Insure Promptness—on the wall beside their entrances. Patrons who wanted their food in a hurry deposited a few coins in the box before they sat down.

AN APPLE FOR THE TEACHER
Now an outmoded custom, it stems from the days when public school teachers were paid with whatever the community they served could afford. Often they were given food or goods in lieu of cash.

THE TOOTH FAIRY
In Germany, where the idea apparently originated, the tooth was not placed under a pillow. Instead, it was put in a rat hole because it was thought that the new tooth growing in would take on the "dental quality" of the animal who found it.

STRIPED BARBER POLES
Barbers were once a lot more versatile than they are today. They not only cut hair, they performed surgery as well. When the barbers finished, the towels used to soak up excess blood were hung outside to dry on a pole. As the wind dried them they wrapped around the pole, making a design, so to speak, of red and white stripes.

ADVICE TO SINGLES
From the 1700s: "If you want to get married, stand on your head and chew a piece of gristle out of a beef neck and swallow it, and you will get anyone you want."

The zipper was invented in 1893, for use in shoes.

MARILYN SAID...

Marilyn Monroe was known for saying exactly what was on her mind. A fascinating collection of quotes is in Marilyn Monroe: A Never-Ending Dream, *by Guus Luijters.*

"I think femininity and beauty are ageless and can't be faked, and that true glamour—I know the manufacturers aren't going to like this—isn't a factory product. Not real glamour, in any case, which is based on femininity. Sexuality is only attractive when it's natural and spontaneous."

"Bobby Kennedy promised to marry me. What do you think of that?"

"A career is a wonderful thing, but you can't snuggle up to it on a cold night."

[*After JFK had surreptitiously slipped his hand under her dress*] "I bet he doesn't put his hand up Jacqueline's dress. I bet no one does. Is she ever stiff!"

"I've noticed that men generally leave married women alone and treat them with respect. It's too bad for married women. Men are always ready to respect someone who bores them. And if most married women, even the pretty ones, look so dull, it's because they're getting too much respect."

"My ass is way too big. They tell me men like it like that. Crazy, huh?"

"Blonde hair and breasts, that's how I got started. I couldn't act. All I had was my blonde hair and a body men liked. The reason I got ahead is that I was lucky and met the right men."

"People are always looking at me as if I were a kind of mirror instead of a person. They don't see me, they see their own hidden thoughts and then they whitewash themselves by claiming that I embody those secret thoughts."

Kotex was first manufactured as bandages, during World War I.

HOLIDAYS

*Beginning in kindergarten, we exchange cards with class-
mates and friends on Valentine's Day. Later, it's flowers
and presents for loved ones. Here's why we do it.*

VALENTINE'S DAY

This "lovers' holiday" is an anomaly. It was actually
an effort by the Catholic Church to *keep* teenagers
from becoming lovers.

Before Christ was born, it was a Roman tradition for teenage
girls and boys to gather every February in the name of the god
Lupercus, and randomly select a "mate" for a year. They were
permitted to do anything they liked together (and what else
would teenagers do?).

When Christians gained power in the Roman Empire, they
wanted to bring this practice to an end. So they selected a substitute for Lupercus (to be the focus of a parallel holiday)—
St. Valentine, a bishop who had reputedly been tortured and
executed by Emperor Claudius II in 270 A.D, for performing
marriages after Claudius had outlawed them in the Empire.
This symbol of more "wholesome" love, was reluctantly accepted by the Romans. But just to be sure no one gave in to
temptation, the Catholic Church made it a mortal sin to worship Lupercus. Eventually, Valentine's Day became a recognized holiday throughout Western Europe.

VALENTINE CARDS

If teens couldn't get together in February, what could they do?
They could send each other respectful notes of affection. And
they did, although it seems like a poor substitute. At any rate,
sending lover's greetings became a part of the Valentine's day
ritual, and when Christian influence grew, the practice of sending notes on February 14 spread with it.

The first greeting cards didn't appear until the 18th century.
Printed cards were common in Germany by the 1780s; they
were called *Freundschaftkarten*, or "friendship cards." The
first American cards were manufactured in the 1870s, at an
amazing cost of up to thirty-five dollars apiece.

If an orangutan belches at you, watch out. He's warning you to stay out of his territory.

ENQUIRING MINDS...

The National Enquirer, "America's most popular newspaper," deals in gossip coupled with oddity. Celebrity "confessions" share space with miracle cures, religious wonders (Jesus's face in a taco), advice on relationships, psychic predictions, UFO/alien kidnap tales, weight loss schemes, interesting trivia and occasionally, a legit news scoop.

VITAL STATS
Circulation: Over 4.5 million weekly
Weekly readership: 15-20 million
Founder: Generoso Pope, Jr., who died on September 25, 1988.

Earnings: Unknown, because the *Enquirer* is privately held.

Headquarters: Lantana, Florida (Pope moved the paper from New Jersey to Florida because he liked the weather.)

Staff: Largely British, Scottish and Australian—writers and editors steeped in the tradition of England's Fleet Street tabloid operations, where they essentially make the news up if it's not exciting enough.

Salaries: Staff is paid on a scale that far surpasses more traditional journalists. In 1981, it was revealed that beginning reporters made over $40,000 and editors could make as much as $80,000; presumably that salary base has risen drastically. However, story editors are paid according to how many of their staff's articles appear in print, so the competition for space in the *Enquirer* is stiff and the burn-out factor is very high. Reporters who last longer than 18 months are a rare breed.

Philosophy: To Pope's way of thinking, the *Enquirer* was not out to win prizes—it is mass entertainment, pure and simple.
In the *Enquirer*'s inner sanctum, the highest compliment Pope could pay an editor was that he had a "Hey Martha!" story—one "so astonishing and compelling" that the reader would stop mid-sentence and turn to his wife or someone nearby and say "Hey Martha, get a load of this!" The rest of the editors had to settle for "Gee-whiz" stories.

How much does an average fashion model weigh? About 120 pounds.

SCOOPS AND STORIES
Some memorable efforts by the Enquirer:

THE SCOOP: A photo of Elvis Presley in his coffin.
HOW THEY DID IT: When Elvis died on August 16, 1977, the *Enquirer* flew staff members to Memphis and set up head-quarters in a boarding house. The reporters were instructed to find a "blockbuster" scoop, something to eclipse the emerging stories about the King's drug habit. One staffer came up with the idea of a photograph of Presley in his coffin, and that was it. The night before the funeral, reporters bought a number of cameras and handed them out to "mourners" along with a liberal sprinkling of cold, hard cash.

The day after the funeral, the command center was littered with snaps of the King lying in state. The next issue of the *Enquirer* went on sale with Elvis' corpse on the cover. It quickly became the newspaper's all-time biggest (at that time) seller.

THE SCOOP: A Photo of Bing Crosby in *his* coffin.
HOW THEY DID IT: This time a reporter dressed as a priest conned his way into the private ceremony held for Bing. As he left the service with his snapshot, the priest/reporter admonished ABC reporter Geraldo Rivera not to bother the Crosby family at such a sensitive moment.

THE SCOOP: Photographs of Democratic presidential candidate Gary Hart in Bimini with Miami model Donna Rice. The photos (snapped by Rice's friend Lynn Armandt) showed Rice sitting on Hart's lap and Hart, surrounded by Rice, Armandt and a male friend, standing on the stage of a Bimini bar holding a pair of maracas.

The story details the long, romantic weekend the two spent aboard the yacht, *Monkey Business*, and quotes Rice as saying to several unnamed friends that Hart had said he loved her, and that he would divorce his long-suffering wife, Lee, *after* he was elected president.

Quotes like this one: "When Gary has a few beers, he becomes a wild and crazy guy, nothing like the straight serious man you see on TV" sank Hart's campaign for good.
HOW THEY DID IT: More than 12 editors and researchers

were involved in tracking down people who had either seen Hart and friends in Bimini or knew Donna Rice and her friend Lynn. Most of the story was drawn from what the loose-lipped Rice later told friends about the weekend. The tab for the photos came to a reputed $25,000.

THE SCOOP: The last hours of John Belushi as told by Cathy Evelyn Smith....and a confession by Smith that it was she who gave Belushi his final "speedball," the injection of cocaine and heroin that killed him.
HOW THEY DID IT: *Enquirer* reporters actually uncovered more information on Belushi's death than the Los Angeles Police Department. Then they tracked Smith down and paid her $15,000 to talk to them. The tell-all interview led police to reopen the case and further investigate her role in the incident. Eight months later, a Los Angeles grand jury indicted Smith for murder along with 13 counts of administering a dangerous drug. The evidence against Smith included the *Enquirer's* interview tapes.

THE SCOOP: Carol Burnett was seen acting "boisterous and disorderly" in a Washington, D.C. restaurant.
HOW THEY DID IT: By stretching the facts. At least, that's what Burnett said as she sued them for big bucks... and won. In a rare retraction, the *Enquirer* admitted the error of its ways, but not without a parting shot.
   The Quote: "As far as we're concerned," said an editor, "the Carol Burnett decision essentially means that Carol Burnett is now the only woman in America officially adjudicated as 'not the life of the party.'"

THE SCOOP: The Three Mile Island disaster was sabotage.
HOW THEY DID IT: According to an ex-reporter, they took a statement by a local cop that an elderly couple at a nearby motel looked a little suspicious to him...combined it with a similar statement that the radio and can opener the old couple had could conceivably be called a "dangerous weapon" and "sophisticated communications equipment," and pieced the rest of the totally misleading story together from there.

ANCIENT RIDDLES

*These old riddles—and hundreds more—have been repro-
duced in the book* Riddles—Ancient and Modern, *by Mark
Bryant, published by Peter Bedrick Books. They're more
"what am I?" than traditional riddles. Some of them are
pretty hard, but they're all very clever.
And all are authentically old.*

1. "The beginning of
eternity,
The end of time and space,
The beginning of every end,
And the end of every
place."
*Hint: It's in front of you right
now.*

2. "I never was, am always
to be,
None ever saw me, nor ever
will,
And yet I am the confidence
of all
Who live and breathe on
this terrestrial ball."
Hint: It never comes.

3. "Runs over fields and
woods all day,
Under the bed at night sits
not alone,
With long tongue hanging
out,
A-waiting for a bone."
*Hint: It's something very
close to you.*

4. "At night they come without being fetched, and by
day they are lost without being stolen."
*Hint: They belong to the
night.*

5. "Fatherless and
motherless,
Born without a skin,
Spoke when it came into the
world,
And never spoke again."
*Hint: If you had no nose,
you'd never know this one.*

6. "What gets wet when
drying?"
No hint.

7. "There was a green house.
Inside the green house there
was a white house.
Inside the white house there
was a red house.
Inside the red house there
were lots of black babies."
Hint: A fruit.

The biggest known pumpkin in history weighed almost 700 pounds.

BYPASS SURGERY

*For a change of pace, here's
some medical history.
Written by Dr. Lisa Berlin.*

Today open heart surgery is performed using a cardiopulmonary bypass pump, a mechanical device that pumps blood and performs gas exchange. It allows surgeons to enter the heart directly without risking damage to other organs through lack of blood and oxygen.

Before mechanical bypass systems were perfected, one of the pioneers in this area, Dr. Walton Lillehei, used the heart and lungs of another living person to perform these vital functions. The patients usually were young children with life-threatening congenital heart defects, and the donors were usually parents. Child and parent lay side by side on separate tables in the operating room, and tubes connected the circulatory systems of each. The tubing went from the superior and inferior vena cavae of the child, major veins draining oxygen-poor blood into the heart, to a large vein in the parent. The blood then went to the parent's heart and lungs, picked up oxygen and released carbon dioxide, and then traveled back to the infant's aorta, or major artery, through a second tube placed in the parent's aorta.

Although this technique allowed for the correction of otherwise inoperable heart defects at a relatively small risk to the child, there were some complications involving the donors. It was eventually replaced by the purely mechanical systems in use today.

TOTALLY UNRELATED NEWS REPORT
A few years ago, someone sent us this article.
Ironton, Ohio. "Church members burned records albums and cassettes, after hearing evangelist Jim Brown of Psalms 150 in South Point say the "Mr. Ed" television theme conveys a satanic message to unwary listeners.

"'A horse is a horse'—when played backwards—contains the message 'the source is Satan' and 'Someone sung this song for Satan,' Brown said."

The theme song to "Mr. Ed" was written by the composers who wrote "Que Sera, Sera."

THE POPE

*It was a tragedy that the Pope passed away. But there
was nothing anyone could have done
about it...or was there?*

THE VICTIM: Pope John Paul I, leader of the Roman Catholic Church for a scant thirty-three days.

THE CIRCUMSTANCES: On September 29, 1978, the deceased Pope was discovered in his own bed; he had apparently died during the night. The cause, according to his doctors, was a heart attack. This didn't come as a surprise, however. Vatican offcials explained that the Pope had been ailing for some time. Fourteen hours later, the Pontiff was embalmed...without an autopsy.

UNANSWERED QUESTIONS: An entire book—*In God's Name: An Investigation Into the Murder of Pope John Paul I*— has been written about them by author David Yallop. A few of the more interesting ones:
•Why would the Vatican doctors claim to know the cause of death without performing an autopsy? Why didn't they do an autopsy? And what was the hurry to get the body embalmed?
•Why did the Vatican claim they anticipated a heart attack when all available evidence indicates the opposite? Three months before his death, for example, the Pope had an EKG which indicated a healthy heart; and his blood pressure was low.
•Why was he reported to have been reading a Medieval religious text when he died, when he had actually been reading some "personal papers"? What were the papers? And why did the Vatican say the Rev. John Magee discovered the corpse when it was really a nun named Sister Vincenza? What did the Sister see?

POSSIBLE CONCLUSIONS:
•It's just another conspiracy theory with no basis in reality.
•The Pope was murdered by conservative elements within the

Einstein couldn't speak fluently when he was nine. His parents thought he might be retarded.

Church because he planned a liberalization of some important rules, particularly regarding birth control.

•He was murdered by forces connected to the Vatican Bank scandals. As it was later revealed, the Vatican Bank was mixed up in a number of shady transactions involving some equally shady characters at that time—including Michael Sindona, a banker whose Mafia connections were exposed after the Franklin National Bank (which he owned) failed.

Sindona was later convicted of hiring hit men to kill an official of the Italian government who was investigating him. Why wouldn't he repeat the approach if the Pope had decided to expose him? Sindona, by the way, died of poisoning in jail.

There were several other questionable characters dealing with the Vatican Bank. Any of them or their associates might have assassinated the Pope if they felt sufficiently threatened. But as one author points out, we'll probably never know what really happened.

DEATH BY WATER BED
Reported by The Realist *in the '60s.*
"Malcolm Coors, a University of Arizona grad student in economics, became the first fatality of the waterbed fad. He had been watching a late-night talk show on his tiny Sony television, which had frayed electrical connecting wires. The set fell into a puddle—the result of his cat clawing at the waterbed—and he was electrocuted. The electrically charged water seeped up and surrounded his body before he could reach safety. Coors would have been 23 years old two days later."

KILLER TALK SHOW
The Realist also reported the rather bizarre circumstances of the death of publisher and health-food advocate J. I. Rodale. Rodale, who created the popular *Prevention* magazine, made an appearance on "The Dick Cavett Show" in the late '60s, confidently discussing his physical well-being. "He said that doctors had given him 6 months to live 30 years ago, but because of the food he ate, he would live to be a hundred." A little later in the show he appeared to have fallen asleep, and Cavett and guest Pete Hamill chuckled about it...until they realized he was dead. The taped show did not air.

CONFUCIUS SAY...

*Yes, there really was a Confucius. He was a Chinese sage
and philosopher who lived from 551 to
479 B.C. Here are a few of the things he actually said.*

"They who know *the truth* are not equal to those who love it, and they who love it are not equal to those who delight in it."

"The superior man has neither anxiety nor fear."

"Without knowing the force of words it is impossible to know men."

"We don't know yet about life, how can we know about death?"

"Being true to oneself is the law of God. To try to be true to oneself is the law of man."

"To be fond of learning is to be near to knowledge."

"Silence is a true friend who never betrays."

"The superior man thinks always of virtue; the common man thinks of comfort."

"He does not preach what he practices till he has practiced what he preaches."

"He who learns but does not think, is lost! He who thinks but does not learn is in great danger!"

"It is only the wisest and the very stupidest who cannot change."

"To see what is right and not to do it is want of courage."

"Our greatest glory is not in never falling but in rising every time we fall."

"True goodness springs from a man's own heart. All men are born good."

"The superior man is firm in the right way, and not merely firm."

"Sincerity and truth are the basis of every virtue."

"The strength of a nation is derived from the integrity of its homes."

Big Bucks: In 1988, Michael Jackson earned an estimated $60 million.

FAMOUS OVERDUBS

*Sometimes a few words can make a big difference in a film.
Here are three examples of voices being added to movies
without the public knowing about it.*

GIANT

James Dean's last film was an adaptation of Edna Ferber's *Giant*. "The last big speech Jimmy, as Jett Rink, made [was] when he addressed all of the Texas crowd who had spurned him. It was a drunken soliloquy, and Dean, in his attempt at accurate excellence, had slurred some meaningful words so badly, they had to be re-recorded." Unfortunately, by this time Dean had had his fatal accident. So his friend Nick Adams stepped in and did the overdub. "Nick, a noted mimic, could imitate anybody from Cary Grant...to Robert Wagner. He was able to redo parts of Jimmy's last speech so perfectly, it was years before anyone knew all those words had not come directly from Dean's own lips."

DR. STRANGELOVE

At the end of Stanley Kubrick's masterpiece of black humor, a B-52 with a doomsday bomb is headed for Russia. "Inside the B-52 Kong [played by Slim Pickens] and his men are opening their survival kits while over the intercom the major itemizes the incongruous contents." Slim Pickens, with his heavy Southern accent, comments: "Shoot, a fellah could have a pretty good weekend in Vegas with all that." Actually, the original line was "a fellah could have a pretty good weekend in Dallas with all that." But Wills went in and overdubbed the name of the city after JFK was assassinated.

THE EXORCIST

One of the most potent scenes in *The Exorcist* is "the voice of the devil emanating from the on-screen mouth of fourteen-year-old Linda Blair." How did she do it? She didn't. The voice turned out to belong to actress Mercedes McCambridge, who commented: "If people had heard her saying some of those obscenities, they would have fallen over laughing."

CAMPAIGN SMEARS

Campaign smears are ugly, but they're a part of American politics, and have been since the first elections. A few notable examples:

THE 1828 PRESIDENTIAL CAMPAIGN

During his second try for the presidency, Andrew Jackson was subjected to vicious slander by incumbent John Quincy Adams.

Jackson was termed "a blood-thirsty wild man, the son of a black and a prostitute and a murderer who had put to death soldiers who offended him." And he was accused of being an adulterer. This hit home. Unfortunately, Jackson's wife Rachel had married him unaware that she was still legally married to someone else; her previous marriage hadn't been officially dissolved. It was merely a technicality, but Adams's supporters relentlessly pursued it, dragging Rachel's name through the mud throughout the country.

By the time the matter was straightened out, Jackson had won the election....But he went to the White House alone. Rachel Jackson died of a heart attack; Jackson and his supporters attributed it to the brutal attacks during the campaign.

THE 1884 PRESIDENTIAL CAMPAIGN

In 1884 the governor of New York, Grover Cleveland, was closing in on the Democratic nomination for president when a Buffalo newspaper accused him of fathering an illegitimate boy ten years earlier.

Had he? Cleveland, a bachelor at the time, had indeed dated the woman. And he had contributed to the support of a child. But Cleveland was never proven to be the child's father; in fact, the woman admitted it could have been any one of a number of men. Nonetheless, when the presidential campaign began, the child was a part of it. Cleveland had to live with the chant: "Ma, Ma, Where's my Pa? Gone to the White House, ha! ha! ha!"

Interestingly, Cleveland's opponent, James G. Blaine, had his own problems—political scandals in his home state of Maine, and anti-Catholic prejudice—and wasn't able to capitalize on Cleveland's vulnerable position. Cleveland won.

THE 1864 PRESIDENTIAL CAMPAIGN

Anticipating the next election, Abraham Lincoln's enemies tried to undermine his presidency. A whispering campaign in Washington suggested that Lincoln's wife, Mary Todd, was secretly aiding the Confederates. It was a spurious charge, but it gained enough credibility to force the president to appear before a secret congressional committee investigating the matter. His prestige was slightly tarnished, but Lincoln was still re-elected.

THE FLORIDA SENATORIAL CAMPAIGN OF 1950

This is a textbook case of a politician using rhetoric to pander to the fears of less-educated people. Congressman George Smathers was challenging incumbent Senator Claude Pepper in Florida's Democratic senatorial primary in 1950. Smathers, the underdog, circulated printed material in the rural towns of central and northern Florida accusing Pepper of the following "indecencies":

• That his brother was a "practicing Homosapien."
• That he had a sister in New York who was a "thespian."
• And that Pepper himself had "matriculated" with young women.

 To top it off, Smathers jumped on the early McCarthy bandwagon and saddled Claude with the nickname "Red" Pepper. Smathers won.

THE PRESIDENTIAL CAMPAIGN OF 1988

It keeps coming back. Sounding every bit like Joseph McCarthy, George Bush accused his opponent, Michael Dukakis, of being "a card-carrying member" of the American Civil Liberties Union—an organization devoted to upholding the Constitution and, ironically, one defending Oliver North at the time. The motive: people who knew nothing about the ACLU would respond to the phrase "card-carrying," identifying it with "commie." It worked.

As a person ages, the first sense to go is the sense of smell.

REAGANISMS

Some of Ronald Reagan's choicest comments.

"I'm not medical. I'm not a lawyer and I'm not medical, either."

"I'm no linguist, but I have been told that in the Russian language there isn't even a word for freedom."

"The taxpayer—that's someone who works for the federal government but doesn't have to take a civil service examination."

"Imagine if people in our nation could see the Bolshoi Ballet again, while Soviet children could see American plays and hear groups like the Beach Boys. And how about Soviet children watching 'Sesame Street'?"

"I'm concentrating on dog heaven."

"Boy, after seeing *Rambo* last night, I know what to do the next time this happens."

[On South Africa] "They have eliminated the segregation that we had in our own country, the type of thing where hotels and restaurants and places of entertainment and so forth were segregated—that has all been eliminated."

"Nuclear war would be the greatest tragedy, I think, ever experienced by mankind in the history of mankind."

"I'm not a lawyer, and I don't intend to get into too many legal areas where I might be caught short."

"If you've seen one redwood, you've seen them all."

"Why should we subsidize intellectual curiosity?"

"Government exists to protect us from each other. Where Government has gone beyond its limits is in deciding to protect us from ourselves."

"The best minds are not in government. If any were, business would hire them away."

SUPERSTITIONS

Many of us secretly believe far fetched legends— that broken mirrors and black cats really do bring bad luck, for example. It's amusing to discover the sources of our silliness.

L ADDERS: The belief that walking under a ladder propped up against a building will bring bad luck comes from the early Christians. They held that the leaning ladder formed a triangle, and that this symbol of the Holy Trinity shouldn't be violated by walking through it. Those who did were considered in league with the devil.

FRIDAY THE THIRTEENTH: Friday, in general, is considered an unlucky day. An old poem goes: "Now Friday came. Your old wives say / Of all the week's the unluckiest day."
  Adam and Eve were supposed to have been kicked out of the Garden of Eden on a Friday; Noah's great flood started on a Friday; and Christ was crucified on a Friday. Couple this with the fact that 12 witches plus the Devil—totalling 13—are necessary for a Satanic meeting, and the resulting combination (of Friday plus 13) is a deadly one.

SNEEZES: The European/American tradition of saying "God bless you" when someone sneezes originated during the sixth century. It was already customary to congratulate someone when they sneezed (the prevalent idea being that a sneeze expelled evil from the body), but when a plague whose symptoms included violent sneezes began spreading around southern Europe, the Pope stepped in. He declared that since a sneeze could be a sign of imminent death, people should bless the sneezer. The phrase caught on and became commonplace.

BREAKING A MIRROR: At one time in the ancient world, mirrors were used to tell fortunes. If a mirror was broken during the reading, it meant the person was doomed. Later, this was amended; a person's image was interpreted as a symbol of health, and a cracked image in a mirror meant imminent ill-

Tarantula spiders have been known to live for over two years without eating.

ness. But ultimately, the superstition of seven years bad luck is common today because it was used to scare European servants in the 1400s and 1500s into using extra care when polishing their masters' expensive mirrors. No servant (or anyone, for that matter) wanted to court a lifetime of bad luck. The belief spread, and became ingrained in European culture.

SALT: The origin of this nearly worldwide superstition is hard to trace, but it logically stems from salt's historic importance as a spice and medicine. If you were the kind of person who could spill something as precious as salt, you were clearly headed for trouble. Some historians attribute the rituals surrounding salt to Judas spilling the stuff at the table during the Last Supper, but that's spurious. The antidote—throwing a few grains over your left shoulder—is a little puzzling. The best explanation: in some cultures, people believed that nasty spirits inhabited the left side, and tossing some salt over the shoulder hit them right in the eyes—thus preventing their evil deeds.

ST. CHRISTOPHER MEDALS: Supposedly the patron saint of travellers. But many authorities don't believe there ever was a Saint Christopher.

BLACK CATS: In ancient Egypt, cats were regarded as spiritual creatures, and among the most exalted Goddesses was Bast, a black female cat. But in European culture, the black cat became an animal to avoid. Apparently in the Middle Ages, when ignorant peasants were convinced that witches and evil demons were living among them, cats were singled out as suspicious creatures (perhaps because of their silent, fluid movements, or the way they stare, or even their occasionally unworldly wailing). The fact that some of the women who cared for the cats were old and grizzled—i.e., witch material—probably added to the legend. Ultimately, people came to believe that a black cat was the nighttime embodiment of a witch.

LADYBUGS: "Ladybird, ladybird, fly away home...." It's considered bad luck to kill one of these orange, spotted insects because it represents the Virgin Mary.

FAMILIAR NAMES

*Some people achieve immortality because their names be-
come commonly associated with an item or activity. You
know the names—now here are the people.*

R J. Lechmere Guppy. A clergyman living in Trinidad.
He sent several species of tropical fish to the British
Museum, including a tiny specimen which now bears his
name.

Dr. J. I. Guillotin. A French physician. Moved by mercy, he en-
dorsed what he thought was a more humane method of execution than hanging. Ironically, the guillotine—which he did not
invent—"is now synonymous with needless and brutal
slaughter."

Jules Leotard. A renowned French acrobat of the nineteenth
century. Designed and introduced the tight-fitting oufit "that
does not hide your best features."

Tom Collins. A nineteenth century English Bartender at Lim-
mer's Old House in London.

Amelia Jenks Bloomer. An outspoken late-nineteenth century
feminist. Did not invent bloomers, but advocated their use by
women (instead of corsets and cumbersome hoop skirts).

Nicholas Chauvin. Fanatically loyal soldier in Napoleon's
army. Inspired the word *chauvinism.*

Cesar Ritz. A Swiss hotelier. Founded a chain of fancy hotels,
which he named after himself.

John Duns Scotus. A respected scholar and theologian of the
thirteenth century. Two hundred years after his death in 1308,
his followers were known as "Scotists, Dunsmen, and Dunses,"
and were reviled for their resistance to the new ideas of the
Renaissance. More enlightened thinkers chided the Dunses for
their ignorance. Eventually *Dunses* became *dunces.*

Pirates thought that wearing an earring in a pierced ear improved their eyesight.

Jean Nicot. French ambassador to Portugal in the 1550s. First brought tobacco to France. When nicotine was found in tobacco leaves in 1818, it was named after him.

Henry Shrapnel. English inventor. Created the shell that helped beat Napoleon in 1815.

Helen Porter Mitchell. A celebrated opera singer whose professional name was Melba (taken from her hometown of Melbourne, Australia). When she was dieting, she ate thin, crisp slices of bread now called Melba Toast. When she wasn't, she ate a dessert called Peach Melba.

Sylvester Graham. A food faddist of the early 1800s. Advocated vegetarianism and high fiber; he was called "the poet of bran meal and pumpkins" by Ralph Waldo Emerson. His followers were called *Grahamites*, and food he recommended included *Graham crackers* and *Graham flour*.

Etienne de Silhouette. Louis XIV's unpopular controller-general in 1759. He made shadow portraits, "recommending them for their cheapness," and they were named after him.

Haile Selassie. The emperor of Ethiopia, known as "The Lion of Judah." His real name was "Ras Tafari"—which explains the origin of the term *Rastafarian*.

Charles Wenburg. A nineteenth century shipping mogul. He discovered a new recipe for lobster and passed it on to Lorenzo Delmonico, who named it after him—*Lobster Wenburg*. Shortly after, Wenburg was ejected from Delmonico's Restaurant for fighting. His punishment: the first three letters of the dish were transposed; *Lobster Wenburg* became *Lobster Newburg*.

Charles Cunningham Boycott. A tyrannical land agent for an absentee owner. The Englishman was overseer of the Earl of Erne's estate in Ireland. When, after two consecutive bad potato harvests, farmers demanded lower rents, Boycott tried to evict them. The result: the farmers banded together and harrassed Boycott until he fled Ireland.

Around 200 people die while watching football games every year.

MYTH AMERICA

Very little of what we are taught about the "taming of the West" is true, and the legend of George Armstrong Custer is a perfect example.

A BRAVE INDIAN FIGHTER?

The Myth: General George Armstrong Custer was one of the U. S. Army's great soldiers during the western expansion. His valiant battle at the Little Bighorn—fighting a horde of renegade Indians that outnumbered his small cavalry unit 1,000 to 1 (Custer's Last Stand)—was an example of the fearlessness that made the white man's victory over the red man inevitable.

At one time so many people believed it that Custer was the hero of several films, and the main character in a prime-time TV series. ("The Legend of Custer" ran for a few months in 1967 on ABC.) Custer was also the subject of a million-selling record, "Please Mr. Custer," in 1958.

The Truth:

•Custer was a lieutenant colonel, not a general. (He had briefly been a major general during the Civil War, but was immediately demoted to captain when the war ended.)

•Custer was far from an exemplary soldier. He finished last in his class at West Point in 1861. And in 1867, he left his command to visit his wife; when he was caught, he was court-martialed and kicked out of the service for a year. He was allowed to return only because the Army needed help fighting Indians.

•Custer's Last Stand wasn't heroism, it was stupidity. Custer's division was supposed to be a small part of a major attack, led by General Alfred Terry—who was planning to meet Custer in two days with his troops. Custer was instructed to wait for Terry. Instead, he led his 266 men into battle, where they were all slaughtered. Historians speculate that the foolishly ambitious Custer believed a victory would earn him a presidential nomination, or that he had unwarranted contempt for the Indians' fighting ability.

According to one study: people who eat hot dogs are extroverts, burger-eaters are introverts.

WHAT AM I?

In the late twenties, America's intellectual elite devised a word game called "What Am I?" The idea was to offer literate clues to the identity of a common object or phenomenon without giving the answer away. These four examples are from the 1920s book about the game. Answers are on page 223.

1. ◆ I wear the face of a leader of men. My financial worth is small and my appearance not impressive, yet my presence is a passport to any country and society. I have the entrée alike to the boudoir and the armed camp; I penetrate to royal palaces and to the far corners of the earth. In my youth I am bright and fresh-looking; later, my face is marred and disfigured and I am cast aside as nothing; but when I am very old I am eagerly sought, and a safe refuge is provided for me, where I am exhibited to admiring visitors. What am I?

2. Everything that is presented to me I return at once. Although helpless I can wound; although speechless I can encourage. People are afraid of my fabled revenge so I am seldom hurt. Children adore me. A widely known character once went through me and discovered an amazing country. What am I?

3. Changeless through uncounted centuries, I am still the symbol of inconstancy. I am dead and cold in death, yet I exercise irresistible power, renewed every day, over that which is thousands of miles distant from me. I cause strange sensations in dogs and lovers and once inspired athletic ambitions in the domestic cow. I am a symbol of mania and of a formidably rising nation. Though I have a well-rounded character nobody has ever seen more than one side of me. What am I?

4. I am positively the worst ever. I am absolutely the best on record. I am always surpassing myself. My past is negligible, my future a matter of universal concern and infinite conjecture. Most people profess a prophetic vision of me, but birds and animals know more about me than they do. Everybody complains of me, but nobody ever does anything to correct or improve me. What am I?

A Swiss scientist named A. E. Fick invented contact lenses in 1887.

NIXON SEZ

It's probably been a while since you've thought about Tricky Dick. Just in case you're beginning to wonder why you didn't trust him in the first place, here's a refresher.

"I'll speak for the man, or against him, whichever will do him most good."

"We cannot judge it before it is concluded, and we cannot judge it even after it has been concluded."

"I rate myself a deeply committed pacifist."

"You won't have Nixon to kick around any more, gentlemen. This is my last Press Conference."

"Let us begin by committing ourselves to the truth, to see it like it is and to tell it like it is, to find the truth, to speak the truth and live with the truth. That's what we'll do."

"You can say that this Administration will have the first complete, far-reaching attack on the problem of hunger in history. Use all the rhetoric, so long as it doesn't cost money."

"I never made the [football] team…I was not heavy enough to play the line, not fast enough to play halfback and not smart enough to be a quarterback."

"When the President does it, that means it is not illegal."

"I like the job I have now, but, if I had my life to live over again, I'd like to have ended up as a sports writer."

"I would have made a good pope."

"I hear that whenever anyone in the White House tells a lie, Nixon gets a royalty."

"I'm not a lovable man."

"Call it paranoia, but paranoia for peace isn't that bad."

"Once you get into this great stream of history, you can't get out."

The first stewardesses were on United Airlines, in 1930. They had to be registered nurses.

M*A*S*H

*"M*A*S*H" was the first comedy on television to deal directly with the ugly facts of war, as well as the funny ones. The American public responded by making it one of the most popular programs in the history of the medium.*

HOW IT STARTED: When Richard Hornberger [pen name: Richard Hooker] completed the memoirs of his days with the 8055th MASH unit in Korea, he hardly expected he'd have a best-seller on his hands. And for the next eight years, his expectations were borne out—by rejection slips. He couldn't even get it published.

Finally in 1968, after securing a partner to polish up the manuscript, M*A*S*H was published by William Morrow and Co. Initially the book was a flop. But it caught the eye of Ingo Preminger (Otto's brother), who bought the movie rights and commissioned a screenplay (adapted by Ring Lardner, Jr.). Directed by Robert Altman, and starring Eliot Gould and Donald Sutherland, M*A*S*H was a phenomenal success—which caused M*A*S*H (the book) to become a surprise best-seller. 20th Century Fox elected to further capitalize on the movie by creating a low-budget television pilot using sets and props from the film.

When CBS decided to give the series a shot (or at least finance a pilot), nothing had been written yet. So producer Gene Reynolds called his friend Larry Gelbart in England and asked for a script. Gelbart whipped one out in two days.

M*A*S*H (the TV show) premiered in September, 1972 to low ratings and poor reviews. But CBS didn't lose faith. It allowed the show to struggle through its first season and, in an unusual act of foresight, kept it going into the next season—when it became a hit.

INSIDE FACTS:

Just the facts. More than half of the M*A*S*H storylines were the product of painstaking research. Larry Gelbart worked with photocopies of '50s issues of *Time* magazine and kept a master list of Korean names, a map of Korea, and an Army handbook on his desk.

Ladies' man. Alan Alda's support of the feminist movement is a tribute to Sister Elizabeth Kenney, whose cure for infantile paralysis (discovered during World War I) wasn't recognized by the male-dominated medical profession for nearly 20 years. The application of her theories cured Alda's childhood case of polio.

The real thing. The model for the M*A*S*H 4077th was the 8055th. In real life, the 8055th had a staff of 10 doctors and 12 nurses, and treated roughly 200 patients at a time.

The last show. The final 2 1/2 hour episode, *Goodbye, Farewell, and Amen*, was broadcast on February 28, 1983. Commercial time for the episode sold briskly at $450,000 per 30 second spot ($50,000 more than for the Super Bowl telecast), and over 125 million viewers were on hand (35 million more than watched *Roots*).

Funnier than fiction. Many of the episodes were based on stories purchased from Korean War MASH unit veterans.

Right Flank. Richard Hornberger (author of M*A*S*H) is actually a conservative Republican who fashioned Hawkeye after himself (real hometown: Crabapple Cove, Maine)—and didn't like the way Alda portrayed him at all. In fact, he was offended by the anti-war message of the show.

Korea or Vietnam? Make no mistake—the apparent anti-Vietnam bent of the early M*A*S*H wasn't coincidental. It was specifically written that way. Reynolds and Gelbart managed to air a weekly vilification of U.S. involvement in Southeast Asia by pre-dating it 20 years. Neat trick.

The set. M*A*S*H outdoor scenes were shot at the 20th Century Fox Ranch (now Malibu Canyon State Park). But most of the footage was shot at Fox Studios, where the M*A*S*H compound measured only 45' x 90', and came complete with a Korean landscape backdrop and a **rubber** floor!

THE POLITICS OF OZ

This fascinating story of how The Wizard of Oz might really
be a political allegory comes from the Utne Reader,
"The Best of the Alternative Press."
Written by Michael Dregni.

W ho would believe that the battle between the gold
and the silver standard in turn-of-the-century U.S.
politics would make a good plot for a children's
fantasy book?

And who would believe that a story as delightful as *The
Wizard of Oz* could also have meaning for adults?

In These Times (Feb. 18, 1987) exposes *Oz* as a parable of
populism, the 1890s Midwestern political movement led by
William Jennings Bryan. The populists challenged Eastern
banks and railroads, which they charged with oppressing farmers and industrial workers. Bryan felt that farmers were being
crucified on a cross of gold; a switch to silver-backed currency
would make money plentiful for all.

Oz author L. Frank Baum was a populist—and also a bit of a
fantasizer. As editor of a South Dakota newspaper, he advised
poor farmers to feed wood shavings to starving livestock, after
fitting the beasts with special green glasses so they would
think they were eating grass.

After Bryan's 1896 bid for the presidency failed, Baum was
so moved to write the first of his long-running Oz series.

The allegory begins with the title: Oz is short for ounce, the
measure for gold. Dorothy, hailing from the populist strong-
hold of Kansas, represents the common person. The Tin
Woodsman is the industrial worker who is rusted solid, referring to the factories shut down in the 1893 depression. The
Scarecrow is the farmer who lacks the brains to realize his own
political interests. And the Cowardly Lion is Bryan himself,
with a loud orator's roar but little else.

After vanquishing the Wicked Witch of the East (the Eastern
banker) Dorothy frees the Munchkins (the little people). With
the witch's silver slippers (the silver standard), Dorothy starts
down the Yellow Brick Road (the gold standard) to the Eme-

The LaCoste shirt is named after French tennis star Rene LaCoste, Davis Cup winner in 1927.

rald City (Washington). There the group meets the Wizard (the president), who, like all good politicians, appears as whatever people wish to see. When the Wizard is defrocked, the Scarecrow denounces him as a humbug, which is the core of Baum's message, writes Michael A. Genovese in the Minneapolis *Star Tribune* (March 22, 1988).

Dorothy saves the day by dousing the Wicked Witch of the West with water, evoking the drought that was plaguing Midwestern farms at the time. The Wizard flies away in a hot-air balloon, the Scarecrow is left in charge of Oz, the Tin Woodsman rules the East, and the Cowardly Lion returns to the forest—Bryan had lost the election.

In the 1939 movie starring Judy Garland, the populist parable lost out to Hollywood escapism, and Dorothy's silver slippers were inexplicably changed to ruby. However, Baum might have applauded the use of black and white film depicting the grim reality of Kansas farm fortunes and color stock for the fantasy world of Oz. And the song "Somewhere Over the Rainbow" suited well the populist dream.

∞   ∞   ∞

TOTALLY UNRELATED GOSSIP
According to Ed Lucaire in *Celebrity Trivia*:

• Clark Gable had no teeth; he wore dentures—which bothered the actresses he worked with. "His false teeth were just too much," complained Grace Kelly. And Vivian Leigh swore she would quit doing love scenes with him in *Gone With the Wind* "unless he washed out his mouth."

• Hugh Hefner was still a virgin on his 22nd birthday.

• Charles Bronson got his first part in a movie, *You're In the Navy Now* (1951), because "he could belch on cue."

• Adolf Hitler owned about 9,000 acres of land in Colorado. Hitler's favorite film was *King Kong*. His favorite song was Walt Disney's "Who's Afraid of the Big, Bad Wolf?"

• Jerry Lewis never wears the same pair of sox twice.

In Los Angeles, there are fewer people than there are automobiles.

QUOTES FROM JFK

Some better-known remarks made by our 35th president.

"There is no city in the United States in which I get a warmer welcome and less votes than Columbus, Ohio."

[*To his brother in 1960, before the election*] "Do you realize the responsibility I carry? I'm the only person standing between Nixon and the White House."

"When we got into office, the thing that surprised me most was to find that things were just as bad as we'd been saying they were."

[*At a press conference prior to the 1960 election*] "I have just received the following telegram from my generous Daddy. It says, 'Dear Jack: Don't buy a single more vote than is necessary. I'll be damned if I'm going to pay for a landslide.'"

"When power corrupts, poetry cleanses."

Question: "The Republican National Committee recently adopted a resolution saying you were pretty much of a failure. How do you feel about that?"
Pres. Kennedy: "I assume it passed unanimously."

"When written in Chinese, the word "crisis" is composed of two characters: one represents danger, the other represents opportunity."

"In a free society, art is not a weapon."

"Failure has no friends."

"Conformity is the jailer of freedom and the enemy of growth."

"Let us never negotiate out of fear. But let us never fear to negotiate."

"We must use time as a tool not as a couch."

"The war against hunger is truly mankind's war of liberation."

"The blessings of liberty have too often stood for privilege, materialism and a life of ease."

The first bra was created by a French designer in 1902. But bras didn't catch on until 1913.

THE LOUIE, LOUIE STORY

"Louie, Louie" is arguably the most recorded rock 'n' roll song of all time. The following history is from Behind the Hits, *by Bob Shannon and John Javna. The authors credit the "extensive liner notes" written by Doc Pelzell for Rhino Records' "Louie, Louie" album—an album consisting completely of different versions of the song.*

Besides groupies and recording contracts, what do Frank Zappa, Julie London, Iggy Pop, Barry White, Tom Petty and the Heartbreakers, Blondie, the Beach Boys, David McCallum, Toots and the Maytals, and the Kinks have in common? You guessed it. They—and thousands of other artists—have all performed versions of "the most easily recognizable rock 'n' roll song of all time"—"Louie, Louie." This three-chord wonder has been singled out by many critics as *the* definitive rock 'n' roll song. Yet it wasn't until seven or eight years *after* it was originally recorded that most American teens heard it for the first time.

In 1955, Richard Berry, a young black musician, was playing in Los Angeles with a Mexican group called Ricky Rivera and the Rhythm Rockers. One of the band's songs, "El Loco Cha Cha Cha," had a contagious rhythm figure in it that Berry just couldn't get out of his mind. And while he was waiting backstage to perform at the Harmony Club Ballroom one night, the words "Louie, Louie" popped into his head and superimposed themselves around the persistent riff; "the rest just fell into place." His main lyrical influence: a composition called "One for My Baby," which was sung from the viewpoint of a customer who was speaking to a bartender named Joe. In it, the singer said: "One for my baby/One for the road/Set 'em up Joe." In Berry's composition, the bartender became Louie, and the customer was telling Louie how he intended to sail to Jamaica to find his true love. The speech patterns and the use of Jamaica in the song were inspired by Berry's exposure to Latin music, and by Chuck (no relation) Berry's "Havana Moon," a similarly styled song that was popular at the time.

When Berry wrote "Louie, Louie," he was under contract to

Modern Records. But because of a dispute over the royalties for the sixty-plus songs he had written for the label, he saved the tune until his contract expired and he could record it for Flip Records. Flip released it in 1956 and it became a respectable R&B hit, selling (according to Berry) around 130,000 copies. A year later, however, sales had tapered off, and Berry needed some money for his upcoming wedding. So he sold the record sales publishing rights to "Louie Louie," retaining only the radio and television performance rights. He philosophically chalks this sale up to "experience." After all, who could have predicted the bizarre set of circumstances that would, a few years later, turn this song into a monster hit?

About five years later in Seattle, Washington, an obscure singer by the name of Rockin' Robin Roberts discovered Berry's recording of "Louie Louie" while browsing through the bargain bin of a local record store. "Louie" soon became Roberts' signature song and he took it with him through a succession of local bands. Finally, he joined one of the area's more popular groups, the Wailers (no relation to Bob Marley's contingent), and they decided to cut the song for their own Etiquette Records label. It was a regional hit in the Northwest, but when Liberty Records released it nationally, it flopped.

Kids in most of America still didn't know the song, but in Portland, Oregon, "Louie, Louie" was hot. One night, a Portland Top 40 band called the Kingsmen were playing a local dance with friendly rivals Paul Revere and the Raiders. During one of their breaks, they happened to notice that a lot of their audience had gathered around a juke box, and were dancing enthusiastically to the Wailers' record. Since this reaction was exactly what the Kingsmen were looking for in their own performances, they decided to include the song in their act; each member agreed to learn the song by their next rehearsal. But the only one to follow through on the pact was lead singer Jack Ely. Consequently, he had to teach it to the rest of the group; when he remembered it incorrectly, no one knew it. He taught the band a 1-2-3, 1-2, 1-2-3, 1-2 version, rather than the Wailers' 1-2-3-4, 1-2-, 1-2-3-4, 1-2 rendition. The result: he made the tune faster. It's interesting to speculate: would the song have been as successful if Ely hadn't accidentally altered it?

Nearly half the American population never reads books.

Anyway, the group got the response they were looking for. They were asked to play it as much as eight or nine times a night. One Friday in May, 1963, the band decided, just for kicks, to do a marathon version of the song to see who could last longer, the dancers or the band. Even bass player Bob Norby, who didn't sing, warbled a few verses just to keep the song going for approximately forty-five minutes. Despite the band's boredom, audience response was so positive that arrangements were made that night to record "Louie, Louie" the next day.

Actually, the Kingsmen had been wanting to get into the studio for some time. Their reason: a summer job. "That's really what 'Louie, Louie' was intended for," members of the band admit now, "an audition tape for a job on a steamship line for the summer. To Australia. We never got there, though. We had this hit record instead and had to go play the White House. And Wyoming. And Iowa." After pooling their money to come up with the $50 they needed for the two-hour session, the group went to the only recording studio in Portland and made their demo. Facilities were, at best, primitive. Mikes were placed next to amps that had been muffled with coats and blankets. Jack Ely's lead vocal was yelled up to a mike that was suspended near the studio's fifteen-foot ceiling—which explains the garbled lyrics that ultimately helped make the Kingsmen's record so successful. Strange twist: the very next day, Paul Revere and the Raiders, with Mark Lindsay on Sax, went into the same studio to record *their* version of "Louie, Louie."

Both the Kingsmen and Paul Revere's versions got local airplay, and Revere's actually did much better at the outset.

THE KINGSMEN: "Radio stations in those days used to promote their own shows—dances, record hops, local supermarket openings...and the Kingsmen were the house band for a station called KISN—y'know, we'd go out and do all the shows with all the jocks. And so, as soon as we recorded 'Louie, Louie,' of course, they put it on the air...Paul Revere's version got instant play all up and down the West Coast as soon as it was released; ours was only played in the Portland area, basically. But after a few months, toward the end of '63, a copy of two of our records got back to Boston. A disc jockey named Earl

Bird on an FM R&B station started playing it, thinking that we were an East Coast Rhythm and blues group or something. There was no precedent for this type of sound east of the Rockies. Eventually, Arnie 'Woo-Woo' Ginsberg on WBZ started blasting it all over the Northeast. Then it spread out all over the East Coast, into New York City. And then it became a national hit."

Going back a few months: after "Louie, Louie" began getting airplay in Boston, it was picked up for pressing and distribution by Wand Records. It fared well; by September, the record had reached #94 on the *Billboard* charts, and was climbing rapidly. But the final shot-in-the-arm that boosted the record to the top of the charts for four months caught even the Kingsmen off-guard; someone, somewhere, decided that the words were dirty. Without warning, rumors spread that Ely's slurred vocals were laced with obscenities, and soon every teenager in America was trying to figure out what Ely was "really" saying. They even did it at the band's live performances.

THE KINGSMEN: "It was kind of disheartening at first. Before we knew that there was this 'dirty lyrics' controversy, we thought that something was wrong with the band because we'd be playing all night long and when we'd hit our closer, which was 'Louie, Louie'—at the time our only hit—everyone would stop watching us. No one would pay attention any longer; they'd all pull these pieces of paper out of their pockets and start reading along...and singing. And they're going, 'Y'know, which version is right?' It was weird, having all these people come up to you like that." J. Edgar Hoover certainly wasn't going to stand for obscenity on the airwaves (neither was the state of Indiana, which banned "Louie"). The FBI and FCC launched a "Louie, Louie" investigation, playing the record at every speed from 16 to 78 rpm. They called in both Jack Ely and Richard Berry to testify about the lyrics. And in the end: the FCC concluded that, "We found the record to be unintelligible at any speed we played it." They hadn't found what they were looking for, but the FCC's efforts weren't entirely fruitless—they helped create a rock 'n' roll classic. With all that "negative" publicity, the record took off. It sold over eight million copies. "Well, you know," a member of the Kingsmen laughs today, "when the FBI and Lyndon Baines Johnson say, 'You can't do this,' that really does wonders for record sales."

The average American eats about 1 1/2 tons of food every year.

MOST COMMON WORDS

How's your vocabulary? Not particularly good,
according to one etymologist.

One of the most entertaining books to peruse in the bathroom is Stuart Flexner's *I Hear America Talking*, an examination of America's speech. According to Flexner, there are an estimated 600,000 words in our English language—but the average American only understands around 2%-3% of them...and actually uses only *half* that amount. "Of these," Flexner says, "just 10 basic words account for over 25% of all speech and 50 simple words for almost 60%, with between 1,500 and 2,000 words accounting for 99% of everything we say." The most commonly used word is *I*, followed by *you, the,* and *a*. Of our written language, Flexner says: "[It] is only a little more varied than our spoken one, 70 words making up 50% of it....We are more likely to qualify our words and to use *but, or, if, so, which,* and *who*. In general, too...we use shorter sentences, fewer auxiliary verbs, and more active verbs."

The 50 Most Common Words

I	A	About	Do
You	An	Now	Are
He	On	Just	Want
She	To	Not	Can
It	Of	That	Would
We	In	This	Go
They	For	Is	Think
Me	With	Get	Say
Him	Out	Was	Be
Her	From	Will	See
Them	Over	Have	Know
What	And	Don't	Tell
The			Thing

The first sound recording ever made was "Mary Had a Little Lamb," in 1877 by Tom Edison.

HULA HOOPS

The Hula Hoop was a pioneer, the first major fad created and fueled by the new power in America—TV ads.

The Hula Hoop originated in Australia, where it was simply a bamboo exercise ring used in gym classes. In 1957, an Australian company began selling the ring in retail stores—which attracted the attention of a small California toy manufacturer named Wham-O.

Wham-O's owners made a few wooden rings for their kids ("They just wouldn't put the hoop down"), took them to cocktail parties ("Folks had to have a couple of drinks in them to take a whack at it")...and then decided they had a hot item on their hands. They began producing a plastic version, naming it a Hula Hoop after the motion it resembled—the Hawaiian hula dance.

Wham-O introduced it to the American public in January 1958, and it quickly became the biggest toy craze in history (up to that time). During the year over 20 million—$30 million worth—were sold. The Hula Hoop was the quintessential fad item, though; by November 1958 the Wall Street Journal was already announcing: "Hoops Have Had It." A brief comeback occurred in 1965, when Wham-O introduced the "Shoop-Shoop" Hula Hoop, with a ball-bearing in it to make noise, but it just wasn't the same.

HOOP FACTS:

• According to the *British Medical Journal*, the Hula Hoop was responsible for an increase in back, neck, and abdominal injuries.

• Indonesia banned Hula Hoops because they "might stimulate passion." Japan forbade them on public streets.

• The official news agency in China called Hula Hoops "A nauseating craze." In the Soviet Union the hoop was seen as a "symbol of the emptiness of American Culture."

• Hula Hoop Endurance records: longest whirl—four hours (over 18,000 turns), by a 10 year old Boston boy; most hoops twirled simultaneously—14, by an 11-year-old in Michigan.

You're more likely to catch people's colds from shaking hands with them than their sneezes.

THE
HUNTING ACCIDENT

To people who noticed it in the obituaries on November 10, 1977, it seemed like just another unfortunate accident. But it may have been something more....

THE VICTIM: William C. Sullivan, former third-in-command in the FBI under J. Edgar Hoover, "the only liberal Democrat ever to break into the top ranks of the Bureau." For a decade, he ran the FBI's Domestic Intelligence division (including the investigation following JFK's assassination). In 1971 he was summarily fired by Hoover. Sullivan subsequently emerged as an active—and effective—critic of the Bureau.

THE CIRCUMSTANCES:
On November 9, 1977, shortly after daybreak, Sullivan went to meet two hunting companions near his Sugar Hill, New Hampshire home. He never made it. On the way, he was shot to death by the eighteen-year-old son of a state policeman. The young man claimed that (despite the fact that his rifle was equipped with a telescopic sight) he had mistaken Sullivan for a deer.

Two months later, the killer received his sentence in court: a $500 fine and a ten-year suspension of his hunting license.

UNANSWERED QUESTIONS:
Was it an accident, or the elimination of an adversary who knew too much? Consider these coincidences:
• As the FBI's illegal activities came to light in the mid-'70s, Bureau men were being brought to trial. At the time of his death, Sullivan was scheduled to be the chief witness against ex-agent John Kearny, who had been indicted for illegal wiretapping.
• At the time of the accident, Sullivan was writing a tell-all book about his years in the FBI. The book was ultimately com-

---

A baby kangaroo is only one inch long.

pleted by his co-author and was published by W. W. Norton and Company. But it had no author to champion it to the media, and no one to do a sequel—the author was dead.

•In 1976, Congress voted to open its own investigation of the JFK and Martin Luther King assassinations. "Sullivan would have been questioned by the Assassinations Committe in 1978," says Anthony Summers in his book about the death of JFK (*Conspiracy*). He goes on: "Sullivan had been head of the FBI's Division Five, which handled much of the King and Kennedy investigations....In 1975, Sullivan responded in opaque fashion to a question from a Congressional committee about Oswald. Asked whether he had seen anything in the files to indicate a relationship between Oswald and the CIA, Sullivan replied, 'No, I think there may be something on that, but you asked me if I had seen anything. I don't recall ever having seen anything like that, but I think there is something on that point....It rings a bell in my head.' Sullivan's fatal accident occurred before the Assassinations Committee could ask him to be more specific about the source of that bell in his mind."

POSSIBLE CONCLUSIONS:

•*It was a hunting accident.* Sullivan's co-author on *The Bureau*, Bill Brown, says he flew to New Hampshire and checked it out—and was satisfied that the incident really was an accident.

•*It was an assassination.* We asked several hunting enthusiasts about the probability of the shooting being an accident, based on their experience. The conclusion: they're skeptical that an experienced hunter with a telescopic sight could confuse a man with a deer. Among other things, the hunter would have to look carefully to verify that the "deer" was old enough—and the right sex—to shoot legally. If it wasn't a hunting accident? Two possibilities: either people associated with the FBI who would be damaged by Sullivan's testimony/revelations decided to eliminate him; or someone associated with the Kennedy assassination wanted him silenced.

What's your guess?

CAR NAMES

*They're a part of your life; you know them as well
as you know your own name. But do you
know where they come from?*

SOME REAL PEOPLE

Chevrolet. Louis Chevrolet, a race car driver and designer who co-founded the company which later merged with GM.

Oldsmobile. Ransom Eli Olds, an auto pioneer who started the Olds Motor Vehicle company in 1897.

Rolls-Royce. A combination of Sir Henry Royce's and Charles Rolls's names. Royce founded the company in 1903, Rolls promoted the car.

Mercedes-Benz. The *Benz* is Karl Benz, believed by many to be the inventor of the automobile in 1879. *Mercedes* comes from a young girl named Mercedes Jellinek, whose father was a German diplomat and an investor in the company.

Dodge. John and Horace Dodge. Set up the Dodge Brothers Machine Shop in Detroit in 1901, and were immediately hired to make transmissions for Ransom Olds. In 1914, they started their own car company, building low-cost autos to compete with Ford.

Buick. David Dunbar Buick, a Scotsman. Gave up his failing Buick Motor Car Company to William Durant, who in 1908 turned it into the nation's most successful—and used it as the cornerstone of the General Motors empire. Buick died broke; he was "so poor he could afford neither a telephone nor a Buick."

Chrysler. Walter Chrysler. A huge man, all of his Chrysler cars were designed extra-large, so they'd be comfortable for him to sit in.

SOME INSTANT WORDS

Caravan. A car combined with a van—a Car-a-van!

Nissan Sentra. According to one of the men who named it: "It's

---

Life Span: Dolphins live for about twenty-five years.

the company's mainstream, or central, car, and they wanted consumers to understand that it was quite safe, even though it was small. The word *Sentra* sounds likes *central*, as well as *sentry*, which evokes images of safety."

Corvair. A combination of the sporty Corvette and the family-oriented Bel Air.

Volvo. Means *I roll* in Latin.

Camaro. According to GM in 1967, it meant pal in French, a fitting title because "the real mission of our automobile is to be a close companion to its owner." But a French auto executive corrected them: "It doesn't mean anything in English, and it doesn't mean anything in French, either."

Toronado. Literally means, in Spanish, *floating bull*. But that has nothing to do with the car; GM just thought it sounded classy and exciting.

SOME SECOND CHOICES

Mustang. Original name: Torino.

Ford expected to appeal exclusively to young sports car lovers with this vehicle. The name *Torino* was chosen because it sounded like an Italian sports car; the projected ad campaign called it "the new import...from Detroit." But last-minute market research showed that the car could appeal to all buyers, and a new name had to be chosen. Colt, Maverick, and Bronco (all used for later cars) were considered. But Mustang seemed best, bringing to mind cowboys, adventure, and the Wild West. As one Ford man put it, "It had the excitement of the wide-open spaces, and it was as American as all hell."

Pontiac Firebird. Original name: the Banshee.

The press releases were out, the initial announcement had been made, and then someone at Pontiac discovered that in Irish folklore, a Banshee is "a supernatural being whose wailing foretells death." That, of course, would have been a public relations disaster; it would have been like calling a car "the Grim Reaper." Who would dare buy it? The firebird, a creature of Native American legends, was chosen instead.

BIRTH OF THE BIKINI

Conservatives have long pointed to the bikini as an example of our moral decline; yet history shows that the bikini is related to the A-bomb and war, not simply sex.

The atomic bomb is responsible for many terrible things and at least one attractive thing—the bikini.

In July 1946, the American government announced that it would be exploding an atomic bomb. It was just a test, but this was the first *announced* atomic bomb blast, and people's imaginations ran wild. Rumors spread that it was going to be a "super bomb" that could easily get out of control, start a massive chain reaction, and blow up the world.

Party Time.
These rumors were especially prevalent in Paris, which had recently suffered through the trauma of German occupation in World War II. Parisians simply couldn't take any more pressure....So instead of protesting the impending explosion, they celebrated. Hostesses used the bomb threat as an excuse to hold "end-of-the-world" parties; young men used it as an excuse to convince reluctant girl friends to give in (if the world was going to end, why not break *all* the rules?). And when it was revealed that the test would take place in the then-unheard-of Bikini Atoll, the parties became "Bikini" parties.

A Publicity Stunt
Meanwhile, a fashion show was being planned for the Piscine Molitor in Paris on July 5, 1946 (note: *piscine* is French for swimming pool). Its promoters wanted to attract attention, and since people seemed to be throwing modesty to the wind, the promoters came up with the idea of a "Bikini" costume—one that would go as far as anyone dared go with a bathing suit. So in the middle of the fashion show, Paris model Micheline Bernardini suddenly stepped out before the audience wearing a scanty two-piece bathing suit—the world's first "bikini." Of course the scandalous suit got international publicity...and a new style was born.

Nothing new under the sun: Archaeologists have now found evidence that bikinis were worn in Sicily as early as 2000, B.C.

STAR TREK

This is the show that started the cult TV boom. It has now spawned an industry that includes movies, toys, videos, etc. Here are some facts about it, from Cult TV, *by John Javna.*

HOW STAR TREK BEGAN: Gene Roddenberry, the head writer for a popular western called *Have Gun, Will Travel*, was also a science fiction buff. He saw a lot of similarities between space exploration and the experiences of the American pioneers—so he conceived of a TV space fantasy that would be similar to a western series, complete with continuing characters (which hadn't ever been done). He based his idea on a popular show named *Wagon Train*. He called his idea a "wagon train to the stars." A star trek.

In 1964, while producing an MGM series *The Lieutenant*, Roddenberry created a workable format for his space show. MGM turned it down, but Desilu bought it and sold the idea to NBC. The network financed the pilot called "The Cage." This was filmed in November and December. It cost $630,000—an outrageous amount for the time—and featured only two members of the final cast—Majel Barret and Leonard Nimoy. The captain's name wasn't Kirk—it was Pike. he was played by Jeffrey Hunter.

The pilot was submitted to NBC in February, 1965. They rejected it. But the project wasn't canned; NBC still saw promise in the series and authorized an unprecedented second pilot—including an almost entirely new cast. The new film was entitled "Where No Man Has Gone Before." It featured Shatner as Kirk, Nimoy as Science Officer Spock, Doohan as Scotty, and Takei as Physicist Sulu. For the record, the doctor's name was Mark Piper. He was played by Paul Fix.

The second pilot was submitted in January, 1966. A month later NBC accepted it for their coming fall schedule.

INSIDE FACTS
Easier than landing. The Enterprise's "transporter" was developed as a cost-cutting measure. It provided an inexpensive means to transport characters from the ship to the next set

(landings are expensive). The "glittering" effect (as the transporter dissolved and relocated the passengers' atoms) was provided by aluminum dust.

The Starship Enterprise. Three models of the Enterprise were used in filming: a 4-inch miniature, a 3-foot model, and a 14-foot plastic model that now hangs in the Smithsonian.

Those Ears. Spock's pointed ears were originally included as a throw-in when Roddenberry contracted with a special-effects house to produce three monster heads.
•The first pair were "gruesome," according to Nimoy. "They were rough and porous, like alligator skin." But two days before shooting, they were finally modified to everyone's satisfaction.
•Nimoy objected to wearing the ears, but Roddenberry offered a compromise—wear them for a while, and if they didn't work out, Spock could have "plastic surgery" and have them altered. Nimoy agreed.
•A typical pair of ears lasted from three to five days.

On the air. Believe it or not, the highest *Star Trek* ever ranked in a year's prime time rating was #52.

Logical thinking. One of Leonard Nimoy's contributions was the Vulcan nerve pinch. In one scene, he was supposed to sneak up behind a character and whack him on the head with a gun. But he objected that Vulcans wouldn't be so crude. As a substitute, he made up the legendary maneuver on the spot.

The Source. Incipient Trekkies who want a first-hand look at the inspiration for many of *Star Trek's* distinctive features should view the 1956 film *Forbidden Planet*, which starred Walter Pidgeon, Anne Francis, and Leslie Neilsen. Some of the "similarities" are amazing.

Fat City. Alert fans can tell in what part of the season an episode was filmed just by observing William Shatner's stomach. Always in top shape before shooting began, Shatner appeared trim and fit in early-season episodes. But as the season wore on, time to exercise became harder to find, and his waistline expanded.

In Germany more people have the last name of Schultz than any other name.

WORD PLAY

What do these familiar phrases really mean?
Etymologists have researched them and come up with
these explanations.

SMELL A RAT
Meaning: To sense that something is wrong.
Background: In earlier times, it was fairly common for people to have rats infesting their houses. And if a rat died in a place where it wasn't visible—inside a wall, for example—the person who lived in the house didn't know about it until he could literally smell the decaying rodent. That's how he could tell something was amiss.

HAM ACTOR (HAM)
Meaning: Someone who enjoys putting on a show, or who plays rather obviously to an audience (though not necessarily on stage). *Background:* An American phrase originating in the 1880s. Minstrel shows, mass entertainment of the time, often featured less-than-talented performers who overacted. They frequently appeared in "blackface," and used ham fat to remove their make-up. Thus they were referred to as "ham fat men," later shortened to "ham."

WHIPPING BOY
Meaning: A scapegoat, or someone who is habitually picked on. *Background:* Hundreds of years ago, it was normal practice for a European prince to be raised with a commoner of the same age. Since princes couldn't be disciplined like ordinary kids, the commoner would be beaten whenever the prince did something wrong. The commoner was called the prince's *whipping boy*.

RAINING CATS AND DOGS
Meaning: Torrential rain
Background: In the days before garbage collection, people tossed their trash in the gutter—including deceased house pets—and it just lay there. When it rained really hard, the garbage,

---

Cutting remark: "There is one chance out of ten you'll undergo surgery this year."

including the bodies of dead cats and dogs, went floating down the street. So there had to be a hell of a lot of water for it to rain cats and dogs.

HIT THE PANIC BUTTON
Meaning: "Speaking or acting in unnecessary haste."
Background: Coined during World War II, by men in the Air Force. According to Lt. Col. James Jackson, in American Speech magazine: "The actual source seems...to have been the bell system used in [B-17 and B-24] bombers for emergency procedures such as bailout and ditching. In case of fighter or flak damage so extensive that the bomber had to be abandoned, the pilot rang a 'prepare to abandon' ring, and then a ring meaning 'jump.' The bell system was used since the intercom was apt to be out if there was extensive damage. The implications of the phrase seem to have come from those few times when pilots hit the panic button too soon and rang for emergency procedures over minor damage, causing their crews to bail out unnecessarily."

HACK WRITER
Meaning: Writer who churns out words for money.
Background: In Victorian England, a hackney, or "hack," was a carriage for hire. (The term is still used in reference to taxi drivers, who need their "hack's licenses" to work.) It became a description of anyone who plies their trade strictly for cash.

PIE IN THE SKY
Meaning: An illusion, a dream, a fantasy. An unrealistic goal.
Background: Joe Hill, a famous labor organizer of the early 20th century, wrote a tune called "The Preacher and the Slave," in which he accused the clergy of promising a better life in Heaven while people starved on Earth. A few of the lines: "Work and pray, live on hay, you'll get pie in the sky when you die (That's a lie!)."

HARD AND FAST
Meaning: "Unalterable."
Background: "Refers to a vessel that is stuck on the bottom, which is hard, where it is held fast."

The animal with the largest eyes on earth: the giant squid, with eyes as big as pie plates.

ROCK CHARACTERS

Many pop songs are about real people, although most of the public never knows exactly who. Here are a few examples, from Behind the Hits, *by Bob Shannon and John Javna.*

DONNA, Ritchie Valens. 1959/Top 5. Donna Ludwig was Ritchie's high school girlfriend. Valens quit high school to go on tour when his record was released. It hit #2 in December, 1958, and Ritchie was killed a few months later in the February, 1959, plane crash with Buddy Holly and Big Bopper Richardson.

LET IT BE, the Beatles. 1969/#1. Who is "Mother Mary"? Paul McCartney: "My mother's name was Mary, so that was probably what that was about."

CATHY'S CLOWN, the Everly Brothers. 1960/#1. Cathy was Don Everly's high school girlfriend in Knoxville, Tennessee.

KILLING ME SOFTLY WITH HIS SONG, Roberta Flack. 1973/#1. The singer referred to in the song is Don McLean, composer of "American Pie." Songwriter Lori Lieberman saw him perform in Los Angeles, and was so knocked out that she wrote a ten-minute song about it. Roberta Flack rewrote the tune and had a hit with it.

DIANA, Paul Anka. 1957/#1. Diana Ayoub was an older girl with whom 15-year-old Paul Anka was infatuated. "She was a girl I saw at church and saw now and then at functions," he says. "She was a little out of my league. She was twenty and I was fifteen—and she really didn't want anything to do with me, which made it even worse." Worse still, Diana was babysitting for Anka's younger brother and sister, so it was hard to avoid her. Anka wrote a poem about her and set it to music. It became a #1 hit and a million-seller, and launched his show business career.

OH! CAROL, Neil Sedaka. 1959/Top 10. Carol was Carole Klein, whom singer Neil Sedaka described as "a scrawny girl,

---

Elvis Presley was thrown out of the Grand Ole Opry in 1954.

with dirty blonde hair, a long nose, and funny buck teeth." She was a fan of Sedaka's Brooklyn high school group, the Tokens, and used to hang around with Sedaka. After "Oh! Carol" hit, the real Carole put out an answer record called "Oh Neil," which flopped. Later she married Gerry Goffin and after changing her name to Carole King, she wrote classic pop songs like "Up on the Roof."

ROSANNA, Toto, 1982/#2. It's about actress Rosanna Arquette.

SEXY SADIE, the Beatles. 1968/"The White Album." Not a single, but worth mentioning. Sadie was the Maharishi Mahesh Yogi, father of "Transcendental Meditation" ("TM"), whom the Beatles followed to India in 1967. John Lennon dubbed him "sexy" after he found out the Maharishi had tried to make it with Mia Farrow, a disciple who was staying at the Maharishi's retreat at the same time the Beatles were.

WINDY, the Association. 1967/#1. Although the Association sang about a *girl* named Windy, the song was actually written about a man. The composer was Ruthann Friedman and Windy, her boyfriend, was an original hippie, living in San Francisco's Haight-Ashbury district. In that context the lyrics make a lot more sense. Example: he's "tripping" down the streets of the city. The song was originally written in waltz (3/4) time.

HEY JUDE, the Beatles. 1968/#1. Jude is Julian Lennon. In 1968, John Lennon had fallen in love with Yoko Ono and wanted to divorce his wife, Cynthia. It was messy at first—Cynthia retreated to Italy with her mother and son, Julian. But finally she returned to England to discuss terms of the divorce. "The only way I could get in touch with John was through Peter Brown at Apple," she says, "and when I finally did meet him, Yoko was there. He insisted she should stay." Julian was feeling the effects of the battle, and Paul McCartney, who was good friends with the boy, went to see him. As McCartney drove he began improvising a consoling melody. The words that went with it were "Hey Jules..." McCartney: "Then I thought a better name was Jude. A bit more country and western for me." Ironically, John Lennon thought that McCartney had written the song for *him*.

ST. LENNY SAYS...

*No one explained the innate contradictions of society
better than Lenny Bruce.*

"All my humor is based on destruction and despair. If the whole world were tranquil, without disease and violence, I'd be standing in the breadline—right back of J. Edgar Hoover."

"Every day people are straying away from the church and going back to God. Really."

[About drugs] "I'll die young …but it's like kissing God."

"[The Crucifixion] was just one of those parties that got out of hand."

"People should be taught what is, not what should be."

"There's nothing sadder than an old hipster."

"If the bedroom is dirty to you, then you are a true atheist, because…if anyone in this audience believes that God made his body, and your body is dirty, the fault lies with the manufacturer."

[*The dedication to his autobiography*] "I dedicate this book to all the followers of Christ and his teachings; in particular to a true Christian—Jimmy Hoffa—because he hired ex-convicts as, I assume, Christ would have."

"We're all the same people….And it discourages me that we try so desperately to be unique."

[*On his legal problems*] "What I need is a lawyer with enough juice to get Ray Charles a driver's license."

"I'm not original. The only way I could truly say I was original is if I created the English language. I did, man, but they don't believe me."

"Marijuana will be legal some day, because the many law students who now smoke pot will some day become Congressmen and legalize it in order to protect themselves."

According to one poll, nearly 3/4 of all American women wear a bra that is the wrong size.

CONGRESSIONAL WIT

*Even congressmen can be funny—albeit sometimes uninten-
tionally. Bill Hogan and Mike Hill scoured the Congressional Record and came up with Congress's most amusing
moments for their book,* Will the Gentleman Yield?*,
published by* **Ten Speed** *Press.*

SHEA A LITTLE LONGER

Mr. *Domenici.* Will the Senator yield for a question without
losing his right to the floor?
Mr. *D'Amato.* Certainly.
Mr. *Domenici.* If the Senator is going to stay here and talk until Saturday night, would he give me his ticket to the Mets
game? He can stay here and I will go.

—*Sens. Pete V. Domenici (R-N. Mex.) and*
Alfonse M. D'Amato (R-N.Y.)
October 16, 1986

POTATO, GRENADA

Mr. Speaker, some 40 years ago, George Gershwin popularized a little ditty that went like this:

"You like po-ta-to and I like po-tah-to,
You like to-ma-to, and I like to-mah-to,
Po-ta-to, po-tah-to, To-ma-to, to-mah-to!
Let's call the whole thing off!"

At about the same time that Mr. Gershwin was writing his tune,
Mr. Reagan was starring in the kind of movies that recent inci-
dents in Grenada cannot help but remind one of. Think about
it for a moment—a small Caribbean island, a band of beard-
ed local militia, a lot of beautiful and confused residents, and
throw in a few angry tourists for comic relief. Unfortunately,
this is not a grade B movie, it is not even a very good script—
two American marines have already lost their lives.

But if that is the way Mr. Reagan persists in looking at these
issues maybe he will listen to a little advice from Mr. Gersh-

---

The flu was first described by Hippocrates, in 412 B.C.

win. If Gershwin were alive today, perhaps he would consider this rewrite:

You like po-ta-to, I like po-tah-to,
You say Gre-na-da, I say Gre-nah-da,
Po-ta-to, po-tah-to, Gre-na-da, Gre-nah-da,
Let's call the whole thing off.

—*Rep. James M. Shannon (D-Mass.)*
October 26, 1983

TEED OFF AT THE POST OFFICE? REMEMBER LARRY

Mr. Speaker, a recent item in the *Washington Star* told of one Larry Ryan who scored a hole-in-one while playing in the Pittsfield, Mass., Post Office Golf Tournament. But his was a dubious achievement. He drove from the third tee and the ball went 180 yards away—into the cup on the first green.

Some would find this an apt analogy to the operations of the Postal Service. So, whenever you receive mail intended for another—a not uncommon occurrence—it is a safe guess that our Postal Service is using the Larry Ryan method of delivery.

—*Rep. Charles H. Wilson (D-Calif.)*
June 10, 1975

OH GOD

I recall something that involved my good Baptist friend, Bill D. Moyers....

President Johnson called on Bill one day to open a Cabinet meeting with prayer. Bill was sitting at the end of the Cabinet table, and when he had finished the prayer, the President said, "Bill, we couldn't hear you up here."

Bill said, "I wasn't talking to you, Mr. President."

—*Rep. Brooks Hays (D-Ark.)*
May 19, 1977

CONE HEAD

Mr. Speaker, I have introduced a resolution declaring July Ice Cream Month and July 15 as Ice Cream Day....Ice cream is good for you.

If you feel dejected or frustrated, eat ice cream; if the legis-

---

The African Queen was originally supposed to star David Niven and Bette Davis.

lative processes frustrate you, eat ice cream; if you are happy and want to celebrate, eat ice cream. Not only will you help an industry and American workers but it is good, it is just plain good.

—*Rep. E de la Garza (D-Tex.)*
June 7, 1984

GOLDEN OLDIE

I am reminded of the time when Emanuel Celler was in the House, and I served with him. Emanuel Celler was the oldest Member of that body at that time. He was...speaking in support of a measure I had introduced, and he forgot certain facts about which I reminded him.

He said, "Oh yes, yes. How clearly I recall that now. You know, there are three signs of aging. The first is that you tend to forget things rather easily—and for the life of me, I don't know what the other two things are."

[Laughter.]

—*Sen. Spark M. Matsunaga (D-Hawaii)*
March 12, 1980

STARK DIFFERENCES

Mr. Speaker, the *Washington Post* reports that the Army has granted a $139,000 contract to the University of Maryland to conduct a study of how to prepare healthy food that tastes good. I submit that the Army asking a college food service about healthy, tasty food is rather like Phyllis Diller asking Joan Rivers about beauty aids....

—*Rep. Fortney H. (Pete) Stark (D-Calif.)*
October 10, 1986

UPS AND DOWNS

Mr. Speaker, after careful and scholarly study I have concluded that the principal cause of congressional inefficiency is the elevator system in the Longworth Building.

—*Rep. Andrew Jacobs, Jr. (D-Ind.)*
June 15, 1976

The first all-talking movie was called *The Lights of New York.*

BUTCH AND SUNDANCE

*Butch Cassidy and the Sundance Kid, starring Paul
Newman and Robert Redford, is the highest-grossing
cowboy film of all-time. For those of you who assume that
the pair's wild on-screen exploits were
pure fantasy, here's a surprise.*

Of all the outlaws, desperadoes and personalities of
the West, perhaps none have captured the fancy of
Americans more than Butch Cassidy and the Sundance
Kid. They were master bank and train robbers, outlaws who
seldom used their guns, and among the very few who lived to
spend and enjoy the enormous wealth they captured in the
waning days of the Wild West.

Cassidy, whose real name was Robert Leroy Parker, was born
in 1866 to Mormon parents in Utah. Harry Longabaugh, the
Sundance Kid, probably hailed from New Jersey or Pennsylvania sometime in the late 1860s. Both Cassidy and Sundance
were products of the times, when small ranchers and businessmen were often overwhelmed by the well-financed "robber
barons" of the era. Some historians believe their robbery exploits were a reaction to the emerging monopoly capitalism
mentality, while others feel it was simply a case of "bad
company."

At any rate, Cassidy, Sundance, and their gang—known both
as the Hole in the Wall Gang and the Wild Bunch—were
masters of the big heist. They perfected the technique of the
three-man robbery—one man to hold the horse, one to hold the
gun, and of course, one to grab the cash. The gang was particularly famous for their stylish technique. When the boys took a
train, they blew up the baggage cars with dynamite...but *never*
hurt the passengers or crew. And the robberies were always

Only 2% of American homes don't have a Bible in them.

well planned out from start to finish—which accounts for their long and lucrative careers.

In 1900, with the Wild Bunch's numbers diminishing (due to the steady pursuit of the famous Pinkerton Detective Agency), Cassidy, Sundance and a third man robbed a bank in a remote part of Nevada and netted over $32,000 in cash. They split up to meet again in Texas, where a wild spending spree ensued.

In 1901, the two discussed plans to go to South America, then pulled a final train robbery, demolishing a baggage car and making off with thousands in bank notes. After a brief visit to New York City, the pair and Sundance's lover went to Argentina and bought a ranch. There they apparently led a quiet life. But in 1906, probably because they were running out of money, they robbed a bank in a nearby town.

After a trip back to the United States by Sundance and his ailing mistress, the pair met up again, sometime around 1909 in Bolivia. A violent shoot out with the Bolivian cavalry (probably during a robbery) ensued, and it was from that point on that their legend began to really take shape. Accounts of what happened during and after the shootout vary: Some say both men died; some think Cassidy survived; but most are now convinced that both outlaws actually escaped, with Sundance rejoining his long-time lover and living quietly in Wyoming until 1956. As for Cassidy, he probably changed his name and died in a nursing home in Washington state in 1937.

Whatever the real story, it's clear that Butch Cassidy and the Sundance Kid were among the cleverest and shrewdest outlaws ever to emerge from the Old West.

FACTS ABOUT THE WEST
- Billy the Kid was from Brooklyn, New York.
- The most common causes of death for old-time cowboys: pneumonia and riding accidents.
- Most cowboys didn't like carrying guns—they got in the way when they were riding, and scared their horses or cattle.

TOP TEN BABY NAMES

What's in a name? Sugar and spice? Or the herd instinct?
Here's what parents have been naming
their kids for the last fifty years.

Most popular baby names in 1925:

For Girls:	For Boys:
1. Mary	Robert
2. Barbara	John
3. Dorothy	William
4. Betty	James
5. Ruth	Charles
6. Margaret	Richard
7. Helen	George
8. Elizabeth	Donald
9. Jean	Joseph
10. Ann	Edward

Most popular baby names in 1974:

For Girls:	For Boys:
1. Jennifer	Michael
2. Michelle	John
3. Christine	Robert
4. Lisa	David
5. Maria	Christopher
6. Melissa	Anthony
7. Nicole	Joseph
8. Elizabeth	Jason
9. Jessica	James
10. Erica	Jose

Most popular baby names in 1948:

For Girls:	For Boys:
1. Linda	Robert
2. Mary	John
3. Barbara	James
4. Patricia	Michael
5. Susan	William
6. Kathleen	Richard
7. Carol	Joseph
8. Nancy	Thomas
9. Margaret	Stephen
10. Diane	David

Most popular baby names in 1987:

For Girls:	For Boys:
1. Jessica	Michael
2. Jennifer	Christopher
3. Ashley	Matthew
4. Amanda	Daniel
5. Christine	Joseph
6. Sara(h)	David
7. Nicole	Andrew
8. Stephanie	Steven
9. Melissa	Brian
10. Danielle	Robert

The Statue of Liberty was originally built for the Suez Canal.

MONOPOLY

Monopoly is the best selling game in history. It has been published in twenty-eight countries and nineteen different languages and is more popular in the eighties than ever.

I f there was ever a way to introduce the concept of capitalism to children, this game is it.

Background: In 1904, "The Landlord's Game," a board game which included the purchasing of property, utilities and a "public park" space, was patented. Apparently Charles Darrow, the father of Monopoly, "borrowed" much of this game.

The Origin. Following the stock market crash of 1929, Darrow—an engineer by trade—found himself unemployed and short of cash like the rest of the country. To kill time (and keep his spirits up), he began devising a game involving "plenty of money for the player to invest or speculate with." Because he was interested in real estate he made that the primary focus; and because he personally didn't believe in credit or borrowing money, he made the whole thing a cash proposition.

Darrow had visited Atlantic City shortly before the stock market crashed, so he transferred his fond memories of the town to the board—thus the Boardwalk, railroad lines and property of the New Jersey resort are represented there.

The original version of the game was crudely painted on a piece of linoleum. But that didn't stop family and friends from getting hooked on it—and demanding their own sets. "I hadn't anything better to do, so I began to make the games," Darrow explained. "I charged people $4.00 a copy." Although Darrow did no advertising, he soon began to receive orders from all over the country. He was shocked but excited. Looking for more distribution, he took the game to Parker Brothers...and was turned down cold. Says one writer: "George and Charles Parker thought Monopoly took much too long to play, the rules were hopelessly complicated, and there were at least fifty-two

---

The most common street name in America is "Park Street."

other weak points they believed ruled the game out as far as they were concerned."

Darrow was upset by the decision, but decided to distribute the games on his own. He took them to two major retailers—Wanamaker's Department Store in Philadelphia, and FAO Schwartz, New York's most prestigious toy store—and convinced them to stock Monopoly. When both quickly sold out their entire stock, the Parker brothers reconsidered. They purchased the rights to make the game…and watched, astounded, as Monopoly sold so fast that it kept the toy company—which was on the edge of insolvency—from going under.

Parker Brothers sold every Monopoly set they could manufacture for Christmas, 1934, and the demand didn't die down after the holidays. They were soon literally inundated with requests for more; orders were so plentiful they had to be stacked in laundry baskets and stored in hallways. The company had never even heard of a product being so much in demand.

By mid-February of the following year, Parker Brothers was selling more than twenty thousand sets of Monopoly per week. Darrow, as one would imagine, was financially set for life. And the reluctant toy company had its hands on the most lucrative game in the history of the toy industry.

GUINNESS ON MONOPOLY

•Largest Monopoly game in history: Took place on full-size sidewalks and streets in Huntington, Pennsylvania, on a board that was bigger than a square city block. Sponsored by students at Juniata College, who cast huge foam dice from a third-story fire escape and kept players informed of their moves by using walkie-talkie-equipped bicycle messengers. April, 1967.
•Longest Monopoly game underwater: 1,008 hours, by the Lodi, California, Diving School. That's forty-two days, one hundred forty players.
•Longest Monopoly game in a moving elevator: sixteen days.
•Longest Monopoly game ever: 1,416 hours. Players: McCluer North Games Club, Florissant, Missouri.
•Longest Monopoly game in a bathtub: 99 hours.
•Longest anti-gravitational Monopoly game: 36 hours.

In 1985, "The Cosby Show" was the highest-ranking TV program in South Africa.

10 COOL BOOKS

From Gene Sculatti, here's a list of ten obscure but hip books which may be suitable for future bathroom reading.

BEEN DOWN SO LONG IT LOOKS LIKE UP TO ME —*Richard Fariña*

The fact that he may inadvertently have invented Tom Robbins should not be held against this late great. This ...is *the* missed link between the beatbooks of Kerouac, Brossard, etc. and the great hippie novels that were never written. Maybe the flower kids took one look at *Been Down So Long* and gave up.

CONFESSIONS OF A HOAXER —*Alan Abel*

OK, there've been odder political candidates than Yetta Brosten, more ludicrous rock stars than Count Von Blitzstein, social protests every bit as ill-founded as the campaign to clothe nude animals. But they didn't all have a single mastermind behind them. Alan Abel got away with the above and more (including staging the debut of the world's first topless string quartet). *Confessions* makes it look easy, as well as eminently worthwhile.

A CONFEDERACY OF DUNCES —*John Kennedy Toole*

The coolest American hero of recent years wore earflaps, caroused with b-girls in a Bourbon Street dive called the Night of Joy, and contended with a mad world and a mother who feared he'd become "a communiss." They don't make 'em like this anymore. A Pulitzer Prize winner.

FLASH AND FILIGREE —*Terry Southern*

The brilliant comic writer's first novel, containing the boss TV game show "What's My Disease," a seduction scene comprised solely of grappling maneuvers, and "Onono-pleaseno's." Surpassed only by his short story "Blood of a Wig" (in *Red Dirt Marijuana and Other Tastes*).

GORMENGHAST TRILOGY —*Mervyn Peake*

One critic described *Titus Groan, Gormenghast*, and *Titus Alone* as "Charles Dickens on opium." Psychologically rich, koo-koo characters live in a huge crumbling castle located somewhere in Peake's brain. The first two novels are great, the third isn't. A companion novella *Boy in Darkness,* is even more unreal.

MINE ENEMY GROWS OLDER —*Alexander King*

By 1958, the man Lenny Bruce christened "the junkie Mark Twain" had seen it all and done most of it twice. Long before he became a high-watt fixture on Jack Paar's TV show, Alex the Great had painted covers for Mencken's *Smart Set* magazine, scrawled Chinese murals on the walls of kosher deli's and been photo editor of *Life*....He'd also been a morphine addict, submitted to bagel therapy at an asylum as batty as Kesey's cuckoo's nest, and played chess with A-bomb "spy" Alger Hiss. Bonus: King explains why, between 1917 and 1948 he only wore pink neckties.

OZZIE —*Ozzie Nelson*

Dedicated to Harriet. It takes 309 pages, but Daddy-O spills it all in this 1977 autobio: what he did for a living all those years on *Ozzie and Harriet*, his days on the road, that time at Rutgers when a young student presented him with a lit marijuana cigarette. (Oz put it in his pocket. It burned.)

THE SECRET LIFE OF SALVADOR DALI

A Forties autobiography from the twentieth century's most profound comedian. Mind-boggling anecdotes, opinions, and self-analysis spill out over the page, filtered through Dali's aristo-punk attitude. (He once shellacked his hair.) Always outrageous, *never* dull.

THE WANDERERS —*Richard Price*

The coolest, craziest juvenile delinquent trip ever put down. Noo Yawk at its most fearsome, funniest. Irish Ducky Boys roam their gang turf like midget dinosaurs, Chinese Wongs take no shit, and everybody listens to Dion.

WRITE IF YOU GET WORK: THE BEST OF BOB & RAY

Worth hunting for if you remember their insane commercials, *Mad* articles, or the deadpan dada of their radio comedy. Reprints classic bits—"Spelling Bee," "Lightbulb Collector," and more.

A good memory is an inherited trait.

THE REAL ARTICLE

A random sampling of first-person articles, dialogue, correspondence. You are there.

SOUR GRAPES

In 1957, Frank Sinatra—a teen idol in the '40s—wrote this piece about rock 'n' roll in a magazine called West-ern World:

"My only deep sorrow is the unrelenting insistence of recording and motion picture companies upon purveying the most brutal, ugly, degenerate, vicious form of expression it has been my displeasure to hear and naturally I'm referring to the bulk of rock 'n' roll.

"It fosters almost totally negative and destructive reactions in young people," he said. "It smells phony and false. It is sung, played, and written for the most part by cretinous goons and by means of its almost imbecilic reiterations and sly, lewd—in plain fact—dirty lyrics, it manages to be the martial music of every sideburned delinquent on the face of the earth."

FORGETTABLE FIRST FILM

On September 15, 1937, Variety *reviewed a film called* Love Is On the Air—*which happened to be Ronald Reagan's first movie appearance. Ironically, Reagan starred as a citizen who exposed a corrupt link between businessmen and politicians.*

"In the lead, Ronald Reagan, whom Warners is trying to build up into a juvenile lead, is a spot-newscaster on a radio station. If he exceeds in authority and importance that role played in radio actually, the public probably won't notice. But they are bound to notice that the plot is the one about the newspaperman who, against the advice and even threats from higher-ups, does his community the good turn of dragging into the open the connections between racketeering gangsters and the businessmen and political job-holders who protect the lawless and share the booty....

"Reagan, before the camera all the way, gives rather an in-and-out performance. He's best when in fast physical action...."

Walt Disney won more Oscars than anyone else.

FARTS IN SPACE

*An official NASA transcript of a conversation between astro-
nauts John Young and Charles Duke during the moon launch on
April 21, 1972.*

Young: "I got the farts again. I got 'em again, Charlie. I don't
know what the hell gives 'em to me."
Duke: [unintelligible]
Young: "Certainly not—I think it's acid in the stomach. I really do."
Duke: "Probably is."
Young: "I mean, I haven't eaten this much citrus fruit in twenty
years. And I'll tell you one thing—in another twelve...days, I
ain't never eating any more. And if they offer to serve me po-
tassium with my breakfast, I'm going to throw up. I like an oc-
casional orange, I really do. But I'll be damned if I'm going to
be buried in oranges."

ABE LINCOLN'S BEARD

*A copy of the letter—written to Abraham Lincoln while he
campaigned for president in 1860—which inspired Lincoln to
grow a beard.*

Westfield, Chautauqua Co., N.Y.
October 15, 1860

Dear Sir,
I am a little girl 11 years old, but want you should be President of the United States very much so I hope you won't think
me very bold to write to such a great man as you are.
  Have you any little girls about as large as I am if so give
them my love and tell her to write me if you cannot answer
this letter. I have got four brothers and part of them will vote
for you any way and if you will let your whiskers grow. I will
try to get the rest of them to vote for you. You would look a
great deal better, for your face is so thin. All the ladies like
whiskers and they would tease their husbands to vote for you
and then you would be President.

Grace Bedell

Over 450 million copies of author Barbara Cartland's books have been sold—a record.

REAGAN'S RESOLUTION
In November, 1955, Ronald Reagan wrote an article for The Hollywood Reporter *about his work in TV, films, and politics. Among his comments:*

"I have for the past months been doubling, combining television and motion picture chores. This manifold job has taught me one thing for sure: never again will I allow myself to get into a position where I must make a choice between a seat in Congress and a comfortable position in the arms of my leading lady.

"Actors are citizens and should exert those rights by speaking their minds, but the actor's first duty is to his profession. Hence, you can rest assured that I will never again run for mayor or anything but head man in my own household...."

HANK WILLIAMS' LAST WORDS
Hank Williams died on December 31, 1952, sitting in the back of his Cadillac. When his body was discovered, a piece of paper was found clutched in his right hand. On it were Hank Williams's last words. They were:

"We met, we lived and dear we loved, then comes that fatal day, the love that felt so dear fades far away. Tonight love hath one alone and lonesome, all that I could sing, I you you [sic] still and always will, but that's the poison we have to pay."

MODEL CITIZEN
Twiggy was a hero to millions of girls in the '60s. Esquire magazine quoted this encounter with a reporter who actually asked her a real question.

Reporter: "Twiggy, do you know what happened at Hiroshima?"
Twiggy: "Where's that?"
Reporter: "In Japan."
Twiggy: "I've never heard of it. What happened there?"
Reporter: "A hundred thousand people died on the spot."
Twiggy: "Oh, God! When did you say it happened? Where? Hiroshima? But that's ghastly! A hundred thousand dead? It's frightful. Men are mad."

A beehive hairdo that stood 6 feet, 6 inches is the tallest recorded hairdo in the world.

MARK TWAIN SAYS...

*No one in the history of American literature combined
sardonic wit, warmth, and intelligence
as Mark Twain did in his novels.*

"Adam and Eve had many advantages, but the principal one was that they escaped teething."

"Reader, suppose you were an idiot. And suppose you were a member of Congress. But I repeat myself."

"Get your facts first, and then you can distort them as much as you please."

"It is better to keep your mouth shut and appear stupid than to open it and remove all doubt."

"It is by the goodness of God that we have in our country three unspeakably precious things: freedom of speech, freedom of conscience, and the prudence never to practice either."

"Truth is the most valuable thing we have. Let us economize it."

"A man pretty much always refuses another man's first offer, no matter what it is."

"Be good, and you will be lonesome."

"There are three kinds of lies—lies, damned lies and statistics."

"Noise proves nothing. Often a hen who has merely laid an egg cackles as if she has laid an asteroid."

"The principle difference between a cat and a lie is that a cat only has nine lives."

"Man is the only animal that blushes. Or needs to."

"I believe that our Heavenly Father invented man because he was disappointed in the monkey."

"War talk by men who have been in a war is always interesting, whereas moon talk by a poet who has not been in the moon is likely to be dull."

The biggest tomato on record weighed 7 1/2 pounds.

PLACES' NAMES

*The fascinating history of place-naming in America is
captured in the classic* Names on the Land. *Author
George R. Stewart demonstrates several of
the main sources for common U.S. names.*

RIVERS. "On August 4, 1830, the inhabitants of
an...undistinguished western village filed [to become a
town]. They had previously been known as Fort Dearborn, but Dearborn (the man for whom it was named)...had
merely been Secretary of War under Jefferson, and was no
hero....So, in accordance with the fashion of the time, the town-
founders took the name of the river, and wrote Chicago upon
their [application]. It was a good example of a name adopted
without knowledge of its meaning, for if the founders had known
it to be Onion river, or allegedly Skunk or Smelling River, they
would very likely have kept Dearborn."

HEROES. "At San Jacinto, on April 21, 1836, General Sam
Houston waved his old campaign hat as a signal, and the Texans
charged, shouting 'Remember the Alamo!' Within a few months
a town was laid out near the battlefield; its promoters combined
patriotism with advertisement, and called it Houston."

THE ANCIENT WORLD. "[John Charles] Fremont made his
best stroke in California. The Spaniards had neglected to supply a name to the passage connecting San Francisco Bay with the
ocean. Although Fremont had never been to Constantinople, he
fancied a resemblance between that ancient harbor and the
western strait;...He wrote accordingly: 'I give the name *Chryso-
playe*, or *Golden Gate*; for the same reasons that the harbor of
Byzantium was called *Chrysoceras*, or *Golden Horn*.'"

LANDOWNERS. "One of the five boroughs of New York
City...is always *The Bronx*, never just a naked *Bronx*....This dates
from the 17th century, a time when a man named Jonas Bronck
farmed...land north of Manhattan Island. When people back
then said they were going to the Broncks, they really meant it."

In 1976, a Los Angeles secretary formally married her fifty-pound pet rock.

GLOBAL VILLAGE

*B.R.I. member Eric Lefcowitz contributed this
batch of world statistics. Unfortunately,
stats are generally buried in books that
are too large and cumbersome
for bathroom reading.*

With the advent of computers and lasers, and both digital and satellite technology, Marshall McLuhan's late Sixties version of a "global village" is more relevant than ever. The media's ability to transmit information is just a small part of the development of global consciousness, however. The depletion of the earth's oxygen through the destruction of rain forests, the ozone layer and the "greenhouse effect" have become world issues. As we found out with Chernobyl, one country does not have a nuclear accident—they all do.

So maybe Uncle Walt was right: it's a small world, after all....Actually, if you want to be precise, it's not so small—the land area of the world is 135,841,000 kilometers, or 52,500,000 square miles.

Here are some other world statistics.
There are approximately
- 1.2 billion households
- 5 billion people
- 1.8 billion people working
- 1.5 billion children under 15
- 32 million teachers
- 4 million doctors
- 8,240 daily newspapers
- 72 million movie seats
- 527 million television sets
- 453 million telephones
- 300 million passenger cars
- 250,000 movie theaters

"All in the Family" was the #1 TV show in America from 1972-76.

Here are some world averages:
- Approximate life expectancy at birth: 62 years
- Life expectancy, female: 59 years; male: 53 years
- Literacy rate: 70%
- Daily Calorie Supply per Capita: 2,607
- Size of a Household: 4.1
- Gross Global Product (GGP): $2,633

However, drastic differences come to light when you subject global averages to quantitative analysis. For example, in terms of male life expectancy, the country of Iceland ranks the highest with 73 years. On the low end of the scale are the African nations of Togo (31.50), Chad (29) and Gabon (25). Neither America nor England are in the top 10.

For female life expectancy, Iceland again ranks number one at 79.20 years. Upper Volta, however, brings up the rear with 31.10.

Other global highs and lows:
- Hottest place—Aroune, Mali. Highest recorded temperature: 130 degrees Fahrenheit (54.4 Centigrade).
- Coldest place—Eismitte, Greenland. Lowest recorded temperature: -85 degrees Fahrenheit (-64.8 Centigrade).
- Wettest place—Cherrapunji, India. Highest recorded rainfall (in 1983): 425 inches of rain.

The Media

TV: According to a 1980 poll, Canada has the most hours of TV broadcasting in the world—over 6 million per year. The U.S. is in second place with 5 1/2 million, followed by Japan and Brazil. England is tenth. If you lived in Cyprus , Norway, Pakistan, or about a dozen other countries, you could watch less than 3,000 hours...if you watched TV *every single minute* there was something on the air. Compare that with the viewing habits of (and influences on) the average American, who routinely watches me than 8 hours of television per day.

Movies: People in the U.S.S.R. watch more movies than anyone in the world—about a third of all movie attendance. Among the countries that average the most films seen per capita: Iceland, the Falkland Islands, Singapore, Hong Kong, and Grenada. The least: Uganda, Tanzania, and other African nations.

You have about 10 gallons of water inside you, making up about 60% of your weight.

FIVE BEATLE SONGS

*It's fun to learn the origin of any Beatles song; here is a
random selection of five tunes to read about, from
Behind the Hits, by Bob Shannon and John Javna.*

PLEASE PLEASE ME, 1964
LENNON (in an interview with *Playboy*): "It was my attempt
at writing a Roy Orbison song, would you believe it? I wrote it
in the bedroom in my house at Menlove Avenue, which was my
auntie's place...I heard Roy Orbison doing 'Only the Lonely' or
something. And...I was intrigued by the words of 'Please lend
your little ears to my pleas'—a Bing Crosby song. I was always intrigued by the double use of the word *please*. So it was
a combination of Bing Crosby and Roy Orbison." The Beatles,
by the way, were once the opening act for headliner Roy Orbison on a British tour.

MICHELLE, 1966
McCARTNEY (to Paul Gambaccini): "I just fancied writing
some French words....I had a friend whose wife taught
French...and I just asked her, you know, what we could figure
out that was French. We got words that go together well. It
was mainly because I always used to think the song sounded
like a French thing...I can't speak French, really, so we sorted
out some actual words."

ELEANOR RIGBY, 1966
McCARTNEY (in *Paul McCartney in His Own Words*): "I
think it was 'Miss Daisy Hawkins' originally, picking up the
rice in a church after a wedding....At first I thought it was a
young Miss Daisy Hawkins...but then I saw I'd said she was
picking up the rice in a church, so she had to be a cleaner,
she'd missed the wedding and she was suddenly lonely. In
fact, she had missed it all—she was the spinster type.

"[But] I didn't really like 'Daisy Hawkins'—I wanted a name
that was more real. The thought just came, 'Eleanor Rigby
picks up the rice and lives in a dream,' so there she was. The

---

One company manufactures an edible set of Monopoly, made of chocolate and butterscotch.

next thing was Father Mackenzie. It was going to be Father McCartney, but then I thought that was a bit of a hang-up for my dad, being in this lonely song. So we looked through the phone book. That's the beauty of working at random—it does come up perfectly, much better than if you try to think it with your intellect. Anyway, there was Father Mackenzie, just as I had imagined him, lonely, darning his socks."

NOWHERE MAN, 1966
LENNON: "I was just sitting, trying to think of a song, and I thought of myself sitting there, doing nothing and getting nowhere. Once I'd thought of that, it was easy. It all came out. No, I remember now, I'd actually stopped trying to think of something. Nothing would come. I was cheesed off and went for a lie-down, having given up. Then I thought of myself as a 'Nowhere Man,' sitting in his nowhere land."

DO YOU WANT TO KNOW A SECRET, 1964
LENNON (in *Playboy* again): "My mother...was a comedienne....She used to get up in pubs and things like that. She had a good voice....She used to do this little tune when I was just a one- or two-year-old. The tune was from a Disney movie—[singing] 'Want to know a secret? Promise not to tell. You are standing by a wishing well.'

"I wrote [the song] and gave it to George to sing. I thought it would be a good vehicle for him because it only had three notes and he wasn't the best singer in the world."

MISCELLANEOUS BEATLES STATS
•In less than a decade, they sold over 125 million singles and 85 million LPs.
•They had the most #1 records during the '60s—17—compared to the second-place Supremes, who had 12.
•They had the most Top 10 hits in the '60s—29.
•In one year—1964—they had 31 songs that hit the charts.
•On April 4, 1964, they had all of the top 5 songs on the Billboard charts: 1) "Can't Buy Me Love"; 2)"Twist and Shout"; 3)"She Loves You"; 4) "I Wanna Hold Your Hand"; 5) "Please Please Me."

Your eyes and nose are the warmest parts of your body.

THE FABULOUS '60s

*If you were there, you remember the "topless" controversy
of the mid-'60s. If you weren't, this might
give you an idea of what it was like.*

THE INSIDE STORY: The Origin of the Topless Bathing Suit

The topless suit began simply as a prediction. One day in 1963, in an interview, fashion designer Rudi Gernreich commented that "in five years every American woman will be wearing a bathing suit that is bare above the waist." After saying that, he realized that if *he* didn't make that topless suit immediately, someone else would. But should he?

Before he could decide, Hess Brothers department store in Allentown, Pennsylvania, ordered some. Then other stores across the United States did, too. Gernreich put the suit into production.

One of the things that focused national attention on the topless suit was that 1964 was an election year, and the Republican party seized on it as a symbol of the "decadence" in America.

This produced millions of dollars worth of publicity for Gernreich, who said in amazement: "I never dreamed it would go beyond the fashion business into sociology."

By the way, the topless suit was never popular to wear—only three thousand were sold.

'60s MADNESS
Topless Bathing

June 1964—New York City Commissioner of Parks Newbold Morris said women wearing topless bathing suits on N.Y.C. beaches would be issued summonses by police for indecent exposure. L.A. police issued the same warning.

July 1964—The Vatican newspaper *L'Osservatore Roma* headlined an article on topless bathing suits "The Ultimate Shame," and said it "negates moral sense."

Your fingers and toes are the coldest parts of your body.

June 1964—In an article entitled "Back to Barbarism," the Soviet newspaper *Izvestia* called the topless suits a sign of America's moral decay. "So the decay of the moneybags society continues," it said.

July 1964—The topless suit was modeled in the *San Francisco Chronicle*—by a four-year-old-girl.

THE REVEREND ED WATT

In Dallas, the Reverend Ed Watt and a group of protesters from the Carroll Avenue Baptist Mission picketed a department store that was displaying a topless bathing suit in its window. Their placards read: "We Protest these Suits in the Name of Christ." Watt said that church action was long overdue—topless shorts would be next.

The picketing continued until the department store removed the one topless suit it had from its display.

Were the protesters successful? Not exactly. They attracted so much attention to the suit that someone went into the store and bought it.

MORE '60S MADNESS:

Bottled Eggs

September 3, 1962: "Fresh eggs sold by the bottle are being test-marketed in National Tea Co. stores. The secret (which the developer, Chicago's David Cleaver Produce Co., won't reveal) is in the 'simple but patentable method' of getting the shellless eggs into the bottle without breaking the yolks. The eggs readily pour out of the bottle one at a time, yolks cushioned by the whites. National Tea claims that refrigerated bottled eggs keep longer than eggs in the shell (six to eight weeks vs. four to six) because the capped bottle offers an airtight seal while the shell is porous. The bottles come in one-pound (about ten eggs) and two-pound (twenty eggs) sizes. Cost: About eight cents more per dozen than eggs in the carton."

Puppy Love.

1962: A fallout shelter for pets was put on the market, "to give pets an equal chance for survival."
1966: Upjohn introduced an oral contraceptive for dogs, for "Planned Puppyhood."

Elvis Presley had more records on the *Billboard* charts—107—than any other artist.

DOO-WOP SOUNDS

You've heard classic street-corner rock 'n' roll tunes before—"Why Do Fools Fall in Love," "Come Go With Me," etc. And you've probably noticed the crazy syllables the groups sing in the background. Ever wonder what they'd look like spelled out? Here are 20 great doo-wop syllables from The Doo-Wop Sing-Along Song Book.

1. **Hooodly-Papa-Kow, Papa-Kow, Papa-Kow (YEAH), Hooodly-Papa-Kow, Papa Kow, Papa Kow.** A gem from Frankie Lymon and the Teenagers.

2. **Pa-pa-pa-pa-pa-pa-pa-Oom-A-Mow-Mow, Papa-Oom Mow Mow.** One of the most famous rock syllable combos, from a group called the Rivingtons and a semi-doo-wop tune called—big surprise—"Papa Oom Mow Mow."

3. **Oop-Shoop, Shang-A-Lack-A-Cheek-A-Bock.** One of the all-time greats, a background section from the Earls' "Remember Then" (1961).

4. **Diddle-iddle-iddle-iddle-it (YEAH), Diddle-iddle-iddle-iddle-it.** Notable for its persistence, in a classic doo-wop tune by Herb Cox and the Cleftones, "Little Girl of Mine" (1956).

5. **Neh-neh-neh-neh, neh neh-neh-neh neh-neh-neh, Neh-neh-neh-neh-neh, neh-neh-neh-neh (repeat the whole thing two more times), Werp-A-Tul-Werp, Neh-Neh-Neh-Neh, Neh-Neh-Neh-Neh.** A perfect example of why you have to hear doo-wop to appreciate it. The opening of "The Closer You Are," by the Magnificent Four.

6. **I Su-mokem Boo-eye-ay, I sumokem boo.** Doo-wop's classic drug reference. From "Ling Ting Tong," by the Five Keys.

M&M's were introduced in 1940 for U.S. soldiers, so their hands wouldn't be sticky.

7. (Bom-bom) Cheer-Up, (Bom-bom) Cheer-up, (Bom-Bom) Cheer-Up, (Bom-bom) Cheer-Up. A favorite adaptation of a real word into a doo-wop. From the Pentagons' "To Be Loved."

8. Rama Lama-Lama-Lama-Lama Ding Dong, Rama Lama-Lama-Lama-Lama-Lama Ding. That's the Edsels playing homage to George Jones, Jr.'s girlfriend, "Rama Lama Ding Dong."

9. Rang Tang Ding Dong, Rankety Sing. Weird syllable combination from "Ring Tang Ding Dong (I am the Japanese Sandman)," by the Cellos.

10. Ka-Ding-Dong, Ding-Dong, Ka-Ding-Dong, Ding-Dong, Ding. The sound of the singer's heart in the G-Clefs' thriller, "Ka-Ding-Dong."

11. Yip, Yip, Yip, Yip Boom, Sha-Na-Na-Na, Sha-Na-Na-Na-Na. It's from "Get A Job" by the Silhouettes and it's not only a great doo-wop, it's the symbol of the '70s doo-wop revival. The quasi-greaser band from Columbia University got its name from this background.

12. Sho-Dot'n' Shoby-Doh, Sho-Dot'n' Shoby-Doh. From Fred Parris and the Five Satins' classic "In the Still of the Night." Strangely, although it's sold millions of records, the highest this song ever reached on the *Billboard* charts was #25.

13. Dom-Dooby-Dom Woh-oh, Dooby Dooby, Dom Dooby Dom, Woh-oh, Dooby Dooby, Dom Dooby Dom Woh-Oh, tonight I fell in love. Sort of a white bread doo-wop, but kind of catchy. From the Tokens' "Tonight I Fell In Love."

14. Tuh-tuh-tuh-tuh-tuh-tuh-tuh-aaa-ooo-ooo-ooo-ooo-ooo. A super doo-wop. This is the end of a line in "Unchained Melody," by Vito and the Salutations. The one that starts "Oh my love, my darling, I hunger for your...." Originally, the next word was "touch." In doo-wop it became this 13-syllable creature.

15. A-Wop-bop-A-Loo-bop-A-Bop--Bam-Boom. For sentimental reasons. From Little Richard's "Tutti Frutti."

The first sperm banks opened in 1964; they were located in Tokyo and Iowa City.

16. Iminni-ma-ma-ma-Iminni-ma-ma-ma-gin-A-tion. Imin-i-ni-ma-ima-ima-ma-gin-aaaa-tion. The doo-wop spelling for the word "imagination," as interpreted by the Quotations.

17. Shoh-Be-Doo-Wop-Wah-Da. The controversial last line in "What's Your Name," by Don and Juan. No one seems to agree on what they're saying. Here's my version.

18. Wah-Wah-OOO, Chop Chop Chop. An original from "Tell Me Why," by the Rob Roys.

19. Wop-wop-Doodly-wop-Wop-wop. Wop-wop, Doodly-wop-Wop-Wop. The El Doradoes lead into the instrumental break in "At My Front Door."

20. And of course: Bomp-ba-ba-bomp, Ba-bom-ba-bom-bomp, Ba-ba-bomp-ba-ba-bomp, A-dang-a-dang-dang. A-ding-a-dong-ding, Bluuuue Moooon.

From the Marcels' adaptation of the Rogers and Hart classic, "Blue Moon." Originally, this song was written for a '30s film—Jean Harlow was supposed to sing it! She never did.

The Marcels, from Pittsburgh, Pa., however, made it the #1 song in America in 1961.

SAD NEWS. *Variety,* March 6, 1968
"Frankie Lymon, 26, a click disk artist as a moppet blues singer back in 1956-58, died of an apparent overdose of narcotics in the New York apartment of a friend. A GI, Lymon had come to New York to start a disk comeback with Roulette Records.

"Lymon was among the original youngsters to ride in on the rock 'n' roll cycle early in the 1950s. His big hits included "Why Do Fools Fall In Love," "Goody, Goody," and "I'm Not a Juvenile Delinquent," recorded with a combo called the Teenagers. He clicked both in rhythm and blues and pop grooves for a few years.

"As the youngster grew up and lost his precocity, he also lost impact and faded into obscurity. He was arrested a few times on assorted charges, including narcotics raps. In the last year, he claimed to have rid himself of the dope habit and had written stories about how he had kicked the habit.

"His wife survives him."

California has had the most Miss Americas since the pageant began in 1921.

JUNK FOOD CONTROVERSY

*As junk food has become an integral part of American life,
it has also become the focal point in
issues unrelated to eating.*

FRITOS CORN CHIPS
Background: Invented 1932, by Elmer Doolin. Doolin, a Texan, bought the recipe—and the whole concept of the corn chip—from a cook at a Mexican border cafe. (He paid $100 for it.) Then he began turning out the chips by hand in his mother's kitchen, ten pounds per hour. When demand increased, Doolin invented a machine that would make the chips automatically. As the company grew, it moved into larger quarters in Dallas, Texas. In 1945, the Frito Company merged with H. W. Lay and Co., Atlanta-based maker of Lay's potato chips, and achieved national distribution.

The Controversy: In the '60s, Frito-Lay was accused of anti-Mexican racism (an ironic assertion, considering the origin of the product). The reason: it introduced the Frito Bandito, a mustachioed cartoon character who showed up on TV in 1967, ready to steal your Fritos Corn Chips.

In his prime, the Bandito devised some pretty sneaky ways of fleecing gringos. One commercial showed the Apollo astronauts landing on the moon. Who do you think they found there waiting for them? The Frito Bandito, standing next to a parking meter with his burro. "I ham the moon parking lot attendant," he announced. "Now if you will kindly deposit one bag of cronchy Fritos corn cheeps for the first hour..."

But after Frito-Lay decided to use him in all its commercials, the Mexican-American Anti-Defamation Committee protested publicly that the Bandito was spreading the "racist message that Mexicans are sneaky thieves." Frito vehemently denied any hidden meaning or racist intent. But several California TV stations quickly banned the commercials and the Anti-Defamation Committee announced its intention of asking the FCC for equal time.

Appoximately 50% of the area of the earth is covered by the Pacific Ocean.

Although he was an effective TV salesman, the Frito Bandito was ultimately withdrawn from Frito commercials.

HOSTESS TWINKIES
Background: Invented in 1931 by James Dewar, manager of Continental Bakeries' Chicago factory. He envisioned the product as a way of using the company's thousands of shortcake pans (which were otherwise employed only during the strawberry season) full-time…and as a way of having a low-priced snack to sell during the Depression. The cakes were originally called Little Shortcake Fingers, but during a business trip Dewar and a friend noticed a shoe factory sign that read "Home of Twinkle Toe Shoes." Dewar had been looking for a new name for his product; his friend suggested he call it "Twinkle Fingers," which was shortened to Twinkies. The five-cent snack soon became one of Continental's best-selling items.

The Controversy: In 1979, a San Francisco employee named Dan White went on a rampage and killed two important politicians—Mayor George Moscone and Supervisor Harvey Milk—in City Hall. His case seemed indefensible…but in the ensuing trial White's attorney, Douglas Schmidt, did come up with a palatable defense. He blamed his client's behavior on junk food—specifically Twinkies. Psychiatrist Martin Blinder testified that White had eaten too many Twinkies, and that their high sugar content had resulted in "diminished mental capacity." It sounded preposterous, but to the shock of the grieving city, the jury bought this explanation and convicted White of voluntary manslaughter instead of murder. In San Francisco, people still refer to it as the "Twinkie defense."

PRINGLE'S POTATO CHIPS
Background: The potato chip was invented in 1853 by a chef named George Crum in Saratoga Springs, New York. Apparently, a customer at the restaurant where Crum worked kept sending back French Fries, complaining that they were too thick. Finally, the exasperated Crum cut the potatoes paper-thin…and the customer loved them. "Saratoga Chips" became the specialty of the house, and ultimately a national snack.

For many years, large food companies avoided manufacturing

potato chips, despite their popularity. The reason: potato chips were hard to transport long distances without heavy breakage. And they got stale too quickly.

Then in 1969, General Mills and Proctor & Gamble each introduced "newfangled" kinds of potato chips. General Mills called theirs "Chipos." P & G called theirs "Pringle's Potato Chips."

This new product wasn't a sliced potato (as the traditional chip is), but a wafer made from "reconstituted potato granules." Each chip was made from scratch, so each could be formed in exactly the same shape and size—which meant the chips could now be designed to be stackable, and thus they could be packaged in break-proof cannisters, complete with preservatives. A food conglomerate's dream.

The Controversy: Would this mean the end of the potato chip as we knew it? Potato chip manufacturers were afraid it would—so in 1970, the Potato Chip Institute (the trade organization for potato chip makers around the U.S.) went on the offensive and sued General Mills for calling their Chipos "new fashioned potato chips." Chipos, the chipmakers asserted, were not "authentic" chips, and General Mills had no right to equate them with America's classic snack. "We don't like synthetics riding on the potato chip's reputation," said Francis X. Rice, the president of the organization.

By the time the suit gathered steam, however, it was clear that the new chips would never be as popular as the old ones. So the suit was quietly dropped.

Frito-Lay, the nation's largest potato chip manufacturer, straddled the issue. They joined as a party in the Potato Chip Institute's suit, but also came out with their own new-style chip—Munchos...just in case.

UNRELATED COMMENT

"Being in politics is like being a football coach. You have to be smart enough to understand the game, and dumb enough to think it's important."

—*Ex-Senator Eugene McCarthy*

ELVIS' TOOTHBRUSH

A bizarre—but true—tale of fan weirdness, from the
book How to Meet the Stars, *by Missy Laws.*
Published by Ross Books, Berkeley, CA.

THE SCENARIO: *A rabid Elvis fan called "Sir Mordrid" and two women were visiting Las Vegas. A celebrity they met in a casino invited them "to meet my good friend Elvis."*

"The four of them went to the Hilton Hotel, where Elvis was performing two shows nightly. They entered the backstage area and confronted a mob. Sir Mordrid could feel the pounding of his heart as he grew nearer to the superstar's private dressing room.

"Because he had an enormous collection of Elvis memorabilia and had attended a vast quantity of his concerts, Sir Mordrid considered himself to be the number one fan of the legendary performer.

"Upon seeing Elvis, Sir Mordrid began to feel dizzy and got sweaty palms. In order to hide his nervous behavior, he headed for a table of food in the corner. Nonstop, he crammed lobster, finger sandwiches and strawberries into his mouth. Between bites, he could see across the room where [the celebrity] was introducing the two girls to Elvis.

"'Where's Sir Mordrid?' [the celebrity] questioned. But upon noticing him hunched over the snack table, he continued, 'Sir Mordrid, come on over. I want to introduce you to Elvis.'

"Panic struck Sir Mordrid as he almost choked on an entire sandwich. Hesitantly he walked over to his idol.

"Sir Mordrid meekly said, 'Hi,' but then, without giving Elvis a chance to speak, he chattered on, attempting to cover his anxiety. The only thing he could think of to say was a joke that he had learned the previous day. Elvis quietly listened, certain that there must be some significance to the joke if this guy insisted on telling it at what seemed to be such an inappropriate time.

[Sir Mordrid told the joke and, staring at Elvis, asked him if he knew what the punchline was.]

If you're an average American, you see around 70 commercials for Coke annually.

"Smiling, the singer answered, 'What?'

"Suddenly, Sir Mordrid was so absorbed in his own feelings of anxiety that he couldn't remember the punchline. He panicked. He could feel the lobster, finger sandwiches and strawberries threatening to come up.

"He broke away from the singer and muttered, 'Excuse me.' He sprinted towards a gentleman standing near the doorway. He pleaded, 'Do you know where the rest room is? I feel really sick!'

"The man pointed to Elvis' private bathroom and said, 'I think it's in there.' Although it was obvious that this was designated as an exclusive chamber for only Elvis, Sir Mordrid ignored this minor detail as he hurled himself inside, slamming and locking the door.

"While Sir Mordrid expelled every bit of food from his stomach, there was a knock. A voice firmly called, 'I'm sorry, but you're not allowed in there.'

"Sir Mordrid ignored this remark. After several minutes of screaming and banging on the door, the man stopped trying to get Sir Mordrid out of the rest room.

"Sir Mordrid stood in silence and noticed a disgusting taste in his mouth. Glancing at the sink, he saw a clear, oblong box engraved with the initials 'E.P.' Inside was a toothbrush. A tube of toothpaste rested behind it.

"After checking to make sure the door was indeed locked, he brushed his teeth with his idol's personal toothbrush. Afterward, he dried it off and replaced it exactly as he had found it. He returned to the party, but kept his distance from Elvis for the rest of the evening."

ꝏ   ꝏ   ꝏ

ELVIS FACTS

•For one stretch of two years, the singer reportedly ate nothing but meat loaf, mashed potatoes, and tomatoes.

•His idol was General Douglas MacArthur.

•He memorized every line of dialogue from the George C. Scott film, *Patton*.

Dream on: Every year, the average human being has about 1,500 dreams.

ON THE BALLOT

There's no easier way to get your name into print than to run for office...unless you try to get a laugh at the same time. Some notable politicians' names:

SISTER BOOM-BOOM. A transvestite who dresses as a nun, he/she ran for mayor of San Francsico in 1982...and received 23,121 votes.

JELLO BIAFRA. Lead singer of the Dead Kennedys, a San Francisco-based rock band. Ran for mayor of San Francisco in 1982.

NONE OF THE ABOVE. Never actually made it to the ballot, but his heart was in the right place. Luther Knox changed his name (legally) to *None of the Above* in order to give Louisianans a choice "to say no" to mainstream candidates in their 1979 gubernatorial election.

BANANAS THE CLOWN. Another almost-made-it...onto the ballot, that is. When Lester Johnson decided to run for a seat on the city council in Salt Lake City, he submitted this name. He was rejected, although he accurately protested that "it wouldn't be unprecedented for a clown to be in city government."

LOUIS ABALOFIA. It's not a weird name, and we're not even sure it's the right spelling, but Louis deserves some mention here. Running for president, he passed out leaflets bearing his official campaign photo—a picture of himself stark naked. His campaign slogan, emblazoned at the top: "I have nothing to hide."

TARQUIN FINTIMLINBINWHIMBINLIN BUS STOP-F'TANG-F'TANG-OLE-BISCUIT BARREL. In 1981, a new political party—the Raving Looney Society of Cambridge—nominated this candidate (a real person otherwise known as John Lewis) for a seat in the British Parliament. The media referred to him as "Mr. Tarquin Biscuit-Barrel," and more than two hundred people actually voted for him.

In 1980, the Yellow Pages accidentally listed a Texas funeral home under frozen foods.

CAVEAT EATER

By David Goines
The ten fundamental rules for selecting an eating place
in an unfamiliar environment are simple to remember
and easy to follow.

1. Never eat in anything that moves, i.e., trains, airplanes, and revolving restaurants. As a corollary, never eat any food that can be purchased and consumed without leaving your car.

2. Never eat on the top of anything, i.e., any restaurant situated at the top of any building or structure, such as "The Top of the Mark."

3. Never eat in anyplace with a theme: waitresses dressed as pirates, menus die-cut in the shape of a cowboy hat, cute incomprehensible names for ordinary beverages and dishes. As a corollary, shun foods allegedly prepared by animals, elves, or pixies: Granny Goose potato chips, etc.

4. Never eat anyplace that serves an infinite amount of food at a fixed price.

5. Never eat anyplace that has a name formatted "The (adjective) (noun)," i.e., "The Hungry Hunter," "The Velvet Turtle," etc.

6. Eat the local product. Beef in Kansas City and Chicago, Jewish delicatessens in New York. Seafood in New Orleans. Bread, wine, and salad in San Francisco. If there is no local product, as in Salt Lake City, don't eat. Or pack a lunch.

7. Never eat in an ethnic restaurant in which no people of that ethnicity are eating.

8. Never eat anyplace called "Mom's," or incorporating the concept of motherhood into the restaurant or food product. Doubly to be avoided is the concept of grandmotherhood.

9. Never drink anything with more than two ingredients: Ice is an ingredient.

10. The quality of a restaurant is in inverse proportion to the size of its pepper grinders.

According to *Billboard* magazine, the "Top Artist" of the '70s was Elton John.

JUST THE FACTS

"Dragnet" is the most popular cop show in TV history. It spanned two generations (running from 1951 to 1959, then returning in 1967 for three seasons). Its monotoned hero, Sgt. Joe Friday, became so familiar that thirty-five years after the show debuted, Dan Ayckroyd's film parody of Friday and his exploits was one of the biggest movie hits of 1987.

Dragnet" played an important role in television history. It was the first realistic crime show ever to air, and the first TV show to treat law enforcement as a day-to-day job—portraying the police as normal working stiffs. Other shows like "Gangbusters" glamorized police work—but Sgt. Joe Friday wasn't colorful, didn't wear a snappy costume, wasn't even particularly interesting. He was a guy with a job to do, and he plodded through it day after day ("12:14 PM. We approached the suspect's house. It looked deserted. We rang the doorbell."). "Dragnet"'s enormous popularity inspired other police shows to take the same approach. "We couldn't have shows like 'Hill Street Blues' if it hadn't been for 'Dragnet,'" comments one TV critic.

HOW IT STARTED: In 1948, after struggling to break into the movies, a radio performer named Jack Webb finally landed a small part in a police thriller called *He Walked By Night*. One day during the filming, Webb was hanging around with his friend, Sgt. Marty Wynn of the L.A.P.D. (the movie's technical adviser). Wynn made a suggestion: "Jack," he said, "I can arrange for you to have access to all the cases in the L.A. police files, and maybe you could do something with them."

Wynn went on to explain that he wanted to hear a radio drama that portrayed police work honestly. No "Gangbusters" stuff. Webb insisted that "Gangbusters" was what people wanted and declined the offer.

But the more he thought about Wynn's idea, the better he liked it. About ten months after the conversation, Webb began writing an outline for this "realistic" show. He did research by accompanying Wynn and his partner in their patrol car.

In Elizabethan England, spoons were so rare that people brought their own.

When Webb had a format, characters, and a title, he made a radio audition record of the show and brought it to NBC...which signed him as a summer replacement at $150 a week, starring and directing. *Dragnet* premiered on June 3, 1949; within two years, it was the top show on radio. The jump to TV was inevitable, but Webb held out until NBC gave him $38,000 to film a pilot (instead of doing it live). The pilot aired on December 16, 1951, and the series began its official run about four weeks later. It immediately became the #2 show on television (behind "I Love Lucy"), and remained popular for 11 years.

INSIDE FACTS

Smoky places. The early '50s shows were sponsored by Chesterfield cigarettes, and Webb and others in the cast often took time to elaborately light up and smoke, to plug the sponsor's product. The '60s shows are much less smoky.

Police Disguise. Each episode of *Dragnet* was based on an actual case. It was selected from the files provided to Webb by a special detail of three L.A.P.D. officers. After Webb picked the case, he adapted it to a script, altering enough details to make it unrecognizable—even to the criminal—but retaining the basic facts.

It's only TV, lady. Sgt. Friday was so real to the public that people often went to L.A.P.D. headquarters to meet him. At first the department was at a loss about how to deal with them. But later, they came up with a standard answer: "Sorry, it's Joe's day off."

Sgt. Everyman. Webb on the name: "Some (people) have said I was thinking of Robinson Crusoe and his man Friday. Or that I thought of it on Friday. I really didn't know where it came from, except that I wanted a name that had no connotations at all. He could be Jewish, or Greek, or English, or anything. He could be all men to all people in their living room."

Friday's return. "Dragnet" was going to return as a 1967 TV movie-of-the-week. But the film came off so well that it was used as a pilot for a new series instead. Retitled "Dragnet '67," it became a virtual parody of itself, with anti-drug preaching, and embarrassing Hollywood hippies. It was "camp" humor to much of its audience.

There is enough phosphorus inside you to make about 250 matchheads.

RUMORS

*Why do people believe wild, unsubstantiated stories?
According to some psychologists, "rumors make things
simpler than they really are." And while people
won't believe just anything, it's surprising what
stories have flourished in the past. Many
of these tales are still in circulation today....*

RUMOR: McDonald's adds earthworms to its hamburger meat.
HOW IT SPREAD: Apparently the stories began in Atlanta in 1979 and were originally aimed at a competitor, Wendy's. "But," as a psychologist commented, "industrial rumors tend to gravitate to the industry leader." Another possibility: an article in *Reader's Digest* about worm farms mentioned that such farms tend to attract animals that like to eat worms, making the farm "a veritable McDonald's" for such animals.
WHAT HAPPENED: To fight it, McDonald's held a press conference in Atlanta and produced a letter from the U.S. Secretary of Agriculture stating that the burgers were, and always had been, 100% beef.

THE RUMOR: Sweaters at K-Mart are infested with hatching baby snakes.
HOW IT SPREAD: The story—that a shopper was trying on sweaters, felt something prick her skin, and discovered she'd been bitten by a rare poisonous snake from Taiwan—was probably started by a competitor.
WHAT HAPPENED: K-Mart has chosen to ignore it.

THE RUMOR: Mikey, the cute kid in the Life cereal commercials, died by exploding after ingesting a combination of "Pop Rocks" candy and soda pop.
HOW IT SPREAD: Unknown.
WHAT HAPPENED: This rumor was so prevalant that Life Cereal redesigned their box to include a photo of several kids

and Mikey, now grown up. The object was to identify Mikey, and of course, reassure us that he hadn't exploded after all.

THE RUMOR: A teenage girl was squeezed to death while sitting in the bathtub in cold water trying to shrink her new Levis.
HOW IT SPREAD: Unknown.
WHAT HAPPENED: No action taken, but a great story.

THE RUMOR: A woman attempted to dry her poodle in a microwave oven and the dog exploded.
HOW IT SPREAD: A classic example of how a rumor reflects fears, this one stemming from concerns about new technology.
WHAT HAPPENED: The public's awareness of microwave ovens was increased, and as people realized the story was just a rumor, they relaxed and accepted the product as safe.

THE RUMOR: Bubble Yum gum, made by Life Savers, had spider eggs in it.
HOW IT SPREAD: Apparently this story began in New York City, where kids began telling each other not to buy Bubble Yum because it contained the aforementioned additive.
WHAT HAPPENED: Life Savers at first paid little attention to the story, but a senior vice president wanted to find out how the story began, so he ordered a phone survey and asked consumers and their parents if they'd heard the rumors. He next checked with retailers to see what they knew....In fact, many were upset and wanted the company to reassure them. In the end, Life Savers published a full-page newspaper ad which said, "Somebody is telling your kids very bad lies about a very good gum." It worked, and the story died. Bubble Yum maintained its position as the #1 selling bubble gum.

THE RUMOR: Another Soviet nuclear accident—similar to the 1986 disaster at Chernobyl—occurred.
HOW IT SPREAD: Apparently it originated in either Stockholm or Moscow and reached world financial markets.
WHAT HAPPENED: The dollar surged in value, but only temporarily. The following day, February 4, 1988, the *Wall*

Street Journal reported that the "accident" was just a rumor. Nonetheless, its effect on world economic markets was undeniable. When the truth became known, the dollar then eased back to its relative value against other currencies.

THE RUMOR: A leper worked in the factory where Spud cigarettes—the first king size menthol filter brand—were manufactured in the 1940s.
HOW IT STARTED: Unknown.
WHAT HAPPENED: Within six months, the brand vanished from stores.

THE RUMOR: Procter & Gamble's company trademark is a satanic symbol signifying a pact with the devil.
HOW IT STARTED: Surfaced in 1980. Refers to the profile of a man-in-the-moon and 13 stars in the trademark, which was created in 1850.
WHAT HAPPENED: In June of 1982, P & G received 15,000 telephone inquiries. The company responded by filing lawsuits against individuals linked to the story and recruiting religious leaders, including Rev. Jerry Falwell, to refute the rumor and publicly declare the company "pure."

THE RUMOR: Xerox copy machine toner gives you cancer.
HOW IT STARTED: 1978, a research team found that extracts of a copier toner caused mutations in bacteria cells and another team reported mutations in mouse cells. The story was picked up by a newspaper which inflated the results from mutagenic to cancer-causing. Though the toner was not Xerox's, the company's name became associated with the findings. An Australian newspaper featured the headline, "Tens of Thousands at Risk."
WHAT HAPPENED: Thousands of customers called Xerox. Every query was answered by company representatives. Health records of 60,000 Xerox employees were reviewed for cancer. A Xerox Vice president presented facts in defense of his company to the Environmental Protection Agency, which resulted in an EPA news release assuring copier users not to be concerned.

ELVIS: WAR ON DRUGS

The secret life of "The King" included a secret visit to the
FBI and a desire to meet "the greatest living American,"
J. Edgar Hoover. Totally bizarre.

After Elvis Presley's death in 1977 we learned about his tragic drug problems. Coroners found a veritable pharmacy in the King of Rock 'n' Roll's bloodstream. The revelations of Elvis' drug abuse were shocking to his loyal fans but not to insiders. Presley's bodyguard, Red West, described him as a "walking pharmaceutical shop who took pills to get up, pills to go to sleep, and pills to go out on the job."

The supreme irony of his drug habit is that Presley, himself, was a dedicated antidrug crusader. According to Penny Stallings book, "Rock 'n' Roll Confidential": "At one time he'd even turned his home into an arsenal, with the idea of meting out backwoods justice to local drug pushers whose names he'd obtained from the Memphis narcs. He sometimes had to be physically restrained from carrying out his plan."

The most bizarre twist in this story is Presley's visit to Washington D.C. in late 1970. During his visit, Presley (who was already addicted to barbiturates and amphetamines) received a special agent's badge of the Bureau of Narcotics and Dangerous Drugs from then-President Richard Nixon.

After his meeting with Nixon, Presley requested a personal audience with the man he considered "the greatest living American": J. Edgar Hoover. Thanks to the Freedom of Information Act, the files of this event are now available.

From the available data it seems that the FBI—always conscious of its image—was quite concerned with Elvis' visit. In an official memorandum dated 12-30-70, the question of whether Presley should meet the Director was discussed. "During the height of his popularity," the memo stated, "during the latter part of the 1950s and early 1960s, his gyrations while performing were the subject of considerable criticism by the public and comment in the press."

An African ostrich egg weighs about 30 lbs. A 200-lb. man can stand on it without breaking it.

The memo concluded: "Presley's sincerity and good intentions notwithstanding, he is certainly not the type of individual whom the Director would wish to meet. It is noted at the present time he is wearing his hair down to his shoulders and indulges in wearing all sorts of exotic dress."

Although a meeting with Hoover was ruled out (Presley's entourage was told he was out of town), the FBI did arrange for a special tour of their facilities on December 31, 1970.

The following is an account of his tour from FBI files:

"Presley...and six individuals who provide security for Presley visited FBI Headquarters and were afforded a very special tour of our facilities in accordance with plans approved by the Director.

"Regrets were expressed to Presley and his party in connection with their request to meet the Director. Presley indicated that he has long been an admirer of Mr. Hoover, and has read material prepared by the Director including 'Masters of Deceit,' 'A Study of Communism' as well as 'J. Edgar Hoover on Communism.' Presley noted that in his opinion no one has ever done as much for his country as has Mr. Hoover, and that he, Presley, considers the Director 'the greatest living American.' He spoke most favorably of the Bureau.

"Despite his rather bizarre personal appearance, Presley seemed a serious minded individual who expressed concern over some of the problems confronting our country, particularly those involving young people. In this regard, in private comments made following his tour, he indicated that he, Presley, is the 'living proof that America is the land of opportunity' since he rose from truck driver to prominent entertainer almost overnight. He said that he spends as much time as his schedule permits informally talking to young people and discussing what they consider to be their problems with them. Presley said that his long hair and unusual apparel were merely tools of his trade and provided him access to and rapport with many people particularly on college campuses who considered themselves 'anti-establishment.' Presley said that while he has a limited education, he has been able to command a certain amount of respect and attention from this segment of the population and in an informal way point out the errors of their ways. He advised that he does not consider himself competent to address

Pogo sticks were first used by sacrificial dancers in Borneo.

large groups but much rather prefers small gatherings in community centers and the like, where he makes himself accessible for talks and discussions regarding the evils of narcotics and other problems of concern to teenagers and other young people.

"Following their tour, Presley privately advised that he has volunteered his services to the President in connection with the narcotics problem and that Mr. Nixon had responded by furnishing him with an Agent's badge of the Bureau of Narcotics and Dangerous Drugs. Presley was carrying this badge in his pocket and displayed it.

"Presley advised that he wished the Director to be aware that he, Presley, from time to time is approached by individuals and groups in and outside the entertainment business whose motives and goals he is convinced are not in the best interests of this country and who seek to have him lend his name to their questionable activities. In this regard, he volunteered to make such information available to the Bureau on a confidential basis whenever it came to his attention. He further indicated that he wanted the Director to know that should the Bureau ever have any need of his services in any way that he would be delighted to be of assistance.

"Presley indicated that he is of the opinion that the Beatles laid the groundwork for many of the problems we are having with young people by their filthy unkempt appearances and suggestive music while entertaining in this country during the early and middle 1960s. He advised that the Smothers Brothers, Jane Fonda, and other persons in the entertainment industry of their ilk have a lot to answer for in the hereafter for the way they have poisoned young minds by disparaging the United States in their public statements and unsavory activities...

"He noted that he can be contacted any time through his Memphis address and that because of problems he has had with people tampering with his mail, such correspondence should be addressed to him under the pseudonym, Colonel Jon Burrows."

The file concludes: "Presley did give the impression of being a sincere, young man who is conscious of the many problems confronting this country. In view of his unique position in the entertainment business, his favorable comments concerning the

A leopon is a cross between a leopard and a lion. Such creatures really exist.

Director and the Bureau, and his offer to be of assistance as well as the fact that he has been recognized by the Junior Chamber of Commerce and the President, it is felt that a letter from the Director would be in order."

☙   ☙   ☙

LITTLE-KNOWN FACTS ABOUT J. EDGAR HOOVER

•Hoover wanted to be president, and believed he could unseat FDR in 1936.

•He had FBI agents conduct a top-secret, unofficial poll in the South and Southwest, where he thought he had the strongest support. "He's a great man," the agents were told to say. "Many people think we'd be better off if Hoover were president." Hoover was shocked to discover that many law enforcement chiefs didn't even want him to continue as director of the FBI.

•Hoover gave up chasing the presidency, and focused his sights on attorney general instead. He planned to use that position as a stepping-stone to become a justice of the Supreme Court. To achieve this goal, he surreptitiously backed and assisted Thomas Dewey in his presidential race against Harry Truman in 1948. Dewey lost.

•He assisted Richard Nixon in his race against JFK in 1960, supplying sensitive data to Nixon for the debates. Nixon lost.

•Hoover once told a top lieutenant that he'd never married "because God had made a woman like Eleanor Roosevelt."

•Whether that's true or not, he rarely fraternized with women, and he and his top aide, Clyde Tolson, went everywhere together.

•In his 48 years with the FBI, Hoover never made an arrest or conducted an investigation.

•Hoover never once left America while he was in charge of the FBI.

•According to a top aide, Hoover didn't even know how to use a gun.

GROUCHO SEZ...

A few choice words from the master.

"I must say I find television very educational. The minute somebody turns it on I go into the library and read a good book."

"Please accept my resignation. I don't want to belong to any club that will accept me as a member."

"I didn't like the play, but then I saw it under adverse conditions—the curtain was up."

"Dig trenches? With our men being killed off like flies? There isn't time to dig trenches. We'll have to buy them ready made."

"Do you suppose I could buy back my introduction to you?"

"I've worked myself up from nothing to a state of extreme poverty."

Mrs. Teasdale: "He's had a change of heart."
Firefly [Groucho]: "A lot of good that'll do him. He's still got the same face."

"Military intelligence is a contradiction in terms."

"Any man who says he can see through a woman is missing a lot."

"A man is as young as the woman he feels."

"She got her good looks from her father—he's a plastic surgeon."

"There's one way to find out if a man is honest—ask him. If he says 'Yes,' you know he is a crook."

[Feeling patient's pulse] "Either he's dead, or my watch has stopped."

"Age is not a particularly interesting subject. Anyone can get old. All you have to do is live long enough."

"Send two dozen roses to Room 424 and put 'Emily, I love you' on the back of the bill."

Life span: A shark lives for about 100 years.

WORD PLAY

What do these familiar phrases really mean? Etymologists have researched them and come up with these explanations.

Fly Off the Handle
Meaning: To get irrationally angry.
Background: Refers to axe heads, which, in the days before mass merchandising, were sometimes fastened poorly to their handles. If one flew off while being used, it was a dangerous situation...with unpredictable results.

Get a Bad Break
Meaning: To be unlucky.
Background: Refers to the game of pool, which begins with a player hitting the cue ball into the rest of the balls and "breaking" them apart (separating them). If the player gets a good break, he pockets several balls. If it's a bad break, he gets nothing. Other terms: "Gets all the breaks," "them's the breaks," etc.

Peeping Tom
Meaning: Someone who looks in the windows of people's homes.
Background: From the legend of Lady Godiva, who rode naked through the streets of Coventry in order to get her husband, Lord Leofric, to reduce taxes. She requested that the citizens stay inside and close their shutters while she rode. Everyone did "except the town tailor, Tom, who peeped through the shutters."

High on the Hog
Meaning; Luxurious, prosperous.
Background: The tastiest parts of a hog are its upper parts. If you're living high on the hog, you've got the best it has to offer.

Pull the Wool Over Someone's Eyes
Meaning: Fool someone
Background: "Goes back to the days when all gentlemen wore powdered wigs like the ones still worn by the judges in British courts. The word wool was then a popular, joking term for hair....The expression 'Pull the wool over his eyes' came from

Cold showers actually increase sexual arousal.

the practice of tilting a man's wig over his eyes, so that he'd be unable to see what was going on."

Hooker
Meaning: A prostitute.
Background: Although occasionally used before the Civil War, its widespread popularity can probably be traced to General Joseph Hooker, a Union soldier who was well-known for the liquor and whores in his camp. He was ultimately demoted, and Washington prostitutes were jokingly referred to as "Hooker's Division."

To Talk Turkey
Meaning: To speak frankly
Background: Derived from a popular, if demeaning, joke in Colonial America:
"A white man and an Indian went out hunting together, agreeing to divide whatever they bagged equally. At the end of the day, they had two crows and two turkeys. 'You can have whichever you like,' the white man told his companion—'Either I'll take the turkeys and you take the crows, or you take the crows and I'll take the turkeys.' The Indian demurred, saying, 'You talk all turkey for you, but you not talk turkey to me.'"

Rack Your Brain
Meaning: Think hard
Background: Refers to a Medieval instrument of torture, the rack, on which people were stretched until—in the worst cases—their limbs were pulled off. When you rack your brain, you subject yourself to a sort of mental torture, stretching it as far as it will go.

Let the Cat Out of the Bag
Meaning: Reveal the truth
Background: Refers to con game practiced at country fairs in old England. "A trickster would try to palm off on an unwary bumpkin a cat in a burlap bag, claiming it was a suckling pig." If the victim figured out the trick and insisted on seeing the merchandise, the cat had to be let out of the bag.

The earliest known board game was used around 3,000 B.C. It is an ancestor of backgammon.

TOY ORIGINS, PART II

*More stories about America's
favorite playthings.*

TWISTER. The first game in the history of the American toy industry "to turn the human body into a vital component of play," enjoyed instant popularity when Milton Bradley introduced it in 1966. Why? TV and sex.

When it first came out, Bradley's PR firm brought Twister to the Tonight Show and showed it to Johnny Carson's writers. They thought it was hilarious, and promised to get it on the show right away.

They were true to their word. **Carson's** guest that night was Eva Gabor, and when millions of viewers saw the two glamorous celebrities climbing all over each other as they played the game on national television, the public understood exactly what Twister was really about—SEX. The next day, toy stores were flooded with demands for the game.

That year, over 3 million games were sold—more than ten times the amount that Milton Bradley anticipated. It became the most popular new game of the '60s, and is still selling over twenty years later.

BINGO. In 1929, a tired, depressed toy salesman named Edwin Lowe set out on a night-time drive from Atlanta, Georgia to Jacksonville, Florida. On the way he noticed the bright lights of a carnival; he decided to stop to investigate. Lowe found only one concession open—a tent full of people seated at tables, each with a hand-stamped, numbered card and a pile of beans. As the emcee called out numbers, players put beans on the corresponding squares on their cards. If they got five beans in a row, they won a Kewpie doll. The concessionaire called his game Beano. Lowe was so impressed that he tried it at his own home, where one young winner became so excited that she stammered out "B-b-b-ingo!" instead of "Beano." So that's what Lowe called it.

Streaking record: 1,200 college students streaked at the same time in Boulder, Colo., 1974.

HOLY PUNCTUATION!

What's the difference between good and evil? Maybe just a little grammar. The following are excerpts from real church bulletins, collected by B.R.I.'s Les Boies.

"This afternoon there will be a meeting in the south and north ends of the church. Children will be baptized at both ends."

"Tuesday, at 4 PM, there will be an ice cream social. All ladies giving milk, come early."

"Wednesday, the Ladies Liturgy Society will meet. Mrs. Johnson will sing, 'Put Me In My Little Bed,' accompanied by the Pastor."

"Thursday, at 5 PM, there will be a meeting of the Little Mothers Club. All those wishing to become little mothers, please meet the pastor in his study."

"This being Easter Sunday, we will ask Mrs. Johnson to come forward and lay an egg on the altar."

"The service will close with 'Little Drops of Water.' One of the ladies will start quietly and the rest of the congregation will join in."

"On Sunday, a special collection will be taken to defray the expense of the new carpet. All those wishing to do something on the new carpet, come forward and get a piece of paper."

"The ladies of the church have cast off clothing of every kind and they may be seen in the basement on Friday afternoon."

"A bean supper will be held Saturday evening in the church basement. Music will follow."

"The rosebud on the altar this morning is to announce the birth of David Alan Belser, the sin of Rev. and Mrs. Julius Belser."

"Altar flowers are given to the glory of God in memory of her mother."

Life span: An average elephant lives for about 55 years.

MYTH AMERICA

*All it takes to create a widely accepted myth is a
popular "historical" movie or television show...
or a damn good liar, like Davy Crockett*

The Myth: Davy Crockett was an American hero, a clean-cut
frontier superman who:
- "Killed him a b'ar when he was only three"
- Was the greatest Indian fighter of his day
- Could shoot a rifle better than any man alive
- Was a respected Congressman who considered running for
president
- Was the last man to die at the Alamo

Background: Much of this "information" was taken from Crockett's autobiography and a series of Crockett *Almanacs* which
were published between 1835 and 1856.

But it was Walt Disney who made the legend stick. In December, 1954 he unveiled a TV mini-series about Crockett with
an episode called "Davy Crockett, Indian fighter." The folk
hero became an instant national fad, surprising even Uncle
Walt. In a matter of months, merchants sold millions of dollars worth of official Davy Crockett coonskin caps, bubble-
gum cards, toy guns, fringed jackets, etc. Fourteen-million copies of Crockett's life story were sold. The Davy Crockett theme
song hit the national top 20 four times in one year, with four
different versions. Sample verse: "Fought single-handed
through the Injun War, Till the Creeks was whipped and
peace was in store, And while he was handlin' this risky chore,
Made hisself a legend forevermore."

The Truth: Crockett was:
- A drunk who deserted his wife and children
- A "scout" who avoided going into battle against the Indians
by hiring a substitute
- A congressman with one of the worst absentee records in
history.

In 1980, a secretary at Deere & Co. was fired "for making a Xerox copy of her bottom."

The only thing that seems to be consistent with the legend is that Crockett did die at the Alamo. But that, says author Paul Sann in *Fads, Follies, and Delusions*, was "more bungling and stupidity than heroism."

During the Crockett craze, several journalists researched the new American hero. Some sample comments:

"He was never king of anything, except maybe the Tennessee Tall Tales and Bourbon Samplers' Association. When he claimed that he had shot 105 bear in nine months, his fellow tipplers refused to believe a word of it, on the grounds that Davy couldn't count that high."

—John Fisher, *Harper's* magazine.

"He was out on the frontier only because it was an easier place to live than in a home with a growing brood. Davy had a flock of children and he left them and never bothered with any of them again. He set the cause of married life back about 200 years."　　**—Harry Golden, syndicated columnist**

"Davy grew up to be a very brave young man, who would bear any hardship to escape a routine day's work."

—Murray Kempton, *New York Post*

Ironically Fess Parker, who played the lead in the Disney version of Crockett's life—and became a star as a result—was also a bit of a fraud. Says Leonard Mosley in *Disney's World*, "Parker hated Wild West roles. As in the case of most minor Hollywood actors, hunger had sometimes forced him to play in Western films, and he found he was allergic to horses and loathed the clothing cowboys wore. His...lip curled in derision and distaste when he saw the drawings of Davy Crockett's outfit.....But eventually hunger won out, and Parker signed up for the film. They had to teach him how to ride a horse, first, and do it without having him come down with a case of hives. His leather breeches were specially sprayed before he wore them, and when he was out of camera range he shied away from them as if they were a bunch of poison ivy, swearing they would give him "crotch rot." Parker later played TV's Daniel Boone for 6 years.

DEAD MAN'S CURVE

*This is one of rock's classic disaster songs. But it's
the only one that was actually fulfilled
by the man who wrote it.*

D ead Man's Curve" was a top ten hit for Jan and Dean in
1964. But it became even more famous when Jan—who
co-wrote the song with Los Angeles disc jockey Roger
Christian—actually had an accident that paralleled the crash
in the song. An eerie prediction? A simple coincidence? A
cursed song? No one will ever know.

But we do know the story behind the song:

ROGER CHRISTIAN: "Dead Man's Curve is in Los Angeles,
right near UCLA, on Sunset Boulevard. It's a downhill, winding
turn that's bowed to the outside, so centrifugal force, comin'
down the hill, will throw you into the opposite lane if you don't
watch it. And that's just what happened. I was a deejay at
KRLA in Los Angeles, and I was reading the news one night. I
read that Mel Blanc had been seriously injured and he was on
the verge of death, from an accident where he was struck at
Dead Man's curve.

"Blanc was like my idol because he was a voiceover man and
could do all kinds of voices [note: Blanc was the voice of Bugs
Bunny, Porky Pig, etc.]. I watched the news copy every hour to
see how he was doing; they didn't think he was gonna live—but
he did. He was in the hospital for six months.

"I thought someone ought to write a song about Dead Man's
Curve. I said, 'Well, we ought to make it into a race,' because
Jan and I were really into racing. Every Saturday night we'd
meet and go to Sunset and Vine...and we'd race. I had a Jaguar
XKE, and Jan had a Stingray—the same cars that are in the
song."

The weirdest part of the story is that Roger didn't intend for
"Dead Man's Curve" to be a "disaster" song at all—he wanted
the race to end in a tie.

But Jan *insisted* that the song end with a disastrous crash. And
in real life, shortly after, Jan was paralyzed in a serious car accident...on Dead Man's Curve.

You can draw a line about 35 miles long with an average pencil.

I LOVE LUCY

I Love Lucy ran from 1951 to 1957. It was the #1 show in
America for 4 of those 6 years.

HOW IT STARTED: In 1948, Lucille Ball became a
radio star in the CBS series, *My Favorite Husband*. It
co-starred Richard Denning as her spouse, a Midwestern bank president.

Two years later, CBS decided to move the show to TV, with
Denning continuing as her "husband." But to their surprise,
Lucy refused. She insisted that the only way she'd do a TV ser-
ies was if her real-life husband—Desi Arnaz—was her co-star.
CBS balked. "Who," they asked, "would believe that a red-
headed movie star and a Cuban bandleader were married?"
But Lucy was determined; she thought it was the only way to
save her marriage.

To prove to CBS that the public would accept them together,
Lucy and Desi put together a vaudeville act and went on the
road, performing live. They were billed as *Desi Arnaz and
Band with Lucille Ball*. They got rave reviews in New York
and Chicago—and interest from NBC.

CBS didn't want to let Lucy get away, so they capitulated
and half-heartedly authorized a pilot. At first they couldn't
find a sponsor for it, and had practically given up on the project when Phillip Morris cigarettes finally agreed to back it.

But there was still a problem. The sponsors wanted the show
done live in New York, (where the biggest audience was), and
the Arnazes refused to leave Hollywood. They came up with a
unique (for the time) compromise: each program was filmed in
front of a live audience in California, then edited and trans-
ported to the East Coast for a "live" broadcast. This made it
the first TV series ever filmed, and gave us *I Love Lucy*
reruns.

INSIDE FACTS:
Sorry about that, chief. On January 20, 1953, two important
events were televised: Lucy's birth to Little Ricky in the "Lucy
Goes to the Hospital" episode of *I Love Lucy*, and Dwight D.

The elephant is the only animal that has 4 knees.

Eisenhower's inauguration. Lucy outdrew Ike by 15 million viewers—44 million to 29 million.

Good timing. When *I Love Lucy* premiered, Lucy was 40, Desi was 35, Vivian Vance was 39 and William Frawley was 64.

Out of sight. After the success of *I Love Lucy*, Desi changed hats again, this time from actor to producer. One of his productions, *The Untouchables*, put mobster Al Capone in such a bad light that a contract was reportedly put out on his life. After selling his share of Desilu to Lucy for $2,552,975 in 1962 (she sold it for $17 million just five years later), he retired to a ranch east of Los Angeles to raise thoroughbred horses. He died in 1986.

Name Game. Coming up with a name for the program was a struggle. Sponsors wanted to call it The Lucille Ball Show, but Lucy wanted Desi's name on it, too. They finally agreed that *I Love Lucy* was acceptable, since the "I" referred to Desi, and it came first in the title. Clever solution to a potentially volatile problem.

Paley's folly. Bill Paley, president of CBS, thought there was absolutely no hope for a series about a dingbat redhead and her Cuban bandleader husband. So he cheerfully handed over all future rights for *I Love Lucy* to Desilu Productions.

Star Wars. While all appeared calm to viewers at home, squabbles on the set were common. Lucy and Desi's tiffs were the stuff of legends, while William Frawley and Vivian Vance really couldn't stand each other. Vance couldn't see why anyone would believe she was married to "that old man"; Frawley often referred to Vance as "that sack of doorknobs."

Red-dy Or Not: During the McCarthy "red scares" in the early '50s, Lucille Ball was accused of being a communist by columnist Walter Winchell, who discovered that she had once joined a leftist organization in the '30s. Believe it or not, this revelation actually threatened her career. Desi went to her defense: "The only thing red about Lucy," he responded, "is her hair. And that's not even real." Lucy is not a true redhead.

THE PRESIDENTIAL CURSE

*From 1840 to 1980, every president
elected in a year that ended in zero died
while in office. Only Ronald Reagan managed
to escape the presidential curse—and
he barely survived an assassination attempt.*

THE VICTIMS: Seven presidents of the United States: William Henry Harrison (the ninth president), Abraham Lincoln (the sixteenth president), James Garfield (the twentieth president), William McKinley (the twenty-fifth president), Warren G. Harding (the twenty-ninth president), Franklin D. Roosevelt (the thirty-second president), and John F. Kennedy (the thirty-fifth president).

THE CIRCUMSTANCES:
- Harrison was elected in 1840. He died of pneumonia on April 4, 1841, one month after taking office.
- Lincoln was elected in 1860. He was assassinated during his second term, in 1865.
- Garfield was elected in 1880. He was shot by a deranged man as he boarded a train in July, 1881. He died two months later.
- McKinley was elected to his second term in 1900. He was assassinated in 1901 by an anarchist who "wanted to kill a ruler."
- Harding was elected in 1920. He supposedly died of pneumonia in 1923, but it is suspected that he was poisoned.
- FDR was elected to his third term in 1940. He died of a cerebral hemorrhage, shortly after being elected to his 4th term.
- JFK was elected in 1960. He was assassinated in Dallas in 1963.

UNANSWERED QUESTIONS: How is it possible that for the last 120 years, *all* of the presidents elected during a year ending in zero died while in office?

POSSIBLE CONCLUSIONS:
No rational ones. A curse? A cosmic sick joke?

In 1977, a 13-year-old boy discovered a tooth growing on his left foot.

NAME THAT FOOD

*We take these household names for granted,
but they had to start somewhere.
Here's where.*

Aunt Jemima: Charles Rutt invented America's first pancake mix, but it bombed without a catchy name. One night in 1889, he saw a blackface vaudeville show featuring a tune called *Aunt Jemima*—which was sung by an actor in drag. Somehow, that inspired the image of Southern hospitality Rutt was looking for...and it worked. Instant success.

Spam Luncheon Meat: Combines the SP from spice and the AM from ham.

Baby Ruth candy bar: Most people think this was inspired by baseball's Babe Ruth. Not true. Originally called Kandy Kake, it was renamed in the 1920s to honor a contemporary celebrity—ex-President Grover Cleveland's daughter, Ruth, the first child born in the White House, and known to the public as "Baby Ruth" despite the fact she was in her late twenties. Within a few years, it was the best-selling candy in America. Footnote: N.Y. Yankee Babe Ruth once tried marketing his own brand of candy, *Babe Ruth's Home Run Candy*; the Curtiss Candy Co. took him to court and enjoined him from using his own name.

Tootsie Roll: Leo Hirschfield, an Austrian immigrant, originally hand-rolled the candies for his daughter, Tootsie.

Crackerjacks: This unnamed combination of peanuts, popcorn and sugar had been around since the 1870s, but was bulk-shipped in wooden crates; when it arrived in stores, it would be stuck together in massive lumps. In 1890, the company finally licked the problem with a new sugar-coating process. A salesman tasted it and exclaimed "That's cracker jack!" The

---

In Switzerland, it is against the law to slam your car door.

phrase was slang at the time for something great or excellent.

Chef Boy-ar-dee Spaghetti & Meatballs: Boy-ar-dee is a phonetic spelling of the inventor's name—Hector Boiardi. An Italian immigrant and restauranteur, Boiardi devised the recipe in a small room above his Cleveland restaurant in 1929. His picture still appears on the label.

Oreo Cookies: Oreo means *hill* in Greek. The original version of the cookie was mound-shaped, not flat.

Fig Newtons: In 1895, a new machine was installed at a Massachusetts cookie company called the Kennedy Biscuit Works. Among the machine's capabilities: it could wrap cookie dough around jam. The first jam the company tried it with just happened to be "made from figs." And since their policy was to name their products after neighboring towns, Newton, Mass. was honored in the title. Hence *Fig Newtons*.

Wonder Bread: Introduced after W.W.I.; it was the successor to *Mary Maid*, a popular brand of bread manufactured by the Taggart Baking Company of Indianapolis, Indiana. They wanted to maintain the appeal of their previous product, and the name *Wonder* filled the bill—it was easy to remember, and implied "goodness." Footnote: the balloons on the wrapper were inspired by the International Balloon Race, held at the Indianapolis Speedway. A Taggart vice president saw the sky filled with multi-colored balloons and decided to incorporate them into a package design.

Coca Cola: Named for two of its original ingredients—coca leaves (yes, the ones that give us cocaine), and Kola nuts.

Budweiser Beer: In the 1870s, German-born Adolphus Busch and his partner produced a light-colored beer, inspired by a beer they'd seen brewed in Budweis, Czechoslovakia.

OFF TO SEE
THE WIZARD

The original Wizard of Oz is one of the most popular children's series ever. L. Frank Baum wrote the first one in 1901, perhaps as a political allegory (see "The Politics of Oz," elsewhere in this book). It was so popular that he wound up writing several more. In modern America, the book's long-term popularity is guaranteed by the lasting appeal of the 1939 film starring Judy Garland. These excerpts are from the original manuscript of The Wizard of Oz.

ON THE ROAD THROUGH THE FOREST
"Tell me something about yourself and the country you came from," said the Scarecrow, when Dorothy had finished her dinner. So she told him all about Kansas, and how gray everything was there, and how the cyclone had carried her to this queer Land of Oz.

The Scarecrow listened carefully, and said, "I cannot understand why you should wish to leave this beautiful country and go back to the dry, gray place you call Kansas."

"That is because you have no brains," answered the girl. "No matter how dreary and gray our homes are, we people of flesh and blood would rather live there than in any other country, be it ever so beautiful. There is no place like home."

The Scarecrow sighed.

"Of course I cannot understand it," he said. "If your heads are stuffed with straw, like mine, you would probably all live in the beautiful places, and then Kansas would have no people at all. It is fortunate for Kansas that you have brains."...

THE SCARECROW
"It was a lonely life to lead, for I had nothing to think of, having been made only the day before. Many crows and other birds flew into the cornfield, but as soon as they saw me they flew away again, thinking I was a Munchkin; and this pleased me and made me feel that I was quite an important person. By and by an old crow flew near me, and after looking at me

In 1983, a Japanese artist made a copy of the Mona Lisa completely out of toast.

carefully he perched upon my shoulder and said:

"'I wonder if that farmer thought to fool me in this clumsy manner. Any crow of sense could see that you are only stuffed with straw.' Then he hopped down at my feet and ate all the corn he wanted. The other birds, seeing he was not harmed by me, came to eat the corn too, so in a short time there was a great flock of them about me.

"I felt sad at this, for it showed I was not such a good Scarecrow after all; but the old crow comforted me, saying, 'If you only had brains in your head you would be as good a man as any of them, and a better man than some of them. Brains are the only things worth having in this world, no matter whether one is a crow or a man.'

"After the crows had gone I thought this over, and decided I would try hard to get some brains. By good luck, you came along and pulled me off the stake, and from what you say I am sure the Great Oz will give me brains as soon as we get to the Emerald City."

"I hope so," said Dorothy earnestly, "since you seem anxious to have them."

"Oh, yes. I am anxious," returned the Scarecrow. "It is such an uncomfortable feeling to know one is a fool."...

THE TIN WOODMAN

"My head is quite empty," answered the Woodman. "But once I had brains, and a heart also. So, having tried them both, I should much rather have a heart."

"And why is that?" asked the Scarecrow.

"I will tell you my story, and then you will know."

So, while they were walking through the forest, the Tin Woodman told the following story:

"I was born the son of a woodman who chopped down trees in the forest and sold the wood for a living. When I grew up I too became a woodchopper, and after my father died I took care of my old mother as long as she lived. Then I made up my mind that instead of living alone I would marry, so that I might not become lonely.

"There was one of the Munchkin girls who was so beautiful that I soon grew to love her with all my heart. She, on her part, promised to marry me as soon as I could earn enough money

---

In the early '80s, a toad was discovered that meows instead of croaking.

to build a better house for her. So I set to work harder than ever. But the girl lived with an old woman who did not want her to marry anyone, for she was so lazy she wished the girl to remain with her and do the cooking and the housework. So the old woman went to the Wicked Witch of the East, and promised her two sheep and a cow if she would prevent the marriage. Thereupon the Wicked Witch enchanted my ax, and when I was chopping away at my best one day, for I was anxious to get the new house and my wife as soon as possible, the ax slipped all at once and cut off my left leg.

"This at first seemed a great misfortune, for I knew a one-legged man could not do very well as a wood-chopper. So I went to a tinsmith and had him make me a new leg out of tin. The leg worked very well, once I was used to it. But my action angered the Wicked Witch of the East, for she had promised the old woman I should not marry the pretty Munchkin girl. When I began chopping again, my ax slipped and cut off my right leg. Again I went to the tinner, and again he made me a leg out of tin. After this the enchanted ax cut off my arms, one after the other; but, nothing daunted me, I had them replaced with tin ones. The Wicked Witch then made the ax slip and cut off my head, and at first I thought that was the end of me. But the tinner happened to come along, and he made me a new head out of tin.

"I thought I had beaten the Wicked Witch then, and I worked harder than ever; but I little knew how cruel my enemy could be. She thought of a new way to kill my love for the beautiful Munchkin maiden, and made my ax slip again, so that it cut right through my body, splitting me into two halves. Once more the tinner came to my help and made me a body of tin, fastening my tin arms and legs and head to it, by means of joints, so that I could move around as well as ever. But alas! I had now no heart, so that I lost all my love for the Munchkin girl, and did not care whether I married her or not. I suppose she is still living with the old woman, waiting for me to come after her.

"My body shone so brightly in the sun that I felt very proud of it and it did not matter now if my ax slipped, for it could not cut me. There was only one danger—that my joints would rust. But I kept an oil-can in my cottage and took care to oil myself whenever I needed it. However, there came a day when I forgot to do this, and, being caught in a rainstorm, before I thought of the danger my joints had rusted, and I was left to stand in the woods until you came to help me. It was a terrible thing to undergo, but during the year I stood there I had time to think that the greatest loss I had ever known was the loss of my heart. While I was in love I was the happiest man on earth; but no one can love who has not a heart...."

THE COWARDLY LION

"You are nothing but a big coward."

"I know it," said the Lion, hanging his head in shame. "I've always known it. But how can I help it?"

"What makes you a coward?" asked Dorothy, looking at the great beast in wonder, for he was as big as a small horse.

"It's a mystery," replied the Lion. "I suppose I was born that way. All the other animals in the forest naturally expect me to be brave, for the Lion is everywhere thought to be the King of Beasts. I learned that if I roared very loudly every living thing was frightened and got out of my way. Whenever I've met a man I've been awfully scared. But I just roared at him, and he has always run away as fast as he could go. If the elephants and the tigers and the bears had ever tried to fight me, I should have run myself—I'm such a coward; but just as soon as they hear me roar they all try to get away from me, and of course I let them go."

"But that isn't right. The King of Beasts shouldn't be a coward," said the Scarecrow.

"I know it," returned the Lion, wiping a tear from his eye with the tip of his paw. "It is my great sorrow, and makes my life very unhappy. But whenever there is danger, my heart begins to beat fast."

"Perhaps you have heart disease," said the Tin Woodman.

"It may be," said the Lion.

"If you have," continued the Tin Woodman, "you ought to be glad, for it proves you have a heart. For my part, I have no heart, so I cannot have heart disease."

"Perhaps," said the Lion thoughtfully, "if I had no heart I should not be a coward."

"Have you brains?" asked the Scarecrow.

Canine Facts: The greyhound has the best eyesight of all breeds of dogs.

"I supposed so. I've never looked to see," replied the Lion.

"I am going to the Great Oz to ask him to give me some," remarked the Scarecrow, "for my head is stuffed with straw."...

"Do you think Oz could give me courage?" asked the Cowardly Lion.

"Just as easily as he could give me brains," said the Scarecrow.

"Or give me a heart," said the Tin Woodman.

"Or send me back to Kansas," said Dorothy.

"Then, if you don't mind, I'll go with you," said the Lion, "for my life is simply unbearable without a bit of courage."

"You will be very welcome," answered Dorothy, "for you will help to keep away the other wild beasts. It seems to me they must be more cowardly than you are if they allow you to scare them so easily."

"They really are," said the Lion, "but that doesn't make me any braver, and as long as I know myself to be a coward I shall be unhappy."

RANDOM GOSSIP:

•Author Margaret Mitchell's only casting suggestion for the film *Gone With the Wind*: She thought Groucho Marx should play Rhett Butler.

•Bob Newhart became a successful comedian without performing at clubs—while he was an accountant in the Illinois State Unemployment Office, he just recorded some wacky phone conversations he made to a friend...and sold them to a record company.

•Peter O'Toole is obsessed with green sox. He always wears them, even while sleeping. In fact, he once almost lost a movie role because he wouldn't take them off. In the end, he agreed to carry them in his pocket instead.

•Comedian Albert Brooks's real name is Albert Einstein.

•Ludwig von Beethoven never took a bath during the time he was writing his Ninth Symphony.

•Attila the Hun was probably a dwarf.

•Charlton Heston, a noted conservative, was once an artists' model who posed in the nude.

About 1 million Americans say they drink Coca Cola for breakfast.

CELEBRITY MANIA

This gets the Ed Wood, Jr. Award for Weirdness. Missy
Laws, a professional celebrity-chaser, has written a book
entitled How to Meet the Stars *(Ross Books, Berkeley, CA).*
The volume offers a glimpse into the mind of a Fan, and boy
is it strange. In case you're scheming to meet the celeb of
your dreams, here's a sample of Missy's advice to you.
Used courtesy of Ross Books.

P**RETEND YOU'RE AN OLD FRIEND.**
To portray an old friend, you must inform your star that
you have met him previously. All you need to know is a
place he has visited and the approximate time he was there.

Your opening line would be, "Hi. I don't know if you remember, but I met you before at (name of place he has been before)."

You may wonder how you can say this if it isn't true. The well-known meet so many strangers that it is simply impossible to remember them all. Therefore, if you insist that the two of you have previously met, your celebrity has little reason to doubt you. Even if he questions your accuracy, it's likely he'll be polite and not dispute your claim.

Perhaps you are certain that your star frequented a particular restaurant in the month of June. You could claim to have met him there. Maybe you know he cut an album at a specific recording studio. You could say that you originally introduced yourself to him there.

However, do not blindly invent a place and circumstance, or your luminary may unravel the lie and label you a fool.

Why is it a good idea to pretend to be an "old friend" by saying that the two of you met before? Partly because it's a good icebreaker. You leave the lines of communication open. In an obscure way, it gives you both something in common.

Also, if your celebrity thinks he has previously met you, he may feel more comfortable in your presence. If the two of you really had come in contact and he doesn't remember, then it's

---

Life span: A gorilla lives to about 40 years of age.

obvious you didn't cause trouble. Your star wouldn't forget if he had a reason to dislike you.

PRETEND TO BE RICH

There are a couple of things to remember when portraying an important person. First, if you dress and act as if you're wealthy, not only will you be more believable in the role, but you may also make your celebrity less leery of you.

Famous people are often suspicious of strangers, and rightly so, for often outsiders have insincere reasons for wanting to know the renowned. Money, for example, may be their objective. Dressing as if you're rich may help alleviate your celebrity's worries.

People are generally more comfortable with those on the same monetary level as they are, and most stars fall into the category of upper-level income citizens. They may more readily accept you as their equal if you outfit yourself to look like you're from the same social class. This could ease you into either a personal or business relationship more rapidly.

It's easy to fake wealth. You could find a classy, expensive-looking outfit at a thrift shop or garage sale. Inexpensive baubles could dangle from your ears and drape around your neck. If someone has the nerve to ask you, "Are those jewels real?" you could skirt the issue by responding, "They were a gift." Perhaps they were a gift to yourself from yourself!

I used to borrow prestigious antique automobiles from my friends or relatives when I really wanted to impress a luminary. If a star was extremely important to me, I'd appear in a different car each time I visited him. On Monday night I might have a Mercedes. On Tuesday I might have a Corvette, and on Wednesday I might have a Ferrari. Some celebrities probably thought I was wealthier than they were!

Mary Tyler Moore: "I know a funny Carol Burnett story. Once a fan followed her into the bathroom. The fan poked her head under the stall and shoved a pen and a piece of paper at Carol [for an autograph]."

According to one poll, 50% of American kindergarteners believe TV commercials.

PERRY MASON

Lawyer shows have always been popular on TV, but without a doubt, this is the most popular of them all. It inspired an entire generation to become attorneys. From Cult TV.

HOW IT STARTED: In the early '20s, a lawyer named Erle Stanley Gardner decided to give up his practice and become a full-time mystery writer. He wrote like a madman. He wrote so much that his fingers started bleeding. But it didn't pay off—no one wanted to buy his stories, not even the lowly pulp magazines he was trying to write for.

Eventually, his style improved, and he began selling literally hundreds of short mystery stories to magazines every year. Then, in 1933, he wrote two novels. One featured a lawyer named Ed Stark. The other was about a detective named Samuel Keene (who doubled as an astrologer). No one bought them, but the head of the William Morrow Publishing Co. suggested that Gardner combine his two heroes into one, creating a lawyer/detective. Gardner obliged. He created *Perry Mason*, whose first adventure, *The Case of the Velvet Claw*, was published in 1934.

By 1955 there were 70 Perry Mason novels, and Perry had become a popular movie and radio character.

But Gardner never liked what movie studios did with his hero. So when he got an offer to sell the TV rights for $1 million, he turned it down. Instead, he and his former agent, Cornwell Jackson, formed Paisano Productions to do their own *Mason* TV show. Jackson's wife, Gail, became executive producer. It aired for the first time on September 21, 1957, and lasted on CBS until the end of the 1965-1966 season.

INSIDE FACTS:

Deja vu. Gardner was so prolific that he couldn't remember what he'd written previously. Sometimes he'd be halfway through a new Perry Mason story before he or his staff realized he'd already used the plot before.

Court is adjourned. In Perry's last case, "The Case of the Final

---

Lifespan: An average lion lives for 25 years.

Fade-Out," the judge was played by his creator, Erle Stanley Gardner. And the killer was...Dick Clark.

Win some, lose some. Surprise! Perry did NOT win every case. He lost at least three of them. But there were extenuating circumstances, of course. And the second was a trick:
  1. In "The Case of the Terrified Typist," the killer was an imposter, pretending to be Perry's real client; the guilty verdict was thrown out.
  2. "The Case of the Witless Witness" opened with Perry losing a civil suit to a judge he later defended for murder in the same episode. Doesn't really count, does it?
  3. And in "The Case of the Deadly Verdict," his client was falsely convicted when she withheld key evidence. They got the *real* killer in the end.

Barbara Hale, 1963: "I occasionally attended meetings of legal secretaries, and the first thing they want to know is 'How do you arrange to go out with the boss every night?' The next is 'Why don't we ever see your typewriter?' "

He can dream, can't he? Erle Stanley Gardner liked Raymond Burr's performance but was particularly fond of Bill Talman as Hamilton Burger. "He actually looks like he expects to win a case," Gardner said, admiringly.

By the book. The *Perry Mason* radio show was more a romance than a detective series. It began with the emphasis on mysteries, but Gardner found that his courtroom dramas didn't adapt well to radio. As a soap opera, however, it was enormously successful. When it moved to television it remained a soap. The name was changed from *Perry Mason* to *Edge of Night*.

Book 'em, Perry. Gardner did not write the teleplays, but almost all of the 70+ Perry Mason novels were adapted for the series.

He's Back: Raymond Burr was so popular as Perry Mason that when he came back as the character in 1985, in a made-for-TV movie called *The Return of Perry Mason*, the show was higher-rated than any TV film of the season.

Liquid Assets: Water is heavier than ice.

THE MAGIC DRAGON

"Puff the Magic Dragon" is probably one of the best-known folk songs in the world. But is it really about drugs? Here's the answer, from Behind the Hits, *by Bob Shannon.*

L enny Lipton's first year of college wasn't easy. Not because he was homesick—he was glad to finally be out of Brooklyn—but for some reason, he was having a hard time getting used to being on his own. There were so many things to think about: girls; money; a career. Growing up obviously wasn't going to be easy. Lenny secretly began to miss his childhood.

The fall of 1958 and winter of 1959 passed. So did Lenny, who managed to survive at Cornell in spite of his emotional turmoil. And then one evening in the spring of 1959, a few days after his nineteenth birthday, Lenny made one of the most important decisions of his life. He decided to go to the library.

He was supposed to have dinner that night with a friend who lived off-campus, but it was still early. So Lenny wandered over to the library in the Cornell Student Union. He scanned the shelves until he found a volume of poems by Ogden Nash, then pulled it from the shelves and retired to a chair with it. Lenny was struck by a simple rhyme about the "Really-o Truly-o Dragon." In fact, he was inspired by it. "If Ogden Nash can write that kind of stuff, so can I," he thought.

Lenny returned the book and left the library and headed for his friend's house. As he walked down the hill that led from Cornell into the town of Ithaca, he thought of Ogden Nash's dragon. And then he thought of his own dragon. As he approached his friend's house, Lenny incorporated his dragon into a little poem about a subject that was never far from his mind in those days—the end of childhood.

When Lenny got to 343 State Street, he knocked on the door. No answer. Apparently neither his friend nor his friend's roommate, Peter Yarrow, was home. But Lenny wanted to get this poem onto paper, so he went inside anyway. He headed straight for a typewriter—which happened be Yarrow's. Lenny sat down and began typing as fast as he could. In three minutes, he typed out his poem—and then he got up and left. He didn't bother taking "Puff the Magic Dragon" with him. He didn't care, he'd gotten it out of his system. He just left it sitting in the typewriter.

Folk music was popular at Cornell in the late '50s, and Peter Yarrow was a big man in the folk scene. Although he was still an undergraduate, he taught a class on folk music, performed, and often organized concerts. As Lipton tells it, Yarrow returned home that night, found the poem sitting in his typewriter, and wrote a melody for it. Eventually Yarrow became part of Peter, Paul, and Mary, and they included the song about "Puff" in their act.

Years went by. And Lipton forgot all about this three-minute poem. Until a friend from Cornell happened to mention that he'd seen Peter Yarrow perform "Puff" with his new group. Yarrow had told him that Lenny had written it. Was it true?

Suddenly, Lenny's little poem came back to him.

In the world of rock 'n' roll, one inevitably runs into stories about unscrupulous operators who've stolen songs from their rightful owners. So it's nice to be able to write about a case in which an honest man went out of his way to find a writer. That's what happened here. When it began to look as if "Puff" was really going to be worth something, Peter Yarrow tracked Lenny Lipton down to let him know about it. And he's always listed Lipton as co-writer—even when Lenny didn't remember having invented the world's most popular dragon.

For years, people have speculated about the meaning of "Puff." But Lenny is quite clear about what was on his mind when he wrote it: "Loss of innocence, and having to face an adult world," he says. "It's surely not about drugs. I can tell you that at Cornell in 1959, *no one* smoked grass." None of the "suggestive" names were thought out—they just popped into his head as he was walking along that night. "I find the fact that people interpret it as a drug song annoying," he says. "It would be insidious to propagandize about drugs in a song for little kids. I think it's a very sentimental tune."

It's had remarkable success for a poem that took three minutes to compose. It reached Number Two on the national charts in 1963, and in the '70s became the basis of a continuing series of children's cartoons.

In 1984, the National Coca Company of Peru introduced toothpaste with cocaine in it.

A-BOMB VS. YOUR CAR

*This article first appeared in a 1957 car magazine which is
now defunct. It revealed the "shocking truth" about a car's
chance of surviving a nuclear blast. B.R. Institute member
Steve Gorlick has been saving it for years, hoping for a
chance to share it. "It's real Atomic Cafe stuff," he says. "In
retrospect, it's preposterous....But people
ate it up in 1957. We were so naive back then."*

The story of "Your Car vs. The Bomb" began on the bar-
ren Nevada desert in the chill gray hours before dawn
of March 17, 1953. At exactly 5:20 AM on that St. Pa-
trick's Day, the rugged landscape suddenly became brighter
than the sunniest day in June. The earth rocked and rolled and
a king-sized shock wave swept across the sand as the awesome
mushroom cloud of a nuclear explosion began its ascent into
the stratosphere.

A split-second earlier, the desert near the site of the blast
had appeared like a small parking lot with 51 automobiles—
some old and some new—standing at various distances from
the tall steel tower which supported the nuclear device. Some
were within one-half mile of the structure—much too close to
escape obliteration from a hydrogen bomb, but near enough to
the atomic weapon to provide a good test of a car's sturdiness.

As the terrific roar reverberated through the Nevada mountain, these same cars stood almost as they had a few moments
earlier, but there was a difference—a difference which can
mean much to millions of American car owners.

A few cars had rolled over, some were on fire, broken glass
was scattered throughout the area and almost all vehicles appeared to have been struck by a giant fist. Tops were dished in
and sides and fenders were crumpled.

Experts Inspect Cars

When experts from the Federal Civil Defense Administration
and the Society of Automotive Engineers inspected the cars,
they found that:

1. Cars which would run before the blast *would* run after the blast, if they had not burned.

2. All cars had survived the blast with *no appreciable structural damage* to frames, front and rear suspensions, and motor mounts.

3. Safety plate glass in cars near ground zero of the weapon was blown out in large pieces which were badly cracked, *but did not shatter.* In most cases, *all cars escaped damage to windows.* There were a number of instances where safety glass gave under the blast impact but did not blow entirely out of the frame.

In a few cars, only a relatively small hole was blown in the center of the caved-in glass!...Curved windshields and rear windows generally resisted the blast better than small or similar sized flat glass surfaces.

4. The percentage of cars lost to fire was very low. Where fire occurred it apparently began with smoldering seat covers, head liners and door panels. There was some scorching of paint, tire sidewalls and other exposed surfaces. There was no evidence that gasoline tanks or fuel systems had contributed to the initial fire hazard. There were no fuel tank explosions, even where the car was burned out.

5. There was no significant difference between makes or models of cars, with exception of wooden-bodied station wagons. These suffered more. No convertibles were tested.

6. The only tire failures were due to fire.

7. In cases where car windows were closed, the greatest damage was done to dished roofs and side panels.

What About Occupants?

All right—so much for the cars themselves. But what would have happened if you had been in one of these crates?

To answer this question, Civil Defense engineers placed

mannequins in many of the cars, all seated as if in driving position. Some of these mannequins showed a great deal of heat flash damage within three-quarters of a mile from the tower. Human skin at this distance would have been badly burned. In many instances the dished tops were pressed down hard on the mannequins' heads, indicating severe or fatal injury if it had been your head.

Thus it was found that while automobiles offered some protection from the bomb—if they were out of the area of complete destruction and if the occupants had had time to duck down below window level—basements and other permanent type shelters would be your best bet for protection from the bomb. However, a brick house standing a few hundred feet further away from the blast than were some of the cars was completely demolished.

One of the most important findings in the test was this:
Cars which could be operated before the blast still would run after the blast.

What does this mean to the average motorist?
The Federal Civil Defense Administration is vitally concerned with this question. Its experts point out that the nation has no guarantee that a potential enemy will not launch an attack against our cities and industries. Nor will we ever have assurance that natural disaster—flood, fire, tornado, hurricane, blizzard and earthquake—will spare us before, during and after attack, if the latter should come. Those who might escape the bombs still could face the threat of natural disaster at any time.

New Cars Would Be Out
If this country ever is hit with nuclear weapons, you can be certain that our automobile plants will be knocked out—if the enemy can do it—stopping production completely. If the plants escape the raids their output most certainly will be diverted to military demands. In any event, *you just won't be able to get a*

new car for no one knows how long. Many cars would be destroyed in such raids and a lot of family jalopies would be damaged. It's the damaged cars which may mean the difference between survival for you and your family, and further disaster.

The surest way to escape any kind of trouble is:
Just don't be there when it happens.

The family car can play an important part in helping you obey this axiom because it provides three essential elements vital to escape from danger.

●**First**, if we are to put distance between ourselves and the source of danger, we must have dependable, speedy transportation from the trouble spot. The family car is a must on this.

●**Second**, no matter where we are the family must have shelter. Despite its relatively small size (but they're growing bigger every year), the American automobile is a sort of house on wheels. It provides a haven from sun, wind, rain, and snow. It can shelter you from insects and even wild animals. It can also shield, to some degree, against the deadly radioactive fallout from a nuclear bomb—the stuff Adlai Stevenson kicked about in the last presidential election campaign.

●**Third**, the family car provides storage for food, clothing and other items vital during an emergency. The roomy luggage compartment of your car can easily accommodate several days' supply of food, clothing and other gear.

However, the car will serve this purpose only if you equip it properly and keep it in good condition. Good luck.

GANDHI SPEAKS

*The fact that Mahatma Gandhi was a man of compassion
and peace makes him unique among the powerful
politicians of the 20th century.*

"Freedom is not worth having if it does not connote freedom to err."

[*Responding to an interviewer who asked what Gandhi thought of Western civilization*] "I think it would be a good idea."

"If non-violence is the law of our being, the future is with women."

"All fear is a sign of want of faith. Cultivate the quiet courage of dying without killing. For man lives freely only by his readiness to die."

"Non-violence is not a garment to be put on and off at will. Its seat is in the heart and it must be an inseparable part of our very being."

"I have known many meat-eaters to be far more non-violent than vegetarians."

"A non-violent revolution is not a program of seizure of power. It is a programme of transformation and relationships, ending in a peaceful transfer of power."

"The slave clings to his chains and he must have them struck from him."

"No sacrifice is worth the name unless it is a joy. Sacrifice and a long face go ill together."

"Honesty is incompatible with amassing a large fortune."

"There is enough for the needy but not for the greedy."

"To a man with an empty stomach food is God."

"Prayer is not an old woman's idle amusement. Properly understood and applied it is the most potent instrument of action."

"There is more to life than increasing its speed."

Life span: A butterfly lives for about 6 months.

WEIRD INSPIRATIONS

*You can find the inspiration
for that great rock song you're trying to write in the
oddest place. These are from* Behind the Hits, *
by John Javna and Bob Shannon.*

ALL SHOOK UP, Elvis Presley. 1957/#1
This story will probably come as a pleasant surprise
to Pepsi Cola. They don't know that their product inspired one of the all-time great Elvis tunes.

1957: Otis Blackwell was sitting in his office at Shalimar Music, desperately trying to come up with a follow-up to his composition, "Don't Be Cruel." It wasn't going to be easy to match;
recorded by Elvis, "Don't Be Cruel" had been #1 on the charts
for *eleven* weeks, making it the top song of 1956. Now Presley
wanted another song and Otis wanted to give him one. But nothing came. Then Al Stanton, one of the partners at Shalimar,
happened to wander in.

Blackwell: "He walked in with a bottle of Pepsi, shaking it as
they did at the time. Al said, 'Otis, I've got an idea. Why don't
you write a song called "All Shook Up?"' A couple of days
later I brought the song in and said, 'Look man, I did something with it!'" So did Presley. It hit #1 and stayed there for
nine weeks, enough to make an Otis Blackwell song the most
popular record of the year *again*! All from a fizzing bottle of
Pepsi.

MONY, MONY — Tommy James and the Shondells.
1968/#3
People who work for the Mutual of New York Insurance Company—also known as M.O.N.Y—probably can't imagine that
the staid, conservative company has something to do with rock
'n' roll. They think it's just a coincidence that the name of their
company is also the title of this song....But it isn't.

M.O.N.Y.'s central office in New York City is a 40-story
building located at 1740 Broadway. On top is a huge old sign
that flashes the company's name in neon at night. This sign inspired Tommy James' 1968 hit.

James: "The night we wrote the song, we were absolutely dev-astated because we couldn't come up with a 'Bony Moronie,' a 'Sloopy' kind of title, and we knew that's what it had to be. It had to be a girl's name that nobody had ever heard of before.

"We were going through the dictionary, but nothing was hap-pening. We were just totally frustrated. I walked out onto my terrace—I lived in Manhattan at the time—and I was just sort of scanning around, looking for just any part of a name, any-thing. I was just kind of staring out into space, and all of a sud-den, I looked up and I saw [what I was looking for]...I said [to my manager], 'Ritchie, c'mere.' He came over and I said, 'Look.'...And all of a sudden, here's this 'M.O.N.Y.' with a dol-lar sign in the middle of the 'O.' The song was kind of etched in stone in New York, I guess. We both just fell down laughing."

Other Weird Ones:

•Paul Simon was inspired to write **"Mother and Child Reun-ion"** by a chicken-and-egg dish in a Chinese restaurant.

•**"Heartbreak Hotel,"** Elvis's first #1 hit, was inspired by a highly publicized suicide note that was printed on the front page of the Miami Herald. It began with the line, "I walk a lonely street...."

•The Teddy Bears' 1958 #1 song, **"To Know Him Is to Love Him,"** was inspired by the epitaph on group-member Phil Spector's father's tombstone.

•Melanie's million-seller, **"Brand New Key,"** came to her after she'd broken a strict vegetarian diet by eating a McDonald's hamburger.

•**"Be-Bop-A-Lula"** was inspired by a Little Lulu comic book.

•Ray Davies of the Kinks got the idea for the chord changes in **"You Really Got Me"** from a performer he saw on TV who "played" half-filled glasses of water with spoons.

•**"Running on Empty"** came to Jackson Browne because, in a tough period of his life, he kept forgetting to fill up his car with gas.

ANDY GRIFFITH SHOW

Although lots of city slickers don't care for the corn-ball world of Mayberry, U.S.A., this show is one of America's cult classics. Here's some info, from Cult TV, by John Javna.

HOW IT STARTED: While he was still riding high in the movies in the '50s, Andy Griffith avoided TV. But when his films started receiving less kind reviews and the quality of the scripts he was offered fell off, he figured it was time to make the jump to the small screen.

In 1960 he let his agents at William Morris know that he was looking for a TV series. They, in turn, contacted Sheldon Leonard, executive producer of *The Danny Thomas Show*, and asked him to devise a show specifically for their client.

Griffith's forte seemed to be playing "hillbillies" (as in *No Time For Sergeants*, where he played fresh-off-the-farm Will Stockdale). So Leonard came up with a rural sitcom featuring Andy as the sheriff, mayor, justice of the peace, and newspaper editor of a small North Carolina town. Andy didn't like the idea—but he liked Sheldon Leonard—so he agreed to give it a try. They decided to air the pilot as an episode of *The Danny Thomas Show*, to showcase it for potential sponsors.

Griffith took ten days off from *Destry*, a Broadway play in which he was starring, went to Hollywood, and shot the pilot (which featured Ronny Howard and Frances Bavier). Called *Danny Meets Andy Griffith*, it aired on February 15, 1960 as the final *Danny Thomas Show* episode of the 1959-60 season.

It was so well received that the sponsor for the *Thomas* show, General Foods, signed up for the *Griffith* show immediately. They were on the air six months later.

INSIDE FACTS:

Mayberry is loosely based on Andy Griffith's North Carolina hometown, Mount Airy. "Andy never left Mount Airy," a resident told *TV Guide* in 1966. "He plain took it to Hollywood with him."

In 1984, a Canadian farmer began renting ad space on his cows.

Fatherly advice. Ronny Howard was only six when he was cast as Opie, so his father, actor Rance Howard, chaperoned him. The first time Ronny had a tantrum about cooperating with the director, his father came up and spanked him right on the set. He rarely complained after that, and developed a reputation with the cast as a great kid.

Going straight. Many of the comic attributes which were originally planned for Andy were shifted to Barney Fife; Andy then became Mayberry's straight man, and Barney its clown.

About Barney. Don Knotts described his interpretation of Barney Fife this way: "I thought of Barney as a childlike man who was funny mainly because he was never able to hide anything in his face. If he was sad, he really looked sad. If he was angry, he acted angry. Children do that—pout, get overjoyed, or whatever. Barney never hid anything. He wasn't able to. In my mind that was really the key to Barney's character."

Communications breakdown. Don Knotts left the show in 1965 because he understood that Andy Griffith didn't want to do the show for more than five years. Knotts had already negotiated a movie contract with Universal Pictures when Andy changed his mind, and couldn't stay on as a regular. He did return, though, to make five more appearances as Barney in the last three seasons.

The real Mayberry. *The Griffith Show* was shot in three locations. The interior scenes were shot at Desilu Studios (the jail, Andy's house, etc.). The exterior scenes of Mayberry were shot at a lot in Culver City (where the main street was constructed). And the bucolic shots (the opening scene, etc.) were shot at Franklin Canyon, a Los Angeles reservoir.

Now you see 'em...
• Jack Nicholson appeared in two episodes.
• Howard McNear (Floyd the Barber) was out of the series for over a year (including the whole 1963-64 season) after he had a stroke. He returned in 1964 and stayed until 1967.
• George Lindsay auditioned for the part of Gomer Pyle and was rejected. Later, he was offered Goober's role.

Phone Crazy: The Pentagon made almost $85 million worth of phone calls in 1986.

INVENTIONS IN THE NEWS

We thought it would be interesting to take a look at the 1st newspaper reports on various inventions that changed our lives. These are excerpts from the actual articles.

The Flashlight...
LIGHT FROM AN ELECTRIC CURRENT
October 22, 1877

"Electricity in a hand-lamp is the most recent fruit of inventive enterprise. Messrs. Voison and Drouier, of Paris, have just patented a new scheme for obtaining light from an electric current. The apparatus consists of a single cell enclosed in a light mahogany case....The whole operation is performed so quickly that it may be said to be almost simultaneous with the pressing of the finger on the plunger.

"The principle of the invention is, of course, well known, but the mode of applying it is altogether novel. The apparatus is very simple, and it is noiseless in its working."

Music over the wire...
MUSIC BY TELEGRAPH
July 23, 1876

"The *Boston Traveller* prints the following statement: A few nights ago Prof. Bell was in communication with a telegraph operator in New York, and commenced experimenting with one of his inventions pertaining to the transmission of musical sounds. He made use of his phonetic organ and played the tune of 'America,' and asked the operator in New York what he heard. 'I hear the tune of "America,"' replied New York; 'give us another.' Prof. Bell then played 'Auld Lang Syne.' 'What do you hear now?' 'I hear the tune of "Auld Lang Syne," with the full chords, distinctly,' replied New York. Thus the astounding discovery has been made that a man can play upon musical instruments in New York, New Orleans, or London, or Paris, and be heard distinctly in Boston! If this can be done, why cannot distinguished performers execute the most artistic and beautiful music in Paris and an audience assemble in Music Hall, Boston, to listen? Prof. Bell's other im-

---

There are 3 times as many astrologers as astronomers in America.

provement, viz., the transmission of the human voice, has become so far perfected that persons have conversed over one thousand miles of wire with perfect ease, although as yet the vocal sounds are not loud enough to be heard by more than one or two persons. But if the human voice can now be sent over the wire, and so distinctively that when two or three known parties are telegraphing the voices of each can be recognized, we may soon have distinguished men delivering speeches in Washington, New York, or London and audiences assembled in Music Hall or Faneuil Hall to listen."

Television...
BELIN SHOWS TELE-VISION
December 2, 1922
"Tele-vision or 'long-distance sight' by wireless, had a preliminary experimental demonstration at the Sorbonne today by Edward Belin, inventor of the transmission of photo-graphs by wire. Flashes of light were directed on a selenium element, which, through another instrument, produced sound waves. These waves were then taken up by a wireless apparatus that reproduced the flashes of light on a mirror.

"This was offered as proof that the general principle of projecting a stationary scene had been solved."

Radio...
TOPICS OF THE TIMES
May 26, 1897
"English electricians, particularly those connected with the army and navy, are much interested in the Marconi system of telegraphy without wires. Some remarkable work has already been done with this machine, and improvements being made are expected to add many miles to the two or three over which it is already effective.

The system, it is thought, will be of especial use to the commanders of fleets at sea by enabling them to communicate with their other vessels without the use of visible signals."

Movie projector...
REALITIES OF ANIMAL MOTION
November 18, 1882
"Prof. Eadweard Muybridge, whose success in instantly photographing the motion of the horse in running has overturned all previous ideas on the subject, lectured last evening in the Turf Club

Theatre under the auspices of the Turf Club....

"Prof. Muybridge's subject was 'The Romance and Reality of Animal Motion,' and he illustrated his lecture upon a large screen by means of a *zoopraxiscope*, which an eminent English writer describes as 'a magic lantern run mad.' With this instrument the Professor produced upon the canvas, first stationary figures of the horse in the different positions assumed in the walk, the pace, the rack, the canter, and the gallop, and afterward displayed the figure of the animal, first at a walk across the canvas, then pacing, cantering, galloping, and even jumping the hurdle... the spectator could almost believe that he saw miniature horses with their riders racing across the screen."

Pocket Calculator...

POCKET COMPUTER CAN HANDLE TASKS OF UNIT 150 TIMES ITS SIZE
October 20, 1961

"Texas Instruments, Inc., has developed a vest pocket computer.

The gadget isn't much bigger than a pack of cigarets and weighs only 10 ounces, but it will do the same tasks as a conventional transistorized computer 150 times its size and 48 times heavier, the company claims.

Texas Instruments built the compact computer for the Air Force, to show it could be done. But it is offering components for sale that could be used to build almost any electronic equipment now using vacuum tubes or transistors.

P.E. Haggerty, president, says the little parts will be competitively priced for 'high reliability, small-run military requirements in 1963.' But their initial offering price runs something like 50 times the equivalent weight in good diamonds. In lots of 1,000 the components will sell for $50 to $65; since it takes 587 components to make a computer, the parts would be priced at $29,350 or more.

Initial use of equipment made from the networks is expected to be in the missile and space field....Future price reductions and development will lead to industrial uses in a few years and perhaps eventual consumer uses, the company feels. At the moment the company can suggest no immediately practical industrial or consumer uses, but officials are in no way perturbed."

THE HIPSTER SAINT

Contributed by Gene Sculatti, one of America's hippest cultural observers, and author of The Catalog of Cool. *Gene believes that the late great Lord Buckley is one of the hippest cats ever to make the scene in America.*

Maybe we shouldn't be talking about Lord Buckley at all.

It's just that, having been a secret so long, could he stand the public acclaim? Besides, words were his axe, and when it comes to that instrument, nobody blew it better.

Richard "Lord" Buckley (1906-60) was the embodiment of life lived coolly. If the coolest one can be is fashioning an accurate expression of what's inside, then Buckley was easily, to borrow a phrase from him, one of "the wildest, grooviest, hippest, swingin'-est, double-frantic, maddest, most exquisite" cats that ever breathed.

It also helps if what's inside is good to start with. Like maybe a huge heart. Tons of compassion. A mind that spontaneously generates material to entertain itself even when there are no audiences around. Or a conviction that language itself is the headiest brew and that staying drunk is divine.

Lord Buckley had all this inside. You'll know that when you hear his records. They're all that survive a life and a "career" that was by all accounts unpredictable and gloriously insane.

Much of the material on albums like *Way Out Humor* and *A Most Immaculately Hip Aristocrat* takes the form of parables. The best known may be his life of Christ "The Nazz" ("The sweetest far-out cat that ever stomped on this Sweet Green Sphere!"). There are also routines on Gandhi ("The Hip Gahn"), Jonah and the whale, Poe's "Raven," and Marc Antony's oration at Caesar's funeral.

The two that made a believer of me are Buckley's profile of the Spanish explorer Alvar Nuñez de Vaca and—best of all—his interpretation of the life of Einstein called "The Hip Einie."

On the multicandle brainpower of this most eminent "sphere-gasser" and his continual job loot predicaments: "Now here was a cat who carried so much *wiggage*—he was gig-less! He *could* not find a wheel to turn! He sounded all the hubcaps within' reach but nathan shakin'. He could *not* connect." Buckley rolls on, in an extrapolation of black jazz-rap, to clue us in on Einstein's subsequent relocation to Switzerland: "Now, not digging the lick, you see, of these double-square kicks the cats were puttin' down, he saved his beans and finally he swung with a Swiss passport, *swooped* the scene and lit in the land of the Coool, to prove and groove with the Alpine-heads!"

Ultimately, the Hip Einie connects with a gig, a pad, a wife and kids. Writing down his scientific theories, he soon becomes "the king of all Spaceheads," flips the physics-chemistry community on its ear, ascends to top dog status at the U of Zurich, and wows the world. Buckley shouts, whispers, wails like an evangelist wired to a generator, stomps through the tale (there is no way to repeat or paraphrase his explication of Einstein's theory—you have to be there) and finally winds down.

Buckley's personal (and sometimes highly public) life was a true trip itself. Born of Indian extraction in California's Mother Lode gold country in '06, he gravitated to Frisco, then to the Texas oil fields. He spent the Thirties doing standup in Capone-style Chicago speakeasies, made it to New York and married "Lady" Buckley. By the mid-Fifties he was reigning hepcat to a circle of admirers that included Sinatra, Robert Mitchum and Stuart Whitman. Ed Sullivan put him on TV; Jonathan Winters, Redd Foxx, and every other comedian dug him. Ultimately, he suffered the Bruce-type fuzz busts—in New York City in '60, where he died in November.

Which is great and dramatic, and somebody should (and somebody else will) make a movie of it someday. But what really counts is first-person Buckley, his work. Here's a sample:

"Now you see in Hip Talk, they call William Shakespeare 'Willie the Shake!' You know why they call him 'Willie the Shake?' Because HE SHOOK EVERYBODY!! They gave this Cat five cents' worth of ink and a nickel's worth of paper and he sat down and wrote up such a breeze, WHAMMMMM!! Everybody got off! Period! He was a hard, tight, tough Cat. Pen in hand, he was a Mother Superior."

FABULOUS FOOD FLOPS

Americans will eat almost anything. We consume billions of Twinkies, drink oceans of Kool-Aid, devour millions of pounds of processed cheese spread. But even we have our limits—some food products are so outrageous that no one will touch them. Like these.

CORN FLAKES WITH FREEZE-DRIED FRUIT. In the '60s, the lure of space-age food technology was too seductive for cereal giants Kellogg and Post to resist.

The year was 1964. Freeze-drying had been "perfected" by NASA, so Post decided to add freeze-dried strawberries to its cornflakes. Just add milk, they told wide-eyed consumers, and these dried-out berries miraculously turned back into real fruit.

"Corn Flakes with Strawberries" took off like a rocket; supermarkets couldn't keep the product on their shelves. Exulting, Post built a multi-million dollar plant to produce the cereal and added two new fruity varieties to their line: "Corn Flakes with Blueberies," and "Corn Flakes with Peaches."

Meanwhile, Kellogg's was test-marketing its own version of high-tech fruit 'n' cereal: "Corn Flakes with Instant Bananas." The Battle Creek cereal giant bought the rights to the song, "Yes We Have No Bananas," and hired Jimmy Durante to croak new lyrics at a piano: "Yes, we now have bananas...." But the prognosis wasn't good. One Kellogg's salesman described the product as "cardboard discs in a box."

It turned out that freeze-dried fruit got soft on the outside, but stayed crunchy on the inside. What's worse: by the time the fruit was soft enough to eat, the cereal was soggy. Millions of families bought "Corn Flakes with Strawberries" once, but never came back for a second helping—leaving both cereal giants stuck with a bountiful harvest of unwanted pseudo-fruit.

OTHER FREEZE-DRIED FLOPS: Freeze-dried mushrooms in a box, from Armour foods; freeze-dried cottage cheese ("with cultured sour cream dressing"), from Holland Dairies.

According to a reliable source, Sammy Davis, Jr. still owns 6 Nehru jackets.

WEIRD BEER

Here are two beer ideas that America refused to swallow:

•In 1965, Dr. Robert Cade came up with the formula for Gatorade. Two years later, he sold it to Stokely-Van Camp. What did he do with the profits? He developed "Hop 'n' Gator," a mixture of beer and Gatorade. The Pittsburgh Brewing Company actually produced it in 1969...but it was canned right away.

•Not to be outdone, the Lone Star Brewing Company retaliated with flavored beer in 1970. It was available in three exciting tastes: cola, grapefruit, and lemon-lime. But of course, it wasn't available too long. Cola-flavored beer?

McDONALD'S MISTAKE

In the '50s, Catholics still weren't permitted to eat meat on Friday's—a problem for McDonald's. Since the fast food giant only had hamburgers on its menu, sales slumped every week in Catholic areas. McDonald's needed a creative alternative...and Ray Kroc, Chairman of the Board, had one. Putting his marketing genius to work, he came up with the "Hula Burger."

Picture a toasted bun, covered with a piece of melted American cheese, mustard, ketchup, a pickle...and a slice of grilled pineapple. Sound appetizing?

The "Hula Burger" had no meat, so it was perfect for Fridays. But it had another problem—Kroc couldn't get anyone to buy it. Customers all said, "I love the Hula, but where's the burger?" McDonald's' vegetarian experiment was abandoned after a few months. It wasn't until 1962 that the religious crisis was solved with the "Filet-O-Fish" sandwich.

A QUICK ONE

In the mid-'60s, Hires developed a brand new product and rushed it out to supermarkets...where it went sour. The product: root beer-flavored milk.

GIMME A LIGHT

Believe it or not, "light beer"—a huge success today—was a dud in 1967. Two light beers were introduced that year.

The first was Gablinger's—also known as "the Edsel of

Research indicates that mosquitoes are attracted to people who have recently eaten bananas.

Beers." Brewed on the East Coast by Reingold, it was named after the Swiss chemist who'd formulated it—Hersch Gablinger. Reingold put his picture on the cans, trying to make him a celebrity, but it was no use. The "no carbohydrate" beer was so watery it wouldn't even hold a head. And the slogan, "It doesn't fill you up," didn't mean anything to beer-drinkers in 1967.

If that wasn't enough, the federal government seized a shipment of Gablinger's because of "misleading" statements on the label, and a Reingold competitor filed a lawsuit, charging that the product was falsely promoted. Reingold made all the necessary changes, but by that time Gablinger's was a lost cause.

The other "light" beer was called...Lite Beer. That's right—the same one that over-the-hill athletes have promoted on television for the last decade. In 1967, it was marketed by a Cincinnati brewery named Meister Brau. They called it "low calorie beer," and their ads featured "Miss Lite," a 21-year-old California blonde in a leotard. But Lite was ahead of its time, and people who were into low-cal foods weren't into drinking beer. Lite lasted for about a year, then disappeared.

IT AIN'T OVER TIL IT'S OVER: In the late '70s, the Miller Brewing Company purchased Meister Brau and its various assets—including the trade name *Lite*. Styles had changed in a decade, and the time was right for "diet beer." So in 1979, Miller launched its "new" beer with a memorable ad campaign featuring aging macho men fighting over whether Lite was more attractive because it tasted good or because it didn't make them feel full. The result: the beer that flopped in '67 was the second-leading beer in America (behind Bud) twenty years later.

BEER NOTES
•Legally, a beer doesn't actually have to be lower in calories to call itself "light" beer. All that's required is for the beer to be light in color.
•In 1986, Anheuser-Busch sold more beer than any brewery in history—72,300,000 barrels.
•Smoke and drink? Tastes good, but doubles your health risk.

ONE-LINERS

Occasionally a random phrase in a conversation inspires a hit record. Here are some examples.

MY BOYFRIEND'S BACK, the Angels. 1963/#1
Abraham Lincoln High School in Brooklyn was fertile ground for musicians and singers. Neil Sedaka and the Tokens went there. So did songwriter/producer Bob Feldman. Bob graduated in 1958 and moved across the East River to Manhattan, where he became a staff writer for April-Blackwood Music.

Five years later he heard that the Sweet Shoppe across the street from Lincoln High, his favorite hangout in the '50s, was being torn down. So he went back for a last look. "While I was there," Feldman recalls, "an altercation started between a young girl and a hoody-looking young man with a leather jacket and a great D.A. [duck's-ass hairstyle]. She was pointing a finger at him and screaming, "My boyfriend's back and you're gonna be in trouble. You've been spreading lies about me all over school and when he gets ahold of you, you're gonna be sorry you were ever born.""

That night Bob told his writing partners, Jerry Goldstein and Richard Gotterher, about the incident and they sat down and wrote a song about it. The Angels recorded the tune a few weeks later, and it became a million-seller—one of the biggest hits of 1963.

OH PRETTY WOMAN, Roy Orbison. 1964/#1
Roy Orbison's wife, Claudette, was already a famous rock 'n' roll name by the '60s. Orbison wrote the flip side of the Everly Brothers' 1958 classic, "All I Have to Do Is Dream," as a tribute to her. But the tune she inspired in 1964 meant even more to Roy's career; he sang it himself.

It started with a shopping trip. Roy and Billy Dees, a songwriter Orbison collaborated with, were sitting in the Orbisons' house when Claudette announced she was going into town to

---

In 1647, New York became the first city in America with a paved street.

buy some groceries. "Do you need any money?" Roy asked. Dee said, "A pretty woman never needs any money." Then he turned to Roy and said, "Hey, how about that for a song title?" Orbison liked the idea of a "pretty woman," but not the part about the money. After Mrs. Orbison left, Roy and Billy began turning the phrase into a song. And when she returned, carrying her bags of food, she was greeted by the debut performance of Roy's second #1 tune.

In 1982, Van Halen remade the song.

OTHER ONE-LINERS

•Otis Redding and drummer Al Jackson were discussing the problems of going on tour, and Redding started complaining too much. Jackson said, "What are you griping about? You're on the road all the time. All you can look for is a little respect when you come home." Redding took the line and wrote **"Respect"** from it.

•**"He Ain't Heavy, He's My Brother"** was inspired by Father Flanagan's Boy's Town poster. The poster had a picture of a priest on one side, and a two kids facing him, one sitting on the other's shoulders. The caption read, "He ain't heavy Father, he's my brother."

•Marvin Gaye's biographer visited Gaye in Belgium, where the singer was living in 1982 after a bitter divorce. The biographer noticed sado-masochistic magazines in Gaye's apartment, and suggested that Gaye needed some "sexual healing." It inspired the tune **"Sexual Healing,"** Gaye's first top 10 hit in five years, and a Grammy-winner.

•"The Jack Benny Show" occasionally featured a used car salesman who swore that every car had been owned by "a little old lady from Pasadena." Jan Berry, of Jan and Dean, was studying geriatrics at the time; he based a million-selling song on the phrase—**"The Little Old Lady From Pasadena."**

•Lamont Dozier was having a fight with his girlfriend. He shouted at her, **"Stop in the name of love!"**

EINSTEIN SAYS...

A few words of wisdom from the white-maned genius.

[Explaining the concept of relativity] "When you are courting a nice girl an hour seems like a second. When you sit on a red-hot cinder a second seems like an hour. That's relativity."

"The most beautiful thing we can experience is the mysterious. It is the source of all true art and science."

"Imagination is more important than knowledge."

"The hardest thing in the world to understand is the income tax."

"God is subtle, but he is not malicious."

"An empty stomach is not a good political adviser."

"Nothing is more destructive of respect for the government and the law of the land than passing laws which cannot be enforced."

"We should take care not to make the intellect our god; it has, of course, powerful muscles, but no personality."

"I don't believe in mathematics."

"The release of atom power has changed everything except our way of thinking, and thus we are being driven unarmed towards a catastrophe."

[When asked how he felt about seeing his ideas used in the atomic bomb] "If only I had known, I should have become a watchmaker."

"Art is the expression of the profoundest thoughts in the simplest way."

"Everything should be made as simple as possible, but not simpler."

"Science without religion is lame, religion without science is blind."

"Whoever is careless with the truth in small matters cannot be trusted with important matters."

Thomas Edison demonstrated the first practical electric lightbulb on December 20, 1879.

THE FBI: WATCHING TV

According to a former ranking agent, the FBI spends an extraordinary amount of time and money on p.r. ...and not nearly enough on solving crimes. A case in point:

In 1986, it was revealed that between 1959 and 1963 the FBI employed agents to watch, report on, and try to influence the content of the TV series "The Untouchables." The reason: Director J. Edgar Hoover was incensed that it portrayed Treasury Agent Eliot Ness as the major crimebuster of his era, ignoring the FBI completely.

"Hoover fumed when episodes showed Ness solving a crime that fell under the FBI's regular jurisdiction," wrote William Barret in *Rolling Stone*. "'We must find some way to prevent FBI cases from being used,' [he] wrote. His staff launched an immediate investigation into published reports—apparently false—that ex-FBI agents were writing scripts for the show."

Actually, J. Edgar Hoover's monitoring of "The Untouchables" barely scratched the surface of the FBI's elaborate surveillance of Hollywood scripts during his tenure as director (48 years). Hoover's obsession with Hollywood's depiction of the Bureau in films and on television led to some strange investigations. FBI files on Rock Hudson, Groucho Marx and Walt Disney reveal the paranoid scope of the Bureau's efforts to reshape its image for public consumption.

As an unelected government official at the whim of periodic presidential reappointments, Hoover—who served as director from 1924 until his death in 1972—had every reason to protect the G-Man's glorified position in popular culture. FBI-sanctioned projects, such as "The FBI" TV series (1965-73) starring Efrem Zimbalist, Jr., helped solidify the Bureau's pre-Watergate public standing and thus Hoover's stranglehold as director.

Hoover himself admitted in a posthumously published article written for *TV Guide* (May 20, 1972) that the Bureau had final approval rights over the scripts, sponsors and actors portraying FBI agents in "The FBI" TV series. The Director also

---

Life span: Average age for a parrot is 120 years.

collected a neat $500 per episode. "We know," Hoover wrote in *TV Guide* "that a less than first-rate program could cheapen the FBI's name and have an adverse effect on its image....Perhaps we are inclined towards Puritanism in an increasingly permissive world."

Only after Hoover's death and the post-Nixon flurry of bureaucratic reform—such as the re-amended Freedom of Information Act of 1974 which subjected FBI documents to declassification—did the truth behind the FBI's Hollywood surveillance become known.

During his almost 50-year reign as Bureau chief, Hoover had been rumored to have amassed a Personal and Confidential file on every major player in both political and entertainment circles, including intimate (but often unsubstantiated) details of drinking, drugging and sexual peccadillos. Unfortunately, the contents of Hoover's P&C files will never be known, thanks to his private secretary Helen Gandy, who shredded every file upon Hoover's death, except one: the pedigree of his terriers, G-Boy and Cindy. (That file, incidentally, had been saved for Clyde Tolson, Hoover's right hand man—some say literally—and brief successor at the Bureau.)

Fortunately, various bits of Hooverana in the form of Official and Confidential files managed to survive the purge. These documents—available for public scrutiny (and cheap thrills) at the FBI's Freedom of Information Act Reading Room in Washington—have revealed the methods by which Hoover managed to meddle into any film production or television series that included a portrayal of an FBI agent.

The following are some examples:

WALT DISNEY

Not even Uncle Walt could escape the Bureau's dragnet. The movie in question was *Moon Pilot*, a harmless Disney pre-*I Dream of Jeannie* comedy about an astronaut who meets an alien before a space mission.

After learning that *Moon Pilot*'s script portrayed FBI agents as ineffectual bumblers, Hoover ordered the chief of the Bureau's Los Angeles division to contact Disney for a meeting, where he was asked to change the film's reference from FBI agents to Federal security agents. Despite Disney's protestations that the change was "unrealistic," dialogue changes were tailored to meet Hoover's specifications.

The real snafu started when Hoover was sent a newspaper review of *Moon Pilot* which referred to the bureau's portrayal "as a mass of dolts." On the margin of the review (which is included in Disney's FBI file), Hoover scrawled "I am amazed Disney would do this. He probably has been infiltrated."

Apparently, the squabble carried over to another Disney production, *That Darn Cat* (1964), which was also closely monitored by the Los Angeles division for references to the FBI. The matter was dropped—according to an FBI memorandum in Disney's file—after "an established source at the Disney studios" confirmed that the script depicted "the FBI in a most complimentary manner."

ROCK HUDSON

In 1982, Rock Hudson's FBI file was rush-released in the midst of the media circus surrounding his AIDS-related death. The most quoted part of the released documents was as follows: "Rock Hudson has not been the subject of an FBI investigation. During 1965, however, a confidential informant reported that several years ago while he was in New York he had an 'affair' with movie star Rock Hudson. The informant stated that from personal knowledge he knew that Rock Hudson was a homosexual. The belief was expressed that by 'personal knowledge' the informant meant he had personally indulged in homosexual acts with Hudson or had witnessed or received the information of individuals who had done so."

This document had been sent to Mildred Stegall, White House staff-member during LBJ's presidency.

Since Hoover himself had been rumored to be gay (never proven but he was a bachelor all his life), he had particular interest in major figures who were gay. For example, Tennessee Williams' FBI files include this: "Subsequently, in connection with the investigation for the Department in 1961 (expurged) the Bureau ascertained that Thomas Lanier Williams has the reputation of being a homosexual. (Expurged.) Further, the Office of Naval Intelligence, in a separate inquiry, secured statements from individuals who admitted participating in homosexual acts with Williams."

Hoover, then, was particularly alarmed to find out that Rock Hudson might be playing an FBI agent in a movie. According to *Daily Variety* (9/5/67), Hudson had been signed to play "an FBI agent who becomes involved with a jewel thief." This revelation sent shockwaves through the Bureau. An investigation into the movie called *The Quiet Couple* (eventually released as *A Fine Pair*) proved that *Daily Variety's* information was erroneous—Hudson's role was that of an ex-police officer. Still, the Bureau made several follow-up reports (and wasted untold thousands of taxpayers' dollars) to make sure Hudson did not play an FBI agent.

GROUCHO MARX

Obviously, any Jewish celebrity with the name Marx was going to be under Hoover's intense scrutiny. Although Marx's FBI files include inconclusive investigations into his possible Communist affiliations, it is the references to his TV series, "You Bet Your Life," that show the Bureau's sensitivity to every mention of the FBI.

Included in Marx's files are the following entries:

"(Expurged) called on 2/29/60 to advise that he had been listening to the captioned program on last Thursday, 2/25/60, on NBC, Channel 4, and that one of the contestants was an individual described by (expurged) as a 'stumble bum' who admitted being a former pugilist and bootlegger. (Expurged) said that when this contestant, whose name he did not recall, stated he had been a bootlegger, Marx asked, 'You mean you were a bootlegger for the FBI?' in an apparent effort to be funny. (Expurged) said the contestant made some non-committal answer and there was little laughter from the audience. (Expurged) stated that he felt that Marx's question was in poor taste and simply wanted to call it to the Bureau's attention."

"We received a letter from (Expurged) Los Angeles 48, California, suggesting that the director see Romaine Rielding talk Russian to Groucho Marx on the Groucho Marx television show Thursday evening, January 29, 1959.

"The show was monitored and there was nothing on it concerning the Bureau or matters of any interest to us."

About 1/4 of American households are single-parent homes.

WORD PLAY

Common phrases and their origins

To Peter Out
Possibly comes from France, where peter means "fart." According to one expert: "'Peter out' would then be equivalent to 'fizzle out,' since...the original 'fizzle' was a noiseless fart."

A Wild Goose Chase
A game played in Elizabethan England—a crazy version of follow-the-leader, on horseback. People believed wild geese acted this way.

Red Tape
The stuff used by bureaucrats in the 19th century to tie together packets of official documents.

Different Drummer
Coined by Henry David Thoreau. In his own words: "If a man does not keep pace with his companions, perhaps it is because he marches to a different drummer."

To Quit Cold Turkey
"Typically, a person [who quits drugs or drinking] undergoes bouts of sweating and chills, with goosebumps. ....Anyone who has seen a plucked turkey prepared for the oven...will at once understand the image."

The Jig Is Up
"First heard during Shakespeare's time. Jig was then a slang word for *trick*, so the phrase simply meant, 'Your trick or deceit has been found out.'"

Toodle-oo
Derived from the French phrase, *Tout a l'heure*, which means "See you later."

Jerk
In Victorian times, masturbation was considered the road to insanity. People who showed the "results" of self-abuse—stupidity, dimwittedness, etc.—were referred to as *Jerk-offs*. Later, just calling someone a *jerk* was sufficient to get the point across.

Someone's Gone to Pot
Like food that's cooked and eaten....It's gone to (the) pot. It's done, finished, over.

Alexander Graham Bell was 29 years old when he invented the telephone.

FRANKS & DOGS

*Some food is so much a part of our lives that we never stop
to ask where it comes from. Here are some
answers you can chew on.*

THE SAUSAGE: ANCIENT HISTORY
• The Babylonians were the first to come up with the concept over 3,500 years ago by stuffing spiced meat into animal intestines.

• Other civilizations adopted and modified the sausage. The Greeks called it "orya." In the 9th Century B.C., the Greek poet Homer praised the sausage in his epic the *Odyssey*.

• The Romans, whose army marched on its stomach, loved the sausage. It is mentioned in the oldest known Roman cookbook, dated 228 A.D. They called it "salsus"—which ultimately became *sausage*.

THE WEINER. Over the next 1000 years, the popularity of sausages spread throughout Europe. By the Middle Ages, they began to take on regional characteristics; their shape and size varied from country to country, and local creations were named for the towns in which they originated. Austria gave birth to the "Vienna sausage" or *wienerwurst*, from which the term "weiner" is derived.

THE FRANKFURTER. The modern hot dog—the frankfurter—is descended from a spiced, smoked, slightly curved, thin sausage developed in Frankfurt, Germany.

• According to German lore, the shape of this "Frankfurter" was a tribute to a popular pet dachshund that belonged to a local butcher. The result: by the 1850s, it was commonly called a "dachshund sausage." It was customarily eaten with sauerkraut and mustard. But no bun.

• In the 1890s, a German immigrant named Charles Feltman began selling "dachshund sausages" on the street in Coney Island, NY. He became so successful that he was able to open a "frankfurter" restaurant—the first in the United States.

THE BUN. In 1904, at the St. Louis "Louisiana Purchase Exposition," another Frankfurt native sold "dachshund" sausages.

Americans' two favorite foods are steak and potatoes.

The effect was far-reaching: besides popularizing the food nationwide, this entrepreneur improved the package by introducing the bun. Here's how: Gloves were customarily supplied for customers to wear while eating their frankfurters. But at the fair, too many people walked away still wearing them; the vendor soon ran out of spare gloves. In desperation, he convinced a nearby baker to make frank-shaped rolls as a substitute for gloves. The rolls actually worked better; a new tradition was born.

THE HOT DOG. The name *Hot Dog* was coined in 1906. A syndicated cartoonist named Tad Dorgan was enjoying a baseball game at New York's Polo Grounds. Inspired by the vendors' call of "Get your red hot dachshund dogs!" he went back to his office and began sketching a cartoon based on the notion of a real dachshund in a bun, covered with mustard. When he couldn't come up with the correct spelling of dachshund, he supposedly just settled for "hot dog." The name stuck. Ironically, although Dorgan is clearly given credit for the name, the original cartoon has never been found.

THE HAMBURGER

• The hamburger originated with the warring Mongolian and Turkish tribes known as Tatars who shredded low-quality beef before cooking to make it taste better.

• The dish was introduced to Germany sometime before the 14th century where it was spiced and prepared cooked or raw. From the town of Hamburg the dish became known as "Hamburg steak."

• In the 1880's, German immigrants brought the Hamburg specialty to America where it became known as "hamburger steak." It was also known as "Salisbury Steak," named after the English Dr. J.H. Salisbury, who recommended to his patients that they eat beef three times a day.

• The "hamburg" began its ascent to unparalleled popularity when it was served as a sandwich at the 1904 St. Louis World's Fair. Unfortunately, no one knows exactly how its association with ketchup started, or who thought of serving it on a bun.

•Today, the hamburger is *the* most popular entrée in American restaurants.

The average American eats between 15 and 20 pounds of apples annually.

PARTY LINES

*People often ask if there's really any difference between
the two major political parties. To answer the question, Rep.
Andrew Jacobs of Indiana rose in the House of Representatives and offered this delineation. It was recorded in* Will
the Gentleman Yield?, *by Bill Hogan and Mike Hill,
and is reprinted with permission of Ten Speed Press.*

TO BE READ ALOUD BY A DEMOCRAT TO A REPUBLICAN, OR A REPUBLICAN TO A DEMOCRAT:

Democrats seldom make good polo players.

The people you see coming out of white wooden churches are
Republicans.

Democrats buy most of the books that have been banned
somewhere. Republicans form censorship committees and read
them as a group.

Republicans are likely to have fewer but larger debts that
cause them no concern.

Democrats owe a lot of small bills. They don't worry either.

Republicans consume three-fourths of all the rutabaga produced in this country. The remainder is thrown out.

Republicans usually wear hats and almost always clean their
paintbrushes.

Democrats give their worn-out clothes to those less fortunate.
Republicans wear theirs.

Republicans post all the signs saying *No Trespassing* and
These Deer are Private Property and so on. Democrats bring
picnic baskets and start their bonfires with signs.

Republicans employ exterminators. Democrats step on bugs.

Republicans have governesses for their children. Democrats
have grandmothers.

Democrats name their children after currently popular sports
figures, politicians and entertainers. Republican children are
named after their parents or grandparents according to where
the most money is.

Large cities such as New York are filled with Republicans—
up until 5 p.m. At this point there is a phenomenon much like

---

Olympic highjump: Penguins can jump as high as 6 feet in the air.

an automatic washer starting the spin cycle. People begin pouring out of every exit of the city. These are Republicans going home.

Democrats keep trying to cut down on smoking, but are not successful. Neither are Republicans.

Republicans tend to keep their shades drawn, though there isn't any reason why they should. Democrats ought to, but don't.

Republicans fish from the stern of a chartered boat. Democrats sit on the dock and let the fish come to them.

Republicans study the financial pages of the newspaper. Democrats put them in the bottom of the bird cage.

Most of the stuff you see alongside the road has been thrown out of car windows by Democrats.

On Saturday, Republicans head for the hunting lodge or the yacht club. Democrats wash the car and get a haircut.

Republicans raise dahlias, Dalmatians and eyebrows. Democrats raise Airedales, kids and taxes.

Democrats eat the fish they catch. Republicans hang them on the wall.

Democrats watch TV crime and Western shows that make them clench their fists and become red in the face. Republicans get the same effect from presidential press conferences.

Christmas cards that Democrats send are filled with reindeer and chimneys and long messages. Republicans select cards containing a spray of holly, or a single candle.

Democrats are continually saying, "This Christmas we're going to be sensible." Republicans consider this highly unlikely.

Republicans smoke cigars on weekdays.

Republicans have guest rooms. Democrats have spare rooms filled with old baby furniture.

Republican boys date Democratic girls. They plan to marry Republican girls, but feel they're entitled to a little fun first.

Democrats make up plans and then do something else. Republicans follow the plans their grandfathers made.

Democrats purchase all the tools—the power saws and mowers. A Republican probably wouldn't know how to use a screwdriver.

Democrats suffer from chapped hands and headaches. Republicans have tennis elbow and gout.

Republicans sleep in twin beds—some even in separate rooms. That is why there are more Democrats.

SOUNDS OF SILENCE

The unusual history of the record that made Simon and Garfunkel famous, from the book Behind the Hits, *by Bob Shannon and John Javna.*

As late as March 1965, Simon and Garfunkel were still just another unknown folk duo who played at Greenwich Village coffee houses. Their act consisted of a few folk standards, a few Dylan tunes, and a few originals.

Then they got a break; Paul Simon managed to interest Columbia producer Tom Wilson in his material. The result: Simon and Garfunkel's first album, a record called "Wednesday Morning, 3 AM." It featured Simon on acoustic guitar, and included "Sounds of Silence," which Paul had written the previous year.

It bombed, and Simon and Garfunkel broke up. Paul moved to England; Artie went back to college.

That could have been the end of the story. But unknown to the singers, a Boston radio station began playing "Sounds of Silence" regularly...and Columbia suddenly became interested. They'd had Top 40 success with the folk-rock music of the Byrds, so they decided it was worth trying to turn S&G into a folk-rock act, too.

The secret: All Columbia had to do was add electric instruments to the S&G tracks already on tape. That task fell to Tom Wilson. Without telling Simon and Garfunkel about it, he gathered a bunch of studio musicians at the Columbia recording studios in New York City and had them add their own music to S&G's. Vinnie Bell was the guitarist in that session.

Vinnie Bell: "We had no idea what we were going to work on that day—we were just doing a session. So we got there and there were no artists...and we had no music; they just played a ...record of these two guys singing....Well, everybody got out their own paper and we started jotting down music. We each made up our own parts because there was no arranger on it. And then we played along to this existing track."

So, thanks to a handful of anonymous New York sidemen, the acoustic version of "Sounds" became electrified. Then Columbia issued it as the new single from their latest "folk-rock discovery," Simon and Garfunkel. Top 40 stations, unaware that the duo no longer existed, immediately played it and soon it was shooting up the charts.

A few weeks later, Paul Simon got a call in England telling him that his record was the #1 song in America. You can imagine his shock—he didn't even know it existed! Of course, Simon flew back to the States, S&G reunited, and America had two new poet-heroes. Simon, however, apparently had no idea who'd played the electric instruments on his record—which proved embarrassing when he and Garfunkel appeared on NBC's prime time rock 'n' roll TV show, "Hullaballoo." Here's what happened:

Vinnie Bell: "I was working [in the house band] on 'Hullaballoo,' and of course we'd get all the big groups on the show. It was a lot of fun for me, because I would see all my friends. I recorded with all those people. The Stones used to come on—I worked with them. Dionne Warwick was a regular guest....All those people, y'know. Well, now Simon and Garfunkel have a big hit, 'Sounds of Silence,' so they came on the show. And during the rehearsal, Paul Simon talked to the musical conductor, Peter Matz. He said, 'I'd like to show the guitar player how to play this [part].' But Peter Matz knew I did the record; he said, 'I think he knows.' But Paul Simon insisted. He said, 'No, I did a special thing on the record that I want him to do with the sound.' And Peter Matz looked at me, and he said, 'All right, go ahead.' So Simon walked through the orchestra and when he got to me, he said, 'Hi, I'm Paul Simon.' I said, 'Hi, I'm Vinnie Bell.' He said, 'I'd like to show you, if you don't mind, how I did this thing on the record. We have a record out, I don't know if you know it, it's a big hit, "Sounds of Silence."' So I said to him, 'Yes, I know the record. To tell you the truth, I know just what to play.' He said, 'No, here, just watch my fingers,' and showed me with his guitar. 'Paul,' I said, '*I did the record*.' And of course there was silence. And he said, 'Well...okay....Are you sure you did the record?' I said, 'Yeah, it's *this*, right?' And I played [the part for him]. He said, 'Yeah, that's it.' I just told him, "Don't worry.'"

PETER PAN

*This is one of the most engaging works of fantasy you'll find
anywhere. After seeing Walt Disney's sugary
version, you'll be surprised how ironic and
sophisticated the original is.*

BACKGROUND

Peter Pan *was written by Sir James Matthew Barrie, one
of England's most celebrated writers. It was first presented as a play in London in 1904, and was so well received
that in 1906 Barrie wrote a sequel called* Peter Pan in Kensing-
ton Gardens. *In 1911, Barrie finally published* Peter Pan and
Wendy, *the famous prose adaptation of the original play. The
following is excerpted from that work.*

Mrs. Darling first heard of Peter when she was tidying up her
children's minds. It is the nightly custom of every good mother
after her children are asleep to rummage in their minds and
put things straight for the next morning, repacking into their
proper places the many articles that have wandered during the
day. If you could keep awake (but of course you can't) you
would see your own mother doing this, and you would find it
very interesting to watch her. It is quite like tidying up draw-
ers. You would see her on her knees, I expect, lingering hu-
morously over some of your contents, wondering where on
earth you had picked this thing up, making discoveries sweet
and not so sweet, pressing this to her cheek as if it were as nice
as a kitten, and hurriedly stowing that out of sight. When you
wake in the morning, the naughtiness and evil passions with
which you went to bed have been folded up small and placed
at the bottom of your mind; and on the top, beautifully aired,
are spread out your prettier thoughts, ready for you to put on.

I don't know whether you have ever seen a map of a person's
mind. Doctors sometimes draw maps of other parts of you, and
your own map can become intensely interesting, but catch them

trying to draw a map of a child's mind, which is not only confused, but keeps going round all the time. There are zigzag
lines on it, just like your temperature on a card, and these are
probably roads in the island; for the Neverland is always
more or less an island, with astonishing splashes of colour
here and there, and coral reefs and rakish-looking craft in
the offing, and savages and lonely lairs, and gnomes who are
mostly tailors, and caves through which a river runs, and
princes with six elder brothers, and a hut fast going to decay,
and one very small old lady with a hooked nose. It would be
an easy map if that were all; but there is also first day at
school, religion, fathers, the round pond, needlework, murders,
hangings, verbs that take the dative, chocolate pudding day,
getting into braces, say ninety-nine, threepence for pulling out
your tooth yourself, and so on; and either these are part of the
island or they are another map showing through, and it is all
rather confusing, especially as nothing will stand still.

Of course the Neverlands vary a good deal. John's, for instance,
had a lagoon with flamingoes flying over it at which John was
shooting, while Michael, who is very small, had a flamingo
with lagoons flying over it. John lived in a boat turned upside
down on the sands, Michael in a wigwam, Wendy in a house of
leaves deftly sewn together. John had no friends, Michael had
friends at night, Wendy had a pet wolf forsaken by its parents; but on the whole the Neverlands have a family resemblance, and if they stood in a row you could say of them that
they have each other's nose, and so forth. On these magic shores
children at play are forever beaching their coracles. We too
have been there; we can still hear the sound of the surf, though
we shall land no more.

Of all delectable lands the Neverland is snuggest and most
compact; not large and sprawly, you know, with tedious distances between one adventure, but nicely crammed. When you
play at it by day with the chairs and tablecloth, it is not in the
least alarming, but in the two minutes before you go to sleep it
becomes very nearly real. That is why there are night-lights.

Occasionally in her travels through her children's minds Mrs.

Darling found things she could not understand, and of these quite the most perplexing was the word Peter. She knew of no Peter, and yet he was here and there in John and Michael's minds, while Wendy's began to be scrawled all over with him. The name stood out in bolder letters than any of the other words, and as Mrs. Darling gazed she felt that it had an oddly cocky appearance.

'Yes, he is rather cocky,' Wendy admitted with regret. Her mother had been questioning her.
  'But who is he, my pet?'
  'He is Peter Pan, you know, mother.'

At first Mrs. Darling did not know, but after thinking back into her childhood she just remembered a Peter Pan who was said to live with the fairies. There were odd stories about him; as that when children died he went part of the way with them, so that they should not be frightened. She had believed in him at the time, but now that she was married and full of sense she quite doubted whether there was any such person.

'Besides,' she said to Wendy, 'he would be grown up by this time.'
  'Oh no, he isn't grown up,' Wendy assured her confidently, 'and he is just my size.' She meant that he was her size in both mind and body; she didn't know how she knew it, she just knew it.

Mrs. Darling consulted Mr. Darling, but he smiled pooh-pooh. 'Mark my words,' he said, 'it is some nonsense Nana has been putting into their heads; just the sort of idea a dog would have. Leave it alone, and it will blow over.'

But it would not blow over; soon the troublesome boy gave Mrs. Darling quite a shock.

Children have the strangest adventures without being troubled by them. For instance, they may remember to mention, a week after the event happened, that when they were in the wood they met their dead father and had a game with him. It was in this

casual way that Wendy one morning made a disquieting revelation. Some leaves of a tree had been found on the nursery
floor, which certainly were not there when the children went to
bed, and Mrs. Darling was puzzling over them when Wendy
said with a tolerant smile:
'I do believe it is that Peter again!'
'Whatever do you mean, Wendy?'
'It is so naughty of him not to wipe,' Wendy said, sighing. She
was a tidy child.

She explained in quite a matter-of-fact way that she thought
Peter sometimes came to the nursery in the night and sat on the
foot of her bed and played his pipes to her. Unfortunately she
never woke, so she didn't know how she knew, she just knew.
'What nonsense you talk, precious. No one can get into the
house without knocking.'
'I think he comes in by the window,' she said.
'My love, it is three floors up.'
'Were not the leaves at the foot of the window, mother?'

It was quite true; the leaves had been found very near the
window.

Mrs. Darling did not know what to think, for it all seemed so
natural to Wendy that you could not dismiss it by saying she
had been dreaming.
'My child,' the mother cried, 'why did you not tell me of this
before?'
'I forgot,' said Wendy lightly. She was in a hurry to get her
breakfast.

Oh, surely she must have been dreaming.
But, on the other hand, there were the leaves. Mrs. Darling ex-
amined them carefully; they were skeleton leaves, but she was
sure they did not come from any tree that grew in England.
She crawled about the floor, peering at it with a candle for
marks of a strange foot. She rattled the poker up the chimney
and tapped the walls. She let down a tape from the window to
the pavement, and it was a sheer drop of thirty feet, without so
much as a spout to climb up by.

Certainly Wendy had been dreaming.

Tall tale: The average person is about a quarter of an inch taller at night.

But Wendy had not been dreaming, as the very next night showed, the night on which the extraordinary adventures of these children may be said to have begun.

On the night we speak of all the children were once more in bed. It happened to be Nana's evening off, and Mrs. Darling had bathed them and sung to them till one by one they had let go her hand and slid away into the land of sleep.

All were looking so safe and cozy that she smiled at her fears now and sat down tranquilly by the fire to sew. It was something for Michael, who on his birthday was getting into shirts. The fire was warm, however, and the nursery dimly lit by three night-lights, and presently the sewing lay on Mrs. Darling's lap. Then her head nodded, oh, so gracefully. She was asleep. Look at the four of them, Wendy and Michael over there, John here, and Mrs. Darling by the fire. There should have been a fourth night-light.

While she slept she had a dream. She dreamt that the Neverland had come too near and that a strange boy had broken through from it. He did not alarm her, for she thought she had seen him before in the faces of many women who have no children. Perhaps he is to be found in the faces of some mothers also. But in her dream he had rent the film that obscures the Neverland, and she saw Wendy and John and Michael peeping through the gap.

The dream by itself would have been a trifle, but while she was dreaming the window of the nursery blew open, and a boy did drop on the floor. He was accompanied by a strange light, no bigger than your fist, which darted about the room like a living thing; and I think it must have been this light that awakened Mrs. Darling.

She started up with a cry, and saw the boy, and somehow she knew at once that he was Peter Pan. If you or I or Wendy had been there we should have seen that he was very like Mrs. Darling's kiss. He was a lovely boy, clad in skeleton leaves and the juices that ooze out of the trees; but the most entrancing thing about him was that he had all his first teeth. When he saw she was a grown-up, he gnashed the little pearls at her.

Doctors in ancient China were paid when patients were healthy, not sick.

ALLENISMS

Some of Woody Allen's coolest comments.

"Thought: Why does man kill? He kills for food. And not only food: frequently there must be a beverage."

"Showing up is 80 percent of life."

"I'm not afraid to die. I just don't want to be there when it happens."

"If only God would give me some clear sign! Like making a large deposit in my name at a Swiss bank."

"I'm a practicing heterosexual...but bisexuality immediately doubles your chances for a date on Saturday night."

"My brain: it's my second favorite organ."

"I don't want to achieve immortality through my work...I want to achieve it through not dying."

Q. "Have you ever taken a serious political stand on anything?"

A. "Yes, for twenty-four hours I refused to eat grapes."

"Eternal nothingness is OK if you're dressed for it."

"Not only is there no God, but try getting a plumber on weekends."

"Is sex dirty? Only if it's done right."

"Money is better than poverty, if only for financial reasons."

"I want to tell you a terrific story about oral contraception. I asked this girl to sleep with me and she said 'no.'"

"My one regret in life is that I'm not someone else."

"I asked the girl if she could bring a sister for me. She did. Sister Maria Teresa. It was a very slow evening. We discussed the New Testament. We agreed that He was very well adjusted for an only child."

CARY GRANT, ACID-HEAD

We think of Timothy Leary, Jimi Hendrix , etc. as the
quintessential LSD freaks. But Cary Grant—of all
people—was into acid before those guys ever heard of it.

Before Timothy Leary and the counterculture discovered LSD—before it was even illegal—the unflappable, ultimately dignified Cary Grant was tripping out every Saturday.

It was 1957. Grant's wife, Betsy Drake, had been going to the Psychiatric Institute of Beverly Hills to undergo an unusual form of chemical therapy. The Institute's directors believed that the little-known drug LSD "acted as a psychic energizer, emptying the subconscious mind and intensifying emotions a hundred times." Drake had been taking it regularly, and it had done wonders for her. So when she realized that Grant was on the verge of a nervous breakdown, she convinced him to try it, too.

Working with Dr. Mortimer Hartman, whom the actor referred to as "My wise Mahatma," Cary began the sessions under strict medical supervision. First he was given a dose of LSD in the therapist's offices; he spent several hours in treatment. Then he was given a depressant to calm him down. Finally, he was driven home to rest and recover for a day. Grant found the effects of the drug astounding. "The first thing that happens to you," he told friends, "is you don't want to look at who you are. Then the light breaks through; to use the cliché, you are enlightened." Hallucinating under the drug gave the otherwise staid Briton a new freedom. Once, he admitted, "I imagined myself as a giant penis launching off from Earth like a spaceship."

Grant continued this treatment for two years; he took hundreds of acid trips. Previously he had been reluctant to talk about his personal life. (An instructive anecdote: a reporter once cabled this question to him: "How old Cary Grant?"

If a room contains 100 American women, 4 will probably not be wearing panties.

Grant's evasive reply: "Old Cary Grant fine.") Now at age 55, thrilled by the new outlook on life that the drug gave him, he spoke to friends, the media, college students—anyone who would listen—about the benefits of LSD therapy.

"I have been born again," he declared. I have been through a psychiatric experience which has completely changed me. It was horrendous. I had to face things about myself which I never admitted, which I didn't know were there. Now I know I hurt every woman I ever loved. I was an utter fake, a self-opinionated bore, a know-all who knew very little."

A Sampling of Grant's "Acid Revelations"

• "Respect women because they are wiser than men...(they) have an innate wisdom we men try to despoil from the time we're sixteen years old."

• "The only way to remain happy is to know nothing or everything. Unfortunately, it is impossible to know nothing for very long."

• "A man owes it to me—if I have to look at him—to keep his hair combed and his teeth cleaned."

• "Deplore your mistakes. Regret them as much as you like. But don't really expect to learn by them."

• "Don't expect to be rewarded if you...tell the truth. Hypocrisy no longer has any power to shock us. We encounter it every day. But we encounter the truth so seldom that it shocks and embarrasses us, and we run from it."

Unfortunately, Grant's acid-inspired statement that "My next marriage will be complete" wasn't accurate—although he did have the child he said he was now ready to "beget." When he and actress Dyan Cannon (who swore she had only taken acid once before their marriage—and never during) decided to divorce, it turned ugly. She accused him of being an "apostle of LSD," "an unfit father," and said he insisted that she trip out. "He told me the new me would be created through LSD," she declared in court.

In later years, Grant refused to discuss the remarkable drug. "My intention in taking LSD," he finally told a reporter, "was to make myself happy. A man would have to be a fool to take something that *didn't* make him happy."

According to one survey, nearly 3/4 of all Americans believe in vigilante justice.

PRESIDENTIAL QUIZ

Odds and Ends about American presidents.

1) In which state were the most presidents born?

2) The first president not born a British subject was:
a) Martin Van Buren
b) William Henry Harrison
c) Andrew Knox Polk

3) The only president who was never elected to any national office was...

4) Which president was into boxing and jujitsu?
a) Abe Lincoln
b) Teddy Roosevelt
c) John Kennedy

5) The first woman appointed to the cabinet was Frances Perkins. Who appointed her?

6) Who was the first president to weigh over 300 lbs.?

7) The first president to have documented nervous breakdowns (he had five before he became president) was...

8) The only president known to have ancestors who were American Indians was...

9) Which of these presidents was a bowling enthusiast?
a) Herbert Hoover
b) Harry Truman
c) Richard Nixon

10) What is the significance of the film, *Hellcats of the Navy* ?

11) Who was the first U.S. president to appear on national public TV?

12) Who was the first president to be inaugurated in Washington, D.C.?
a) George Washington
b) Thomas Jefferson
c) Andrew Jackson

13) The first bachelor president is considered likely to have been homosexual (his V.P., nicknamed "Miss Nancy," was thought to be his lover). Who was he?

14) More presidents were officially residents of this state when they were elected than any other. Which state?

15) How many presidents have there been?

One in ten truck drivers is a woman.

CAR BOMB: THE EDSEL

In the lore of American business, the name Edsel is synonomous with total failure. Yet hardly anyone knows anything about the Edsel. The story is almost too stupid to believe, but here it is. Judge for yourself.

The story of the Edsel sounds like a *Mad* magazine parody of the auto industry of the '50s: The people at Ford were so intent on using the latest novelty gadgets, super-sophisticated marketing techniques, and "personality surveys" to sell their new vehicle that they forgot to give their customers a car, too. Everything, from beginning to end, was done wrong ....And to top it off, Ford had the bad luck to unveil its up-scale bomb during an economic slump that was responsible for the worst overall car sales in a decade. Things couldn't have gotten much worse.

"How much planning went into the Edsel? In a sense, it must be the most thoroughly planned product ever introduced."
—*Fortune* **magazine, September, 1957.**

THE PLAN: Ford, the #2 car manufacturer in the '50s, was losing too much business to GM in the "trade-up" field. Upwardly mobile consumers who started with an ordinary Ford or Chevrolet eventually wanted something a little more prestigious. Surveys showed that they "traded up" to either an Oldsmobile or a Buick—rarely a Mercury, which was all Ford had to offer in the upper range. So in the early '50s, Ford executives decided to create a whole new line of cars to attract "the young executive or the professional family on its way up." It was to be "the first new line of cars...started from scratch by a major manufacturer" since the Mercury was introduced in 1938. Ford committed $250 million to the project.

THE EXECUTION: Ford concentrated on three key elements: Design, Dealers, and "Personality."

DESIGN: Roy Brown, from the Lincoln division, was assigned the task of styling the Edsel. "His first move," reported one

---

magazine, "was to take his stylists out to a busy intersection to look at cars. To no one's surprise, they decided all American cars looked pretty much alike."

"I wanted a car with strong identity, " Brown explained before the Edsel's unveiling, "one that could be recognized instantly from the front, the side, or rear." An example: Struck by the fact that front grilles on American cars were all "massive and horizontal," Brown decided a vertical grille would set the Edsel apart visually. His 1957 analysis of the result: "It is crisp and fresh-looking. That grille could become a classic." [It did, of course, but not exactly the way Brown foresaw it; the famous "toilet-seat" grille remains a classic example of tasteless excess in car design.]

The interior was next. Neil Blume was assigned the task of "loading it with exciting things for Edsel dealers to talk about." He came up with 23 selling points, most of which were simply cosmetic. Some examples: "A drum-like speedometer that glows a menacing red when the car exceeds a preset speed;" "a thermometer that registers the temperature both inside and outside the car;" "a single-dial heating and ventilating control;" and "gearshift buttons sensibly located in the steering wheel hub."

DEALERS: Ford wanted exclusive dealers for the Edsel—not salesmen who also handled Fords, Mercurys, or any other brand. The reason: they figured the car stood a better chance of succeeding if the Edsel was all a dealer had to offer. So beginning in 1955, they began trying to woo dealers away from their competition, offering the the chance of a lifetime to become the first Edsel dealers. The amazing thing is that it worked. Almost 200 GM dealers jumped to the Edsel; 150 Chrysler-Plymouth dealers took the bait; another 200 dealers from smaller manufacturers went for it. Each had to plunk down over $100,000 (1957 money), and in some cases, they hadn't even seen the car—they took it on faith that Ford was behind the project 100%...and how could Ford miss? It was like buying a ticket on the *Titanic*.

PERSONALITY: The Edsel may have been the first auto to rely on sophisticated marketing profiles to target its potential customers. Ford wanted to know what the car's "personality" should be, so they hired a marketing expert named David Wallace to tell them. Begining in 1955, Wallace worked with the Bureau of Applied Social Research at Columbia University, doing market studies and polling consumers to find out how they *felt* about various makes of automobiles. It was he who determined that the Edsel should be positioned as "the smart car for young families."

But it was a crazy survey. They approached their new car strictly as a status symbol, asking questions about what *impressed* people, without asking what people would *buy*. "The trouble here," commented one critic, "[is] that they didn't ask questions that elicited meaningful replies. Ford asked no questions at all about car prices, cost of upkeep, cost of operation, cars too long for garages, etc. In fact, the consumer research program...completely ignored automobiles as functioning machines of transportation."

In addition, Ford frequently ignored the research and reverted to its standard decision-making techniques..."If you ask how a policy was determined, like the choice of green as the Edsel's color" said one writer at the time, "you may still be told 'Well, So-and-so liked it, and he has the power. That's the way it is.'" The marketing men weren't particularly pleased with the choice of the name Edsel, either. [Edsel Ford was Henry Ford II's father—it's obvious who picked that one.] "Just look at the associations," complained one. "Edsel, diesel, pretzel—Good Lord! It's a wonderful name for a plow or a tractor, but a car? They can make it elegant, but it will take them two or three years and $50 million to do it." [An aside: Wallace corresponded with poet Marianne Moore about names for the new car. The ones she suggested included: Mongoose Cigique, Pastelogram, Pluma Piluma and Utopian Turtletop.]

In the end, Wallace shrugged it off. "All we can do is advise them how to merchandise the car," he said. "We can't tell them how to create it."

THE UNVEILING: "On September 4, 1957, after a year of intensive and elaborate build-up (in which no detail of the car was revealed) and better than a month before any of the 1958 models were out, the public was finally invited to see the dream made real." People couldn't resist the invitation; for the first week, Edsel showrooms were packed. But within a month, it was clear that customers had just come to look. No one was buying the car. Ford announced that "They're simply waiting to see what the other makes will offer; they'll be back," but Ford was dreaming. October's sales were worse than September's, and November's were so bad that dealers started going bankrupt. The main Edsel dealer in New York City quit, declaring that "The Ford Motor Company has laid an egg."

Ford used every trick it knew to lure people into the showrooms—it raised the Edsel ad budget to a record $20 million, offered the car to state highway officials at huge discounts to give the car some road respectability, offered rebates to dealers...But nothing worked.

In retrospect, perhaps the most amazing thing about this new product is the fact that Ford concentrated so much effort on the "sell" that the car itself was overlooked. Not only did it offer nothing new—it was even inadequately supplied with the basics. The brakes, for example, were the same as Ford used on its smaller cars, although the Edsel was considerably heavier than the rest of the Ford line.

TEST REPORTS: Here are a few of the comments *Consumer Reports* made when it test-drove the celebrated new auto:
- "The public expected the new name to be on a new-from-the-ground-up car. CU's answer: the Edsel has no...advantages over other brands. The car is almost entirely conventional in construction, utilizing components from the 1957 Ford...and Mercury."
- "Edsels offer nothing new in passenger accommodations—unless 'contour seats' feel different to you....The interior dimensions are, for the most part, those of the 1957 Ford Fairlane, one of the least roomy of last year's cars."
- "The amount of shake present...on rough roads—which wasn't long in making itself heard as squeaks and rattles—went well beyond any acceptable limit."
- "As a matter of simple fact, combined with the car's tendency to shake like jelly, Edsel's handling represents retrogression rather than progress in design and behavior."
- "The 'luxury-loaded' Edsel—as one magazine cover described it—will certainly please anyone who confuses gadgetry with true luxury."

• "The center of the steering wheel is not, in CU's opinion, a good pushbutton location....To look at the Edsel buttons pulls the driver's eyes clear down off the road."

• "The Edsel instrument panel is a mismanaged dilly."

And so it went. Fundamentally, the magazine had nothing good to say about Ford's new product—except that it had great acceleration.

EVEN MORE REASONS IT FLOPPED:

• It was an effort to get into the mid-sized car market....But in 1956 and 1957, the mid-sized car was in trouble. Anyone in the auto industry knew that. What Ford should have done was to bring out a low-priced, innovative economy model, a car to compete with the German Volkswagen. Instead, Ford produced an instant white elephant.

• Rotten timing. In September 1957, the stock market was in a downturn. In fact, the Edsel and the economic recession hit the market at exactly the same time.

• Ford introduced its new car with its 1958 prices at exactly the same time that the 1957 models were being discounted to clear them out. Consequently, the attention the company had sought for its new baby focused instead on its price. Consumers, dealers and bankers alike, balked at higher car prices in general—but because Edsel was the first car to announce them, the brunt of the public's displeasure landed right at Edsel's doorstep.

• The over-designed status symbol appeared a month before Russia successfully launched its Sputnik. In the wake of the U.S.S.R.'s feat, embarrassed Americans shunned opulent new cars as symbols of a misguided national priority. The emphasis in American culture temporarily shifted to academics and practicality.

THE AFTERMATH

The Edsel lasted for two years. Shortly after it bombed, the *Wall Street Journal* ran this little squib: "Ford Motor has called on the Institute of Motivational Research to find out why Americans buy foreign economy cars."

P.S.: Edsel Ford, the car's unfortunate namesake, was a progressive minded, artistic thinker whose death preceded that of his father. Neither he nor Henry Ford ever saw the Edsel.

Six hours after you brush your teeth, plaque starts forming again.

THE FABULOUS '60S

More odds and ends about America's favorite decade, from 60s!, by John and Gordon Javna

FLASH-IN-THE-PANTIES. In the summer of 1960, Macy's installed a men's underwear vending machine. It was national news; throngs of people swarmed into the store to get a look at the contraption—so many, in fact, that Macy's had to move it from the ground level to the fifth floor to avoid store traffic jams. But it died there; the bare facts were that nobody wanted to buy boxer shorts from a machine.

AUTO MANIPULATION. Ford's Thunderbird was so popular in the early '60s that when John F. Kennedy requested 25 of them for his inaugural parade, Ford had none to supply; they were all sold out, and none of the waiting buyers would relinquish his claim to a new T-Bird (not even for the President). After some desperate juggling, Ford finally decided to make a few of its customers wait until after the inauguration.

UNFRIENDLY SKIES. In 1967 in Ankara, Turkey, farmers marched to the American and Soviet embassies and demanded compensation for flood damages to their crops. The floods, they charged, were caused by Russian and American spaceships, which had torn "holes in the sky." The Russian ambassador suggested that if they really thought there was a hole in the sky, they ought to be trying to figure out how to fix it, not complaining to him about it.

POLITICAL IMAGE. After JFK's election in 1960, Robert J. Donovan's book *PT 109*—an account of the heroic rescue Kennedy pulled off during World War II—became a bestseller. A movie version wasn't far behind; but who would star? JFK, it turns out, wanted Warren Beatty to play him. But the director considered Beatty too unstable, and hired Cliff Robertson for the part instead. Kennedy sent his press secretary, Pierre Salinger, to protest the choice. The director's reply to the president: "Don't tell *me* how to make an exploitation movie."

BRAINTEASERS

*Still more logic puzzles. Remember—no
heavy math or pencils needed.*

Y ou know," said my Uncle Gordon, "an eccentric friend
of mine decided that one of his two sons should take
over his horse-breeding business. Being a sporting man,
he arranged a horse race between the two sons. But being eccentric, he decided that the son who owned the *slowest* horse
would win the business. Naturally each son was worried that
the other would cheat by holding his horse back and not letting
it run freely. So they decided to ask me for advice. I don't
mean to be immodest," he said, grinning, "but I solved their
problem with two words."
What did Uncle Gordon say?

"**Y**ou know," said my Uncle Gordon, "people on Wall Street
say that 1987 dollars are worth more than 1985 dollars."
"Uncle Gordon, you old faker," I said, "everybody knows
that."
Why is it true?

"**I** know a man," said Uncle Gordon, "who lives on the 25th
floor of an apartment building. Every morning he rides the elevator down to the street level, gets out and goes to work. But
when he comes home at night, he only rides the elevator to the
8th floor and then walks up the stairs the rest of the way.
Know why?"
"I haven't the foggiest idea," I answered.
Do you?

"**O**nce in Asia," said Uncle Gordon, "I was captured by ban-
dits. They told me: 'Make a statement—if you speak the truth,
we'll hang you...if you say something false, we'll shoot you.' I
thought it over for a minute, and then uttered a phrase that confused the robbers so completely that they let me go."
What did he say?

Head-lines: Fine hair grows twice as fast as coarse hair.

HOLIDAYS

*We celebrate them every year without having the
slightest idea where they really came from...
Here are a few enlightening tidbits.*

E ASTER
Although we know it as the Christian celebration of the
Resurrection of Christ, the name "Easter" derives from
Eostre, the dawn goddess of Anglo-Saxon myth—who was tra-
ditionally honored with an annual festival at the beginning of
spring. This celebration happened to coincide with Christian
holy days, and so was co-opted by that religion. In America,
Easter was largely ignored until immediately after the Civil
War. The war-torn country needed a holiday which stressed
rebirth, so observance of Easter became important.

EASTER RABBIT
Take your pick: The rabbit is either a traditional symbol of
fertility that represents spring, or the rabbit was the earthly
symbol of the goddess Eostre.

EASTER EGG
The egg represents birth and resurrection. It was apparently
an ancient pre-Christian tradition to give people decorated
eggs as gifts in the spring.

APRIL FOOL'S DAY
Until 1564, it was a tradition to begin the New Year with a
week of celebration, ending with a big party. But the calendar
was different then, and the New Year began on March 25—
which meant that the annual party was held on April 1. In
1564, a new calendar was instituted, making January 1 the New
Year. People who forgot—or didn't realize—what had happened, and still showed up to celebrate on April 1, were
called "April fools."

MOTHER'S DAY
Created in response to the prolific letter-writing campaign of

Only 1% of American women are completely satisfied with the way they look.

a Miss Anna Jarvis, a West Virginia school teacher who wanted to honor her own deceased mother. How could anyone say no? In 1914, six years after Jarvis began her campaign, President Woodrow Wilson signed a bill proclaiming the second Sunday in May as America's official Mother's Day. Jarvis was named the head of the official Mother's Day committee, and greeting card, flower, and candy sellers—thrilled at the opportunity to sell more of their goods—supported the effort with advertising. (In 1986 it was reported that over 150 million cards and 8 million bouquets of flowers were sent on Mother's Day.)

By the mid-'30s, however, Anna Jarvis was so disgusted with the commercialization of the holiday that she disavowed it. This didn't faze American businesses one bit. They set up their own organization to support Mother's Day, and with the backing of the American public, the holiday continues to flourish.

CHRISTMAS

No one knows exactly when Christ was born, but according to accounts in the Bible, it might well not be December 25—the activities of the shepherds described in conjunction with the event are associated with spring, not winter. Nor did Christians celebrate Christ's birth when the religion was new. It wasn't until around the third century A.D. that December 25 was sanctioned as a holy day by the Church. The reason: It seems likely that Christian fathers were trying to compete with another growing religion, Mithraism—the worship of a sun god—whose big day was December 25.

THE CHRISTMAS TREE

Might have begun in pre-Christian Europe, where the Nordic people believed that fruit trees and evergreens were embodiments of powerful spirits, although there are several other equally plausible legends. German families in the 16th century began bringing evergreens into their homes during the holiday season. They were known as *Christbaume* or "Christ trees," and were decorated with fruit, candles, and cookies.

The *Christbaum* was taken to England by Queen Victoria's German husband, Prince Albert. The first American Christmas trees were brought by German immigrants in the 1820s, but it wasn't until the beginning of the 20th century that Christmas trees became a mainstream custom in the States.

Only about 5% of American men say they are satisfied with the way they look.

HANGING CHRISTMAS STOCKINGS

The custom of hanging stockings on the mantel to receive small gifts originated with St. Nicholas, the Turkish version of our own Santa Claus. Long ago, St. Nick was supposed to have provided dowries for the three daughters of a poor nobleman. He threw bags of money through their windows (in one version, down the chimney), where the gifts happened to fall into a stocking that was hung out to dry by the fire.

SANTA CLAUS

The first Santa was the bishop of Myra of Asia Minor, St. Nicholas—who today remains a principal saint of the Eastern Orthodox church. In the 4th Century, he distributed presents to good children on his feast day, December 6.

During the Protestant Reformation, St. Nicholas was replaced in many countries by the Christmas Man, known in England as Father Christmas and in France as Pere Noel. But in the Netherlands, where St. Nicholas was the patron saint of sailors, he remained popular. There he was known as Sint Nikolaas or Sinterclaas, and Dutch children expected him to leave goodies in their wooden clogs on his feast day. Both this tradition and the name were Americanized. Sinterclaas became Santa Claus.

Amazingly, most of the things American kids believe about Santa originated with the 1822 poem, "The Night Before Christmas," by Dr. Clement C. Moore; the image of the tubby, jolly man in the red suit can be attributed to some 1860s illustrations by celebrated political cartoonist, Thomas Nast.

WASHINGTON'S BIRTHDAY

Surprisingly, the Father of Our Country's birthday was first celebrated as a national holiday in 1780, during his lifetime. But it was his real birthday, February 11, they celebrated.

GROUNDHOG DAY

Originally, this was a European planting superstition—if hedgehogs saw their shadows when they emerged from hibernation, planting was put off a few weeks. American settlers adapted the day to the groundhog.

About 1/3 of all Americans ride bicycles.

MONKEE TALES

*In 1987, the Monkees returned, spurred by exposure
on MTV and books like A Monkees
Tale, by Eric Lefcowitz.*

HISTORY

On September 8, 1965, director Bob Rafelson and producer Bert Schneider (together as Raybert Productions) placed an ad in *Variety* magazine that read:

"Madness!! Auditions
Folk & Rock Musicians-Singers
For Acting Roles in New TV Series
Running Parts for 4 Insane Boys, Age 17-21
Want Spirited Ben Frank's Types
Have Courage To Work
Must Come Down For Interview"

The idea was to create an American TV version of the Beatles—a pre-fab four.

In all, 437 applicants showed up at Raybert's offices trying to become the four finalists for a "musical situation comedy" called "The Monkees." Among those rejected were Harry Nilsson, Paul Williams, Danny Hutton (Three Dog Night), Rodney Bingenheimer, Steven Stills and, according to legend, Charlie Manson. Eventually Rafelson and Schneider narrowed it down to four: Davy Jones, Micky Dolenz, Michael Nesmith and Peter Tork. NBC bought the pilot, RCA agreed to distribute the records and almost overnight, the Monkees were a pop phenomenon.

With corporate power and a crack creative team behind them (director Paul Mazursky co-wrote the pilot), the Monkees first single, "Last Train To Clarksville," sold 250,000 copies before the series even debuted—despite the fact that the group did little more than sing on cue. Later it hit number one—as did the group's first album...and the group's second single...and the group's second album...etc.

The show debuted in the 1966-67 season, and never rated

highly. One problem: Many NBC affiliates refused to carry a show that had long-haired "hippie" types as the heroes. But it was a respected program. Most people aren't aware that in addition to having hit records (including the #1 song of 1967, "I'm a Believer"), the Monkees won two Emmy awards for best sitcom.

At the end of the second season NBC cancelled the series, so the group concentrated its efforts on a movie called *Head* (now a cult classic) instead. It was released with little fanfare in 1968.

The group's last project with all four members was a bizarre TV special entitled "33 1/3 Revolutions Per Monkee," which featured Jerry Lee Lewis, Fats Domino and Little Richard as guests. NBC ran the show against the Oscars, dooming it to obscurity. The Monkees themselves soon disappeared, splitting in 1970.

MONKEE FACTS

• In 1965, Peter Tork was playing with Stephen Stills in the Buffalo Fish—an early incarnation of the Buffalo Springfield. It was Stills, in fact, who tipped off Tork—then washing dishes for $50 a week—that TV producers were still casting for the Monkees (Stills auditioned, but lost out due to bad teeth and a receding hairline). Tork was the last hired and the first to quit the group in 1968.

• Micky Dolenz wasn't a drummer. He agreed to play drums only after the other Monkees refused.

• Davy Jones' big break came with the stage musical "Oliver!" where he played the role of the Artful Dodger. When the musical moved from London to New York, Jones became an instant teen star, winning a Tony nomination for his role. Ironically, Jones—along with the rest of the cast of "Oliver!"—appeared on the Ed Sullivan Show which included the Beatles' first American TV appearance.

• In terms of fan mail, Jones was always the most popular Monkee.

•Michael Nesmith's mother, Bette Nesmith, was a commercial artist who invented Liquid Paper (i.e., typewriter correction fluid). Michael inherited millions of dollars from her.

- Jack Nicholson co-wrote *Head*. Nicholson also made a cameo appearance in the movie.

- Frank Zappa made a rare guest appearance on "The Monkees" TV series and in *Head*.

- Due to Davy Jones' popularity, another English singer named Jones was forced to change his real name to...David Bowie.

- Monkeeing Around: Davy Jones was due to be drafted for duty in Vietnam when suddenly (by coincidence?) someone broke into the local Army recruitment branch and stole the file cabinet with Jones' file.

- Jimi Hendrix was the Monkees' opening act on their 1967 summer tour of the States. Micky Dolenz had seen Hendrix perform in a New York club and later signed Hendrix following his historic show at Monterey Pop (where both Dolenz and Tork were stage announcers). Monkees fans, however, were unprepared for the overt sexuality and strange guitar work of the Jimi Hendrix Experience—they kept cheering, "We Want the Monkees." Finally, after the group's show at Forest Hills, New York, Hendrix and the Monkees amicably split company. The official excuse for Hendrix leaving the tour was the Daughters of The American Revolution had banned him for being too sexually suggestive.

- Bob Rafelson and Bert Schneider later went on to form BBS Productions, which produced films such as *Easy Rider, The Last Picture Show* and *Hearts and Minds*.

- In 1980, Michael Nesmith received the first video Grammy award for his one-hour video special, "Elephant Parts." Nesmith has produced such movies as *Tapeheads* and *Repo Man*.

- In 1986, Micky Dolenz, Peter Tork and Davy Jones reunited for a massively-successful 20th Anniversary Monkees Tour. Although Nesmith declined to tour, he did show up for the encore at the group's 9/6/86 appearance at Hollywood's Greek Theatre. Thanks to MTV exposure of the original series, the Monkees experienced a surge in popularity, culminating in the hit single, "That Was Then, This Is Now." In an unprecedented showing on the *Billboard* charts, the Monkees had seven albums in the Hot 200, six of which were reissues of original albums.

The condom—made originally of linen—was invented in the early 1500s.

BRAINTEASERS

A few more simple logic problems to entertain you.
Remember: no heavy math or pencils needed.

T his is a true story," my uncle Gordon said. "When I was living in Vermont, the minister of a local church fell asleep during the services. He dreamed he was a French nobleman during the French Revolution, had been sentenced to die, and was waiting for the blade of the guillotine to fall. Right then, his wife noticed he was asleep and poked him on the back of the neck with a pencil to wake him up. It was a terrible thing—the shock was so great that he had a heart attack and fell over, dead."

"Come on, Uncle Gordon," I replied. "That can't possibly be true."

How could I be so sure that my uncle was kidding me?

One day, Uncle Gordon and I were walking down a busy street, and we noticed four workmen digging. "Hm-m-m," my uncle mused. "If it takes four men four days to dig four holes, how long would it take one man to dig half a hole?"

What's the answer?

Every summer my Uncle Gordon goes to his house in the country. One summer, he asked me to forward his mail to him. I assured him I would. A month went by, and one night he angrily called to ask where his mail was—he hadn't received any yet.

"I'm sorry Uncle Gordon," I replied, "but you forgot to give me your mailbox key."

He apologized profusely, and promised to mail me the key right away. Another month went by, and when he returned, he was fuming.

"I never got a bit of mail!" he screamed. "How could you be so irresponsible?!!"

"Sorry, unk, but it wasn't my fault," I replied.

What did I mean?

The first known contraceptive was crocodile dung, used by Egyptians in 2000 B.C.

THE LASER

Tired of reading about music and TV? Try this.

In a scant 30 years, the laser (short for Light Amplification by Stimulated Emission of Radiation) has become as indispensable to the fields of communication, medicine, industry, manufacturing and the military, as the wheel. The concentrated beam of a laser can bore a hole through a diamond or mend a detached retina. It can slice through a sheet of metal like a hot knife through aged Brie or it can read the price code on a can of creamed corn at your local supermarket check-out counter.

DEVELOPMENT
Lasers were developed in the late '50s and early '60s, growing out of earlier research studies of microwave amplifying devices called masers. Because of this parallel development, early lasers were called *optical masers* because they amplified light in the same manner that masers amplified microwaves. The first laser was produced by Theodore H. Maiman at Hughes Research Laboratory using a ruby crystal as the amplifying medium.

HOW THEY WORK
Simply put, lasers collect and harness light to produce an intense beam of radiation in a single, pure color.

To know something about how lasers work is to have a crash course in the basic nature of the atom. Every atom stores energy. The amount of energy in the atom depends on the motion of the electrons that circle the nucleus of the atom. When the atom absorbs energy, its own energy level increases and the atom becomes "excited."

To return to its normal unexcited state, the atom must release its extra energy in the form of light. This release is called "spontaneous emission." When the atom returns to its lower energy state, it emits a "photon," the basic unit of all radiation.

An ordinary light source, such as the common electric bulb, emits photons of light independently in a random manner. That light is called "incoherent." Wavelengths of light issuing from a laser, on the other hand, are organized or "coherent," and work in conjunction with one another, producing an amplified stream of photons which all have the same wavelength and move in the same direction.

Because of its highly directional beam (unlike radio waves, laser beams spread only slightly as they travel), lasers can transmit information with little interference. And because they operate on a higher frequency than conventional electronic transmitters, lasers can carry more information than radio waves, allowing them to transmit both telephone and television programs at the same time.

THREE DIFFERENT KINDS

The three major types of lasers, based on their light-amplifying medium are solid lasers, gas lasers and liquid lasers:

Solid Lasers: The light-amplifying substance may be a crystal, glass or a semiconductor. For instance, crystal lasers have a fluorescent crystal, such as a ruby. Ruby lasers produce intensely powerful bursts of light that can drill through solid steel. A garnet crystal laser which emits a continuous beam of light may be used as a drill or a range finder. Glass lasers are used by scientists in experiments with plasmas. And semiconductor lasers, which convert electricity into coherent light, are useful in the communications industry.

Gas lasers: The light-amplifying source, a mixture of gases, is contained in a glass or quartz tube. Unlike ruby or glass lasers, gas lasers can produce a continuous beam of light which has a narrow frequency range than the light from a solid laser. Gas lasers are used in communications and in measuring.

Liquid lasers: Chemical dyes dissolved in methanol and contained in a glass tube are the light-amplifying sources for liquid lasers. The only kind of laser that can have its light frequency adjusted, liquid lasers are used by scientists to study the properties of atomic and molecular systems.

The air that leaves your body when you exhale floats out at a rate of about 15 m.p.h.

THE LASER IN YOUR LIFE

In the '60s, people who understood lasers looked forward to the day when they would be a part our everyday lives. In 1963, for example, *Life* magazine reported of a laser test: "This dazzling demonstration only hints at the vast power and versatility of laser beams. Although lasers today are still laboratory tools, scientists foresee a variety of future uses."

Then, in the '70s, the laser came into its own—not only as those eerie green special effects projected during elaborate rock shows, but as technical medical marvels—"bloodless scalpels" used to treat certain types of cancers, to stop bleeding stomach ulcers and, more recently, to perform complicated microsurgeries.

Today, the dreams of scientists two decades ago have largely come true. The impact of laser technology encompasses everything from child care (pricking holes in baby-bottle nipples) and home entertainment (creating audio equipment systems that can reproduce sound with studio or live-performance accuracy) to cost-effective communications (lowering the cost of transoceanic telephone calls through the use of optical fibers) and "national defense" (creating space-based "Star Wars" weaponry).

ఌ   ఌ   ఌ

TOTALLY UNRELATED INFORMATION

Weird Lawsuits: In 1985, a Budweiser radio commercial featured a recreation of the Bill Mazeroski home run that won the 1960 World Series for the Pittsburgh Pirates. It went: "Ditmar delivers...Mazeroski swings...It's going back, back...." The thing is, Ralph Terry was the pitcher who threw that ball for the Yankees, not Art Ditmar—and Ditmar was angry to hear his name mentioned. So he sued Anheuser-Busch for half-a-million dollars, charging "his reputation had been tarnished."

Meat takes longer than other foods to digest.

PRIME TIME PROVERBS

More comments about everyday life in America. From Prime Time Proverbs, a forthcoming book by Jack Mingo.

ON TELEVISION:
"Television has done much for psychiatry by spreading information about it...as well as contributing to the need for it."
—**Alfred Hitchcock,**
Alfred Hitchcock Presents

George: "Gracie, what do you think of television?"
Gracie: "I think it's wonderful—I hardly ever watch radio anymore."
—***Burns and Allen***

ON GROWING UP:
"You don't need any brains to grow up. It just happens to ya."
—**Gilbert Bates,**
Leave It to Beaver

"I used to do a year in 365 days. Now they go by much faster."
—**Dr. Graham,**
Ben Casey

ON MONEY:
The Riddler: "This is my dream come true!...Nothing stands between me and the Lost Treasure of the Incas!...And it's worth millions...MILLIONS!!!
Batman: "Just remember, Riddler, you can't buy friends with money."
—***Batman***

"There's only one thing more important than money— and that's more money."
—**"Pappy" Maverick,**
Maverick

ON PHYSICS:
"A dog can't get struck by lightning. You know why? Cause he's too close to the ground. See, lightning strikes tall things. Now, if they were giraffes out there in that field, now then we'd be in trouble. But you sure don't have to worry about dogs."
—**Barney Fife,**
The Andy Griffith Show

ON EATING RIGHT:
John Burns: "I try to eat only natural things."
Louie DePalma: "How'd you like a sack of dirt?"
—***Taxi***

ALICE TAKES A TRIP

The final selection in our Bathroom Reader—and the longest—is from Through the Looking Glass, by Lewis Carroll. This is a particular favorite, because it is one of the few works of fiction you can pick up and begin anywhere (a bathroom reading requisite). In this passage, Alice meets Humpty Dumpty. Due to space limitations, we've cut out some of the poetry. But if you enjoy what's here, you can pick up an unabridged copy for your bathroom.

Alice finds herself in a grocery store, talking to a sheep.

"I should like to buy an egg, please," she said timidly. "How do you sell them?"

"Fivepence...for one—twopence for two," the Sheep replied.

"Then two are cheaper than one?" Alice said in a surprised tone, taking out her purse.

"Only you *must* eat them both, if you buy two," said the Sheep.

"Then I'll have *one* please," said Alice, as she put the money down on the counter. For she thought to herself, "They mightn't be at all nice, you know."

The Sheep took the money and put it away in a box: then she said, "I never put things into people's hands—that would never do—you must get it for yourself." And so saying, she went off to the other end of the shop, and set the egg upright on the shelf.

"I wonder why it wouldn't do?" thought Alice, as she groped her way among the tables and chairs, for the shop was very dark towards the end. "The egg seems to get further away the more I walk towards it. Let me see, is this a chair? Why, it's got branches, I declare! How very odd to find trees growing here! And actually here's a little brook! Well, this is the very queerest shop I ever saw!"

So she went on, wondering more and more at every step, as everything turned into a tree the moment she came to it, and she quite expected the egg to do the same.

However, the egg only got larger and larger, and more and more human; when she had come within a few yards of it, she saw that it had eyes and a nose and mouth; and, when she had come close to it, she saw clearly that it was HUMPTY DUMPTY himself. "It can't be anybody else!" she said to herself. "I'm as certain of it, as if his name were written all over his face!"

It might have been written a hundred times, easily, on that enormous face. Humpty Dumpty was sitting, with his legs crossed like a Turk, on the top of a high wall—such a narrow one that Alice quite wondered how he could keep his balance—and, as his eyes were steadily fixed in the opposite direction, and he didn't take the least notice of her, she thought he must be a stuffed figure after all.

"And how exactly like an egg he is!" she said aloud, standing with her hands ready to catch him, for she was every moment expecting him to fall.

"It's *very* provoking," Humpty Dumpty said after a long silence, looking away from Alice as she spoke, "to be called an egg—*very*!"

"I said you *looked* like an egg, Sir," Alice gently explained. "And some eggs are very pretty, you know," she added, hoping to turn her remark into a sort of compliment.

"Some people," said Humpty Dumpty, looking away from her as usual, "have no more sense than a baby!"

Alice didn't know what to say to this: it wasn't at all like conversation, she thought, as he never said anything to *her*; in fact, his last remark was evidently addressed to a tree—so she stood and softly repeated to herself:

> *"Humpty Dumpty sat on a wall:*
> *Humpty Dumpty had a great fall.*
> *All the King's horses and all the King's men*
> *Couldn't put Humpty Dumpty in his place again."*

"That last line is much too long for the poetry," she added, almost out loud, forgetting that Humpty Dumpty would hear her.

"Don't stand chattering to yourself like that," Humpty Dumpty said, looking at her for the first time, "but tell me your name and your business."

"My *name* is Alice, but—"

A hard rain falls at the rate of about 20 m.p.h.

"It's a stupid name enough!" Humpty Dumpty interrupted impatiently. 'What does it mean?'

"*Must* a name mean something?" Alice asked doubtfully.

"Of course it must," Humpty Dumpty said with a short laugh: "*my* name means the shape I am—and a good handsome shape it is, too. With a name like yours, you might be any shape, almost."

"Why do you sit out here all alone?" said Alice, not wishing to begin an argument.

"Why, because there's nobody with me!" cried Humpty Dumpty. "Did you think I didn't know the answer to *that*? Ask another!"

"Don't you think you'd be safer down on the ground?" Alice went on, not with any idea of making another riddle, but simply in her good-natured anxiety for the queer creature. "That wall is so *very* narrow!"

"What tremendously easy riddles you ask!" Humpty Dumpty growled out. "Of course I don't think so! Why, if ever I *did* fall off—which there's no chance of—but *if* I did—"

Here he pursed his lips, and looked so solemn and grand that Alice could hardly help laughing. "*If* I *did* fall," he went on, "*the King has promised me*—ah, you may turn pale, if you like! You didn't think I was going to say that, did you? *The King has promised me—with his very own mouth*—to—to—"

"To send all his horses and all his men," Alice interrupted, rather unwisely.

"Now I declare that's too bad!" Humpty Dumpty cried, breaking into a sudden passion. "You've been listening at doors—and behind trees—and down chimneys—or you couldn't have known it!"

"I haven't indeed!" Alice said very gently. "It's in a book."

"Ah, well! They may write such things in a *book*," Humpty Dumpty said in a calmer tone. "That's what you call a History of England, that is. Now, take a good look at me! I'm one that has spoken to a King, *I* am: mayhap you'll never see such another: and, to show you I'm not proud, you may shake hands with me!" And he grinned almost from ear to ear, as he leant forwards (and as nearly as possible fell off the wall in doing so) and offered Alice his hand. She watched him a little anxiously as she took it. "If he smiled much more the ends of his mouth might meet behind," she thought: "And then I don't know *what* would happen to his head! I'm afraid it would come off!"

"Yes, all his horses and all his men," Humpty Dumpty went on. "They'd pick me up again in a minute, *they* would! However, this conversation is going a little too fast; let's go back to the last remark but one."

"I'm afraid I can't quite remember it," Alice said, very politely.

"In that case we start afresh," said Humpty Dumpty, "and it's my turn to choose a subject—" ("He talks about it just as if it was a game!" thought Alice.) "So here's a question for you. How old did you say you were?"

Alice made a short calculation, and said "Seven years and six months."

"Wrong!" Humpty Dumpty exclaimed triumphantly. "You never said a word like it!"

"I thought you meant 'How old *are* you?'" Alice explained.

"If I'd meant that, I'd have said it," said Humpty Dumpty.

Alice didn't want to begin another argument, so she said nothing.

"Seven years and six months!" Humpty Dumpty repeated thoughtfully. "An uncomfortable sort of age. Now if you'd asked my advice, I'd have said 'Leave off at seven'—but it's too late now."

"I never ask advice about growing," Alice said indignantly.

"Too proud?" the other enquired.

Alice felt even more indignant at this suggestion. "I mean," she said, "that one can't help growing older."

"*One* can't, perhaps," said Humpty Dumpty; "but *two* can. With proper assistance, you might have left off at seven."

"What a beautiful belt you've got on!" Alice suddenly remarked. (They had quite enough of the subject of age, she thought: and, if they really were to take turns in choosing subjects, it was her turn now.) "At least," she corrected herself on second thoughts, "a beautiful cravat, I should have said—no, a belt, I mean—I beg your pardon!" she added in dismay, for Humpty Dumpty looked thoroughly offended, and she began to wish she hadn't chosen that subject. "If only I knew," she thought to herself, "which was neck and which was waist!"

Evidently Humpty Dumpty was very angry, though he said nothing for a minute or two. When he *did* speak again, it was in a deep growl.

"It is a—most—provoking—thing," he said at last, "when a person doesn't know a cravat from a belt!"

"I know it's very ignorant of me," Alice said, in so humble a tone that Humpty Dumpty relented.

"It's a cravat, child, and a beautiful one, as you say. It's a present from the White King and Queen. There now!"

"Is it really?" said Alice, quite pleased to find that she *had* chosen a good subject after all.

"They gave it me," Humpty Dumpty continued thoughtfully as he crossed one knee over the other and clasped his hands round it, "they gave it me—for an un-birthday present."

"I beg your pardon," Alice said with a puzzled air.

"I'm not offended," said Humpty Dumpty.

"I mean, what *is* an un-birthday present?"

"A present given when it isn't your birthday, of course."

Alice considered a little. "I like birthday presents best," she said at last.

"You don't know what you're talking about!" cried Humpty Dumpty. "How many days are there in a year?"

"Three hundred and sixty-five," said Alice.

"And how many birthdays have you?"

"One."

"And if you take one from three hundred and sixty-five what remains?"

"Three hundred and sixty-four, of course."

Humpty Dumpty looked doubtful. "I'd rather see that one on paper," he said.

Alice couldn't help smiling as she took out her memorandum book, and worked the sum for him:

$$\begin{array}{r} 365 \\ -\ 1 \\ \hline 364 \end{array}$$

Humpty Dumpty took the book and looked at it carefully. "That seems to be done right—" he began.

"You're holding it upside down!" Alice interrupted.

Ivan the Terrible built the Kremlin—then gouged the architect's eyes out to

"To be sure I was!" Humpty Dumpty said gaily as she turned it round for him. "I thought it looked a little queer. As I was saying, that *seems* to be done right—though I haven't time to look it over thoroughly just now—and that shows that there are three hundred and sixty-four days when you might get un-birth-birthday presents—"

"Certainly," said Alice.

"And only one for birthday presents, you know. There's glory for you!"

"I don't know what you mean by 'glory,'" Alice said.

Humpty Dumpty smiled contemptuously. "Of course you don't—till I tell you. I meant 'there's a nice knock-down argument for you!'"

"But 'glory' doesn't mean 'a nice knock-down argument,'" Alice objected.

"When *I* use a word," Humpty Dumpty said, in rather a scornful tone, "It means just what I choose it to mean—neither more nor less."

"The question is," said Alice, "whether you *can* make words mean so many different thing."

"The question is," said Humpty Dumpty, "which is to be master—that's all."

Alice was too much puzzled to say anything; so after a minute Humpty Dumpty began again. "They've a temper, some of them—particularly verbs: they're the proudest—adjectives you can do anything with, but not verbs—however, *I* can manage the whole lot of them! Impenetrability! That's what *I* say!"

"Would you tell me please," said Alice, "what that means?" "Now you talk like a reasonable child," said Humpty Dumpty, looking very much pleased. "I meant by 'impenetrability' that we've had enough of that subject, and it would be just as well if you'd mention what you mean to do next, as I suppose you don't mean to stop here all the rest of your life."

"That's a great deal to make one word mean," Alice said in a thoughtful tone.

"When I make a word do a lot of work like that," said Humpty Dumpty, "I always pay it extra."

"Oh!" said Alice. She was too much puzzled to make any other remark.

"Ah, you should see 'em come round me of a Saturday night," Humpty Dumpty went on, wagging his head gravely from side

prevent him from ever designing another structure like it.

to side, "for to get their wages, you know."

(Alice didn't venture to ask what he paid them with; so you see I can't tell *you*.)

[*Humpty Dumpty explains Jabberwocky to Alice, and then recites his own poem…*]

> "I sent a message to the fish:
> I told them this is what I wish.
>
> The little fishes of the sea,
> They sent an answer back to me.
>
> The little fishes' answer was,
> 'We cannot do it, Sir, because—'"

"I'm afraid I don't quite understand," said Alice.

"It gets easier further on," Humpty Dumpty replied.

> "I sent to them again to say,
> 'It will be better to obey.'
>
> The fishes answered, with a grin,
> 'Why, what a temper you are in!'
>
> I told them once, I told them twice:
> They would not listen to advice.
>
> I took a kettle large and new,
> Fit for the deed I had to do.
>
> My heart went hop, my heart went thump:
> I filled the kettle at the pump.
>
> Then someone came to me and said,
> 'The little fishes are in bed.'
>
> I said to him, I said it plain,
> 'Then you must wake them up again.'
>
> I said it very loud and clear,
> I went and shouted in his ear."

Humpty Dumpty raised his voice almost to a scream as he repeated this verse, and Alice thought with a shudder, "I wouldn't have been the messenger for anything!"

Holly has never grown in Hollywood—the town was named after an estate in Illinois.

"But he was very stiff and proud:
He said, 'you needn't shout so loud!'

And he was very proud and stiff:
He said, 'I'd go and wake them, if—'

I took a corkscrew from the shelf:
I went to wake them up myself!

And when I found the door was locked,
I pulled and pushed and kicked and knocked

And when I found the door was shut,
I tried to turn the handle, but—"

There was a long pause.

"Is that all?" Alice timidly asked.

"That's all," said Humpty Dumpty. "Good-bye."

This was rather sudden, Alice thought: but, after such a very strong hint that she ought to be going, she felt that it would hardly be civil to stay. So she got up and held out her hand. "Good-bye, till we meet again!" she said as cheerfully as she could.

"I shouldn't know you again if we did meet," Humpty Dumpty replied in a discontented tone, giving her one of his fingers to shake: "you're so exactly like other people."

"The face is what one goes by, generally," Alice remarked in a thoughtful tone.

"That's just what I complain of," said Humpty Dumpty. "Your face is the same as everybody has—the two eyes, so—" (marking their places in the air with his thumb) "nose in the middle, mouth under. It's always the same. Now if you have the two eyes on the same side of the nose, for instance—or the mouth at the top—that would be *some* help."

"It wouldn't look nice," Alice objected, but Humpty Dumpty only shut his eyes, and said, "Wait till you've tried."

Alice waited a minute to see if he would speak again, but, as he never opened his eyes or took any further notice of her, she said, "Good-bye!" once more, and, getting no answer to this, she quietly walked away: But she couldn't help saying to herself as she went, "Of all the unsatisfactory...people I ever met—" She never finished the sentence, for at this moment a heavy crash shook the forest from end to end.

Almost 1/10 of the garbage Americans produce is plastics.

SOLUTION PAGE

PAGE 21, BRAINTEASERS:
1. Friday; 2. An egg; the riddle is by J. R. R. Tolkien; 3. Neither—when they meet, they're the same distance from N.Y.

PAGE 35, BRAINTEASERS:
1. House numbers; 2. He saw the other boy's face and assumed his was just as dirty; 3. June 29, the next-to-last day of the month; 4. The match

PAGE 54, ANCIENT RIDDLES:
1. The Letter "E"; 2. Tomorrow; 3. A shoe; 4. The stars; 5. A fart; 6. A towel; 7. A watermelon

PAGE 68, WHAT AM I?
1. A postage stamp; 2. A mirror; 3. The moon; 4. The weather

PAGE 196, PRESIDENTIAL QUIZ:
1. Virginia; 2. a, Martin Van Buren; 3. b, Teddy Roosevelt; 4. Gerald Ford, who was appointed to the vice presidency before he became president; 5. Franklin D. Roosevelt; 6. William Howard Taft; 7. Warren G. Harding; 8. Calvin Coolidge; 9. c, Richard Nixon; 10. It is the first Hollywood film in which a future president (Ronald Reagan) and first lady (Nancy Davis) co-starred; 11. Dwight Eisenhower; 12. b, Thomas Jefferson; 13. James Buchanan; 14. New York; 15. 41 as of January, 1989.

PAGE 203, BRAINTEASERS:
1. "Trade horses"; 2. $1987 is worth more than $1985; 3. He's a midget, and the highest button he can reach is the one for 8th floor; "I will die by shooting." If they shot him, that would be true, so he would have to die by hanging—but that would make his statement false. Unable to reconcile the two, they gave up.

PAGE 210, BRAINTEASERS:
1. If the minister died without ever waking up, it would be impossible to know what he'd been dreaming; 2. You can't dig half a hole; 3. He mailed me the key, but I couldn't get into the mailbox to get it.

THE LAST PAGE

FELLOW BATHROOM READERS:
The fight for good bathroom reading should never be taken loosely—we must sit firmly for what we believe in, even while the rest of the world is taking pot shots at us.

Once we prove we're not simply a flush-in-the-pan, writers and publishers will find their resistance unrolling.

So we invite you to take the plunge—"Sit Down and Be Counted"—by joining The Bathroom Readers' Institute. Send a self-addressed, stamped envelope to: B.R.I., 1400 Shattuck Avenue, #25, Berkeley, CA 94709. You'll receive your free membership card, a copy of the B.R.I. newsletter whenever it's published, and earn a permanent spot on the B.R.I. honor roll.

ↄ⊕   ↄ⊕   ↄ⊕

**VOLUME II OF *UNCLE JOHN'S*
BATHROOM READER IS IN THE WORKS**
Don't fret—there's more good reading on its way. In fact, there are a few ways you can contribute to the next volume:

1) Is there a subject you'd like to see us cover? Write and let us know. We aim to please.

2) Got a neat idea for a couple of pages in the new *Reader*? If you're the first to suggest it, and we use it, we'll send you a free copy of the book.

3) Have you seen or read an article you'd recommend as quintessential bathroom reading? Or is there a passage in a book that you want to share with other B.R.I. members? Tell us where to find it, or send a copy. If you're the first to suggest it and we publish it in the next volume, there's a free book in it for you.

Well, we're out of space, and when you've gotta go, you've gotta go. Hope to hear from you soon. Meanwhile, remember:
Go With the Flow.